THE
CHRISTIAN PRINCE

PUTTING "CIVIL" BACK INTO CIVIL GOVERNMENT

Gene -

" For the Lord is our Judge, the
Lord is our Lawgiver, the Lord
is our King; He will save us.
                    Jeremiah 33:22

Buddy

Scripture quotations are from the New Geneva Study Bible, NKJV,
1995, Thomas Nelson, Inc.

TABLE OF CONTENTS

What Is "Government?"
Machiavellian Principles 7, 9, 17-18, 20

Chapter One

The Citizen's Role
Machiavellian Principle 6

Chapter Two

Living Large (with a Christian worldview)
Machiavellian Principles 15, 19, 21

Can Culture Be Changed?
Machiavellian Principle 3

Becoming the Change We Seek

Case Studies

Charts

PREFACE

IT'S BEEN APPROXIMATELY 5,000 YEARS SINCE SATAN ASKED Eve if she really needed God to tell her how to live, [1] and everyone since then has continued to struggle with Satan's temptation for us to believe that we are smarter and wiser than our Creator. We should be ashamed at having such a low regard for, and trust in, the very Creator of the universe. Indeed, we should ask ourselves whether such an attitude is blasphemous! Instead, we continue to buy into Satan's myth that God's Word is only relevant inside our homes, churches and minds, (in the "religious" realm of life) while man's word should be trusted outside (in the "real life" realm).

Satan, whose only power over Christians is deception, is at his best when he convinces us to ignore the clear record of history and concentrate exclusively on the issues at hand. In doing so our approach to life mirrors the existential mindset of non-Christians, who do not believe in absolute truth, and if they believe in "truth" at all it is "whatever works now." This means-justifies-the-ends outlook on life has "truth" constantly changing to fit emerging situations, and regards words as merely euphemisms to attract votes and build coalitions.

When we Christians look at life from our own perspective instead of from God's perspective, we begin to frame our goals, motivations and decisions in the identical manner used by non-Christians. "Power and personal prestige" replace "humility and righteousness." Have we forgotten that Jesus' seventh beatitude is "blessed are the peacemakers," [2] not "blessed are the power brokers"?

With no absolute ethical foundation for life, non-Christians conclude that the only "constant" in life is "change." Therefore, civil laws that applied to past generations are seen as "out-of-date" and in need of changing to meet our modern lifestyle. Christians, however, should know better. We know that the various elements of today's cultural agenda are "abnormal," not "normal," because normality is what God's Word describes, and 21st century America is certainly out of sync with that. So while non-Christians seek to bring potential enemies under control through warfare, we seek to transform the world to biblical principles one individual at a time through personal evangelization, discipleship and a civil government that conforms to God's accountabilities and does not ignore nor deny the accountabilities of the God-appointed, self-governing spheres of the individual, family and church. Non-Christians have as their model the Prussian General Karl Von Clausewitz, who states, "War is the continuation of politics by other means." [3] Christians have as our model Jesus Christ, who states, "Glory to God in the highest, and on earth peace, goodwill toward men!" [4] Jesus' half-brother James writes,

> For where envy and self-seeking exist, confusion
> and every evil thing are there. But the wisdom that
> is from above is first pure, then peaceable, gentle,
> willing to yield, full of mercy and good fruits,
> without partiality and without hypocrisy.
>
> JAMES 3.16-17

A great advantage that we have over our non-Christian neighbors is that since we believe in absolute principles, we can look to history for lessons and proof that only God's ways will succeed. Throughout the pages of the Old Testament and the epochs of history we learn that those civilizations that have based their civil government upon biblical principles (the West) have achieved a level of personal liberty and freedom that is unknown in ungodly civilizations (the East). Non-Christians, if they believed in history, which they don't, would chalk that up to "Lady Luck," but we know that it is because of "Father God."

None of this is anything we don't know and agree with, but still we continue to turn to the "words of wisdom" from non-Christians in an effort to improve our vocational performance, our marriages, and our civil government. This is not to say that we can't pick up an insight or two from a street-smart heathen, but the truth is that they have no truth of their own, and whatever "valuable insights" we may learn from them have been stolen from biblical principles. For example, a civil government based upon the 2nd Table of the Law (Commandments five through ten: honor authority, don't kill, cheat, steal, lie, or covet) will provide a society a temporary time of personal liberty and freedom. But unless legislators and judges admit that their civil laws are based upon the unchanging principles of Scripture, such laws will sooner or later be replaced or re-interpreted according to those who are currently in control of the culture. The reason for this is that when a society refuses to admit that God is the authority behind its laws, it must believe that its laws are based upon man's opinion. God's opinion (the 1st Table of the Law; Commandments 1-4), never changes, whereas man's laws are constantly in flux because of the ever-changing whims and fads of that society's citizens.

One of the most influential books on political science was written nearly five hundred years ago by the Italian government official, Niccolo Machiavelli. *The Prince* epitomizes the love man has for Satan's lie, instead of God's truth. Machiavelli served for thirteen years as the Republic of Florence's Second Chancery, carrying out his duties in foreign and military affairs. His 26 "principles" for civil rulers have been studied and applied as gospel not only for politicians, but for business leaders, athletic coaches and military officers. *The Prince* has been both sworn by ("the handbook of modern political science") and sworn at ("a handbook for gangsters").

As mentioned, it is understandable why non-Christians would be attracted to his street-smart counsel, because they do not have an absolute ethical standard to which to conform their daily business, political, and military decisions. When men dismiss the idea of a transcendent Creator God who is in sovereign control of His creation, the only way left to "control" a culture is through coercion or force.

Christians, however, should see through the transparency of Machiavelli's "dog-eat-dog" worldview. We who profess to believe that "it's a Kingdom out there" instead of "it's a jungle out there" should quickly dismiss the option of following a non-Christian's advice. After all, don't we remember how disoriented and clueless we were when we thought that we were "the captain of our ship and the master of our fate?" Aren't we forever grateful that the Holy Spirit has "lifted the veil from our eyes" [5] and enabled us to understand the wisdom of His inerrant instructions on how to live and govern ourselves? Since we now have access to God's knowledge, why should we desire to seek man's knowledge?

Perhaps its time we reminded ourselves just how bad we were before the Holy Spirit changed our heart. Perhaps its time we reminded ourselves that there is much more to Christianity than attending church on Sunday rather than going to the lake. One of the South's literary giants of the 20th century, Robert Penn Warren, in his Pulitzer prize winning *All The King's Men*, provides this insightful declaration by the Southern political fascist Willie Stark to the moralistic Dr. Adam Stanton:

Goodness—yeah, just plain simple goodness! Well,
you can't inherit it from anybody. You got to make
it, Doc, if you want it. And you got to make it out of
badness. And you know why Doc? ... Because there
isn't anything else to make it out of. [6]

Perhaps we need to remind ourselves that the only reason we are "good," is because of the grace of God, and that without His grace and mercy, our non-Christian legislators and judges are "bad." Or, as George Thorogood & The Destroyers sing, they are "BBBB-Bad to the bbbb-bone!"

Do we not remember the words God told Noah and his family as they stepped out of the ark: "I will never again curse the ground for man's sake, although the imagination of man's heart is evil from his youth ..." [7] Aaron made the same point to Moses, when Moses returned from Mount Sinai with the Ten Commandments and found that the Israelites had made a golden calf out of their jewelry.

Do not let the anger of my lord become hot. You
know the people, that they are set on evil.
EXODUS 32.22

Perhaps we need also to remind ourselves how foolish the reasoning of non-Christians is: they are set on evil! Warren's political character, Stark, poignantly presents the hopelessness and the futileness of the non-Christian worldview:

... if as you say, there is only the bad to start with,
and the good must be made from the bad, then how
do you ever know what the good is? Assuming you
have made it from the bad. "You just make it up, as
you go along"

...When your great-great-grandpappy climbed down out of the tree, he didn't have any more notion of good or bad, or right or wrong, than the hoot owl that stayed up in the tree. Well, he climbed down and he began to make things up, as he went along. He made up what he needed to do business, Doc. And what he made up and got everybody to agree on as good and right was always just a couple of jumps behind what he needed to do business on. That's why things change, Doc. Because what folks claim is right is always just a couple of jumps short of what they need to do business. Now an individual, one fellow he will stop doing business because he's got a notion of what is right, and he is a hero. But folks in general, which is society, Doc, is never going to stop doing business. Society is just going to cook up a new notion of what is right. Society is sure not ever going to commit suicide.... [8]

Are humans simply the most evolved animal, that is constantly looking for "new notions to cook up" as Warren so eloquently describes, or are we special creations of God? Of course, we know that answer, but judging by our actions (including our legislative and judicial decisions) we prefer to be in the "cooking up new notions" mode.

Machiavelli bases each of his "principles" on cunning, human logic, and technical skills. Jesus, on the other hand, in His "Instruction Book for Living" (the Bible), provides an absolute and divinely inspired ethical code by which we can live and govern ourselves. For us, the decision comes down to virtue vs. virtuosity, or to put it another way, Jesus' ethics vs. man's ethics. As we continue to reap the fruit of a culture that is based upon man's ever-changing ethics, there is a growing sentiment to once again base our lives and governance upon Jesus' never-changing ethical code.

The *Christian Prince* explains how we can put "civil" back into civil government, and how America can once again attract others-focused statesmen to serve as our representatives, instead of the self-centered politicians with whom we are so familiar.

It should be remembered that it is not the Creator God, but the supposed "evolutionary man" who has the problem of "the missing link." There is no reason for us to attempt to "help God out" by inventing an antidote for ungodly civil rulers. He has already provided us with such an antidote in the pages of the Bible, and *The Christian Prince* exposes and contrasts the failing ideas of man with the divinely guaranteed-to-succeed ideas of our Lord, Savior and King, Jesus Christ.

The goal of The Christian Prince is to contrast the non-Christian worldview that undergirds The Prince with a worldview that conforms to biblical principles, and to provide a biblical framework for civil rulers (legislators and judges) to use in carrying out their duties.

The Christian Prince contrasts each of ten specific principles of Machiavelli's *The Prince*, with a boxed area entitled, "Is It Machiavellian, or Christian?" These succinct and clear contrasts show that Machiavelli's principles limit personal liberty, while God's principles expand personal liberty. The "Legislative Building Blocks" page at the end of each chapter provides a quick review of specific biblical principles that civil rulers can incorporate into their decision-making process.

The content of The Christian Prince is arranged under five headings:

- What is "Government?"
- The Citizen's Role
- Living Large (with a Christian Worldview)
- Can Culture Be Changed?
- Becoming The Change We Seek

Also included are seven case studies that provide a wealth of information on specific issues that civil rulers deal with day in and day out. They are:

- The Importance of Keeping Who You Are in Biblical Perspective: Nebuchadnezzar's Nefarious Narcissism
- Church & State – Distinct Spheres, Related Mission
- The Civil Ruler Model of Behavior
- Whose Money is it? We've Come a Long Way Since Col. Davy Crockett
- A Christian Perspective on Just War
- Biblical Principles of Civil Government

The Christian Prince removes all doubt that our heavenly Father knows best when it comes to providing the prescription for how to make our community, state, region, nation (and the world!) peaceful places in which to live, work, play and raise our families by incorporating biblical principles into the civil law code.

If you are a Christian civil ruler this book will help you evaluate your current approach to legislating or judging. You may be a concerned citizen who wants to do your part in "turning the world rightside up," [9] or a home schooling parent who wants to present the biblical basis for civil government. *The Christian Prince* has been written with you in mind.

There are brothers and sisters who up to now have been restricting their Christianity to the comfortable confines of their homes and churches because they think that's all there is to being a member of Christ's Kingdom. It is my hope and prayer that they may see on these pages that it is time for them to shed their cocoon of inward-focused, culture-abandoning personal pietism—which incorrectly sees Christians as second-class citizens—and stretch out wings of an outward-focused, others-first worldview that correctly sees Christians as first-class citizens whose daily testimonies will cause their non-Christian neighbors to want to live as they do and be, like them, victorious!

Buddy Hanson
Tuscaloosa, Alabama
June 2007

NOTES

1 Genesis 3.1-6

2 Matthew 5.9

3 Clausewitz, Karl Von, War, *Politics and Power*, (Regnery, [1965], 1997)

4 Luke 2.14

5 2 Corinthians 3.12-18

6 Warren, Robert Penn, *All The King's Men*, (Harvest Books, 1949), p. 257

7 Genesis 8.21

8 Warren, *op. cit.*, *Kings*, p.257

9 See *It's Time to Un-Quo the Status*, Buddy Hanson, (Hanson Group, 2006)

INTRODUCTION

WHAT IS "GOVERNMENT?" SOUNDS LIKE A SIMPLE ENOUGH question, yet the answer most people give is for the God-appointed sphere of civil government. That, however, is not all of "government," since God's divinely appointed "division of labor" also includes three other self-governing spheres: Individual, Family and Church. The correct understanding of God's design for how each of these spheres compliment each other to provide a smooth running society is critical for reforming our current tyrannical central government, because our government is usurping the responsibilities of the Individual, Family and Church spheres as fast as it can.

Speaking of civil government, why do you suppose God invented it? It is also important to know where America's form of civil government came from. Did our founding fathers copy the Greeks, as non-Christian revisionist historians say, or did they follow God's instructions? Is our current way of governing ourselves the same as our Founders established, or is it different, and does this matter?

A society's choices of ways of governing itself come down to three:

- Dictatorship
- Democracy
- Republic

The Christian Prince discusses which one is closest to the biblical model and compares the record of non-Christian civil governments with Christian models. There are two sides of every coin, and while The Christian Prince focuses on the conduct and responsibilities of civil rulers, we will also point out the responsibilities of citizens and how we should act toward our legislators and judges. For example, are our ideas all we have, or do we have God's inerrant principles to guide us? Another way of examining this is to identify the source of our power. Limited to their own "self help," non-Christians have three choices:

• The Political Party
• Political Tricks of the Trade
• The Barrel of a Gun

Christians have the unlimited resources of "God's help": the irresistible and sovereign power of the Trinity that assures the success of our obedience. This brings up the foundational question:

> *To whom are we partisan in our politics: a political party, or Christ's party?*

It's common to hear Christians say, "I must be a Republican, because I don't have anything in common with Democrats!" But at some point a somewhat irreverent question must be asked: What's the difference in the legislation of the Republican and Democrat parties? If the answer is "their platform," yet neither platform conforms their legislative policies to biblical principles, then, by the very definition of Christianity (i.e. God's Word is truth), their words are lies and should not be trusted. As Romeo said to Juliet, "A rose by any other name would smell as sweet."

The Christian Prince also emphasizes that as important as the civil government sphere is, we should not expect to be able to legislate our culture into a different worldview. The idea that individuals and our culture can be reformed by changing the conditions of our society via top-down decrees of our civil government is strictly an idea from man. God's idea is to supernaturally change the hearts of individuals who will then be motivated to change their lifestyles, their family's lifestyle, their church's lifestyle, their community's lifestyle and their country's lifestyle. God's idea is a reformation of culture from the bottom up, not from the top down.

It's personal evangelism, missions and self-government, not political parties, focus groups and central government that will truly transform a culture. God's Word and the Gospel is the key, not man's politically correct spin on how special interest groups will be helped by political programs.

It has been said that the fate of the country does not depend on what kind of paper you drop into the ballot box once a year, but on what kind of person you drop from your chamber into the street every morning.

We have staked the whole future of American civilization, not on the power of the government, far from it; we have staked the future ... upon the capacity of each and all of us to govern ourselves, to sustain ourselves, according to the Ten Commandments of God.

JAMES MADISON,
FOURTH PRESIDENT OF THE U.S.

Our lifestyle reflects our worldview, so in order to change culture we must first change our worldview. Legislation can't overcome our lifestyles. Virtuous laws can encourage virtuous lifestyles, but can't cause citizens to automatically act virtuously. The question is, "Upon what authority (God's or man's) do we base our suggestions for a cultural change?"

xxi

It is at this point that the importance of having a developed Christian worldview comes into view. In beginning a self-check of our current worldview we must ask if we are a Christian or merely an upstanding, conscientious, law-abiding, moralistic, "goody two shoes" citizen and/or civil ruler? For civil rulers, the answer would depend on whether they only uphold the second table of the Law, (Commandments 5-10), or whether they also uphold the first table of God's Law (Commandments 1-4). If a legislator says he is against abortion, and for the death penalty (the second table), but refuses to cite as his reason "God commands it," (the first table) then all he has done is offer a conservative (man's) opinion instead of a liberal (man's) opinion. In order to win the cultural debate we must frame the debates between God's ideas and man's ideas. Lacking this, we simply have a "he said, she said" dialogue.

The Christian Prince concludes with the concrete, hands-on chapter entitled, "Becoming the Change we Seek," where we "plan our work, in order to work our plan."

WHAT IS "GOVERNMENT?"

_1_

OUR LEGISLATIVE ROOTS...
ARE THEY BIBLICAL OR TRADITIONAL?

THE *CHRISTIAN PRINCE* IS ABOUT THE NECESSITY OF HOW OUR civil rulers* conform their decisions to biblical principles. Citizens have two responsibilities in this regard:

✔ Elect legislators and judges who are Christians
✔ After the election, assist them in developing their Christian worldview

Any other option goes against God's eternally perfect plan for how we should live and govern ourselves, and will sooner or later fail under the weight of its own foolishness. [1] God established civil rulers to administer justice and protect and defend communities so that the citizens would have the liberty to govern themselves (to practice self-government). The form of civil government that a particular community or country uses is not as important as its conformity to biblical principles. The ethical standards of a community, state, and nation should be based upon the eternal principles of the transcendent triune God of the Bible. Any view of civil government other than this will result in the citizens becoming a law unto themselves. The derisive term America's founders used for this type of civil government was "democracy." America's founders established this country on the basis of

*legislators and judges

3

the biblical model of a representative republic. [2] Not only did they follow the biblical model in setting up a system of checks and balances, but the civil laws themselves were based upon biblical principles. In order to prevent a democracy from occurring, our founders recognized that "law" was more than an independent expression of human will. The Founders established a republic of independent states with laws based upon the idea that our Creator knows the best way for us to live and govern ourselves; by this means, the citizens were protected against being tyrannized by one group of opinions (political party A) pitting itself against another group of opinions (political party B). Political parties are good, and they provide citizens with the opportunity to voice their will in electing their representatives, but the brilliance of the original formation of America is that "man" was removed from the court of appeals dictating the ethical standard by which we live. "God" and His inerrant Word were the "supreme court of appeals" whenever anyone questioned the definition of "good or bad behavior." The biblical model for civil government, then, is based upon citizens' electing candidates to represent them who will legislate in conformity to biblical principles. This means that no matter who is elected, they can be counted upon to carry out God's will "on earth as it is in heaven." [3]

The current collective non-Christian worldview positions civil government as the solution for all problems. This, however, was certainly not the original view of America's founders. Even as late as 1901 the writers of the constitution of my home state of Alabama defined civil government's role as follows:

> *That the sole object and only legitimate end of gov-*
> *ernment is to protect the citizen in the enjoyment*
> *of life, liberty, and property, and when the govern-*

ment assumes other functions it is usurpation and
oppression. ARTICLE I, SECTION 35

This statement, unfortunately, has not prevented Alabama legislators from being as socialistic as legislators in other states, but that is not the fault of the form of the civil government, but rather of the legislators we have been electing.

- Has there been an outcry from Alabama Christians demanding that our representatives legislate in conformity to the constitution? No. Instead, there has been misinformation taught regarding the Christian's role in civil government.
- Has there been a move to replace the current constitution (replacing the biblical principles) with a new and modern (non-Christian) one? Yes.

The esteemed Protestant reformer, John Calvin, wrote an exhortation more than 400 years ago that is as appropriate for today's Americans as it was for his European contemporaries:

> *And ye, O peoples, to whom God gave the liberty*
> *to choose your own magistrates, see to it that ye do*
> *not forfeit this favor by electing to the positions of*
> *highest honor, rascals and enemies of God.* [4]

It is said that it's hard to read the label from the inside of the jar, but that's exactly where we are in the early years of the 21st century. The cultural jar into which we have allowed ourselves to be placed and confined is a result of a century and a half of preferring the world's ways to God's ways. This has so influenced the way we look at life that when we decide

5

to "do something" about our culture, we act according to non-Christian tactics—and don't even realize that we are doing so. With only one in twenty adult Christians having a developed Christian worldview, [5] it's only natural for our proposed solutions to be non-Christian. For example, our tendency is to say, "We need to do what we can to elect conservative legislators and judges to protect us from the cultural agenda of the liberals." This solution, however, continues to fail because it's the natural (ungodly) thing to do. As Christians, we have by the very definition of the term, been given a supernatural heart transplant which motivates us to think our Creator's thoughts after Him. It frees us from the natural condition in which we came into this world. In our former condition we put ourselves first and viewed other humans as people to manipulate as we seek to achieve our goals.

What is not understood is that by acting naturally we are guaranteeing that the non-Christian agenda will continue to influence culture. As the Christian political commentator, Howard Phillips, describes it, "Liberals are going over the cliff at 100 mph and conservatives are going over at 50 mph, but both are going to crash."

The *The Christian Prince* is written to clarify that what our culture needs is not a "slower crash," but to avoid the crash! This means that we cannot assume that our job is complete just because we have helped elect Christians to office. Contact must be made with newly elected and re-elected Christian civil rulers to determine if they know how to connect their Spiritual Dots (their core Biblical beliefs) to their everyday decision-making. If they need help, there are some excellent resources available. [6]

In order to turn our culture around, we must frame the debate in terms of God's ideas vs. man's ideas.

To continue debating issues in terms of conservative (man's) ideas vs. liberal (man's) ideas, means we are leaving God out of the picture. No wonder we continue to lose ground to non-Christians. Our entire approach is Godless! Without a developed Christian worldview, well-intentioned Christians see the Republican Party as their only means of winning the culture war. From man's viewpoint this looks like a logical and pragmatic alternative. For the most part, the Republican party supports the ethics of the second table of the Law (commandments 5-10) far more consistently than the Democratic party. But what needs to be seen is that when God is left out of the debate, Christians lose regardless of whether the winning side is Democrat or Republican. This may sound like a strange statement, but to disagree with it is the same as saying "God's Word is irrelevant to our culture!" Such a statement conforms to the natural thoughts of fallen man, but in our redeemed condition we are commanded to think about all things from a supernatural perspective.

While this sounds like an easy dichotomy to deal with, and indeed should be an easy and obvious alternative, it isn't as cut and dried as one might think. Since we, our parents, and their parents have willingly jumped inside the non-Christian worldview jar, our natural (!) tendency is to see solutions in shades of grey instead of black and white.

So when *The Christian Prince* presents God's antidotes for our culture, the clear contrast between these two prescriptions may, at first glance, be so bright that we will want to shut our eyes, or at least look in another direction. However, if you will resist this temptation, you will find that, just as it is when we exit a theatre on a bright day, you only have to squint for a few seconds until the world comes into clear view. Prepare your attitude, then, for the "bright" biblical solutions you will see and resist the natural temptation to shut your eyes, and you will see God's clear plan for redeeming our culture.

7

Non-Christians rally to the political party of their liking because they view that particular party as having the power to either improve culture, or to keep it from being changed into something else. This is not to say that Christians should not be involved in political parties. We most certainly should be, but in doing so we must be convinced that the party either supports biblical principles, or can be reformed through our efforts to do so. Let's take a few moments to see if there is "power in the party."

PARTY POLITICS

As mentioned, non-Christians approach each day in terms of "What's in it for me," and set each day's priorities to bring attention to themselves so that they will receive honor and recognition. With this as the driving force behind all of their decisions and actions, it should be recognized that the primary purpose of political parties is not to "solve cultural problems," but to get their candidates elected and keep them elected. The reason for this is that when one party holds the majority in a legislative body, it can control committees, which means they can decide which bills come up for a vote. When all of this self-serving demagoguery is stripped away, it should be clear that

> *The issue for non-Christian politicians is not to improve our culture, but rather to get an advantage on their political opponents.*

Today's political parties are not moral defenders, indeed, they are "moral agnostics." The primary reason they support or oppose particular cultural issues is to maintain and/or gain seats in the legislature. In his book *1984*, George Orwell has O'Brien of the Inner Party saying to Winton Smith:

"It is impossible to see reality by looking through the eyes of the Party." Today, we could paraphrase Mr. Orwell by saying, "The final result of any political party's position is 'spin, spin, spin.'" The goal of *The Christian Prince* is to present guidelines to bring political parties back to the truth, so that they and the voters can avoid suffering the negative consequences of legislation based upon man's self-centered and distorted will.

19th Century French economist and statesman Frederic Bastiat provides some excellent observations on the consequences to a society once man begins to make up his own "law." According to Bastiat, the first mistake is when society is looked upon "as an artificial creation of the legislator's genius." [7] Under such an illusion, "The prince is depicted as the soul of this shapeless mass of people who form the nation." [8] He quotes the 17th Century French Enlightenment thinker Baron de Montesquieu's statement that in the eyes of non-Christian civil rulers, "mankind is nothing but materials for legislators to exercise their wisdom upon." [9] This type of elitist attitude, says Bastiat, is brought about because "They desire to set themselves above mankind in order to arrange, organize, and regulate it according to their fancy." [10]

Bastiat points out that once man begins creating his own law, justice becomes a "fallacy." Legislators, he says, "[tell us] that the law should be just; it must be philanthropic." [11] While such political demagoguery sounds good to most fair-minded citizens, as Christians we must ask who's defining the terms. According to the Bible, "justice" means protecting a citizen's property, life and personal liberty, but as 21st Century Americans are well aware, "justice" as defined by current legislators has been perverted to mean transferring wealth from one group of citizens to another. Bastiat notes, "It is impossible to introduce into society a greater change and a greater evil than this: the conversion of the law into an instrument of plunder." [12] Bastiat continues, "The present day delusion is an attempt to enrich everyone at the expense of everyone else." [13]

Once civil government leaves the biblical model of a representative republican form of governance and turns to a democracy,

- Statesmen are replaced by politicians whose top priority is to stay in office, rather than to legislate according to the best interest of his constituents.
- Whenever controversial decisions must be made, the politician shifts his responsibility to others instead of carrying out the responsibilities of his office. In like manner, when something goes wrong, it's always the fault of someone else (i.e., the other party).
- Ideology replaces theology. "Truth" becomes, not what God says, but what "The Party" says, because it is no longer "truth" that is sought, but political objectives.
- Man's wisdom is elevated above God's wisdom, and instead of governing according to God's revealed principles, new laws are passed that are designed to buy votes so "The Party" can stay in power.
- The rights of the individual can be sacrificed whenever the needs of the majority, as determined by the state, require it. The state, according to this view, is an organism, and like all organisms it evolves. It assumes new functions, grows steadily more complex, and gets bigger and bigger, all the while shrinking the liberty and the bank accounts of the citizens.
- "Emergency situations" are fabricated in order to pass legislation that citizens would not otherwise allow to be passed. Many examples could be cited; one is the Patriot Act, under which the state has the intrusive privilege to invade our privacy and set aside our constitutional rights.

- Votes are "bought" by providing social services, roads, schools and healthcare funded by increased taxes.
- The legislative agenda is determined by special interest lobbyists (who donate to the politician's campaign), rather than by the needs of the constituents.

Unlike fallen man, Party Politics are not inherently evil. It doesn't take a supernatural act of grace on the part of God to change their actions. They can be transformed into God-honoring entities simply by the guidance and direction of fellow Christians. Needless to say, this idea will be fiercely opposed by the incumbent political hacks and bureaucrats who would be replaced by Christians and forced to find some other means of employment. Being faithful to a particular political party, then, is not, in itself, a problem. The problem comes when the party is not faithful to biblical principles. The psalmist Asaph and the apostle Paul call civil rulers "gods," because they are appointed by God for our good.[14] According to God's eternally perfect plan for the earth, civil rulers stand in the place of God. Hear the counsel of the apostle Peter:

> *Therefore submit yourselves to every ordinance of man for the Lord's sake, whether to the king as supreme, or to governors, as to those who are sent by him for the punishment of evildoers and for the praise of those who do good. For this is the will of God, that by doing good you may put to silence the ignorance of foolish men—as free, yet not using liberty as a cloak for vice, but as bondservants of God. Honor all people. Love the brotherhood. Fear God. Honor the king.*
>
> 1 PETER 2.13-15

So, when we view the sorry state of today's two major political parties, we can only conclude that God is judging us for our sin of ignoring His instructions on how we should govern ourselves. America's sixth President, John Quincy Adams, states the critical importance of governing according to biblical principles:

> *The highest glory of the American Revolution was this: It connected, in one indissoluble bond, the principles of civil government with the principles of Christianity.* [15]

The founder of Pennsylvania and America's first great champion of liberty and peace, William Penn, proclaims that we should not replace biblical principles with partisan principles:

> *Men must choose to be governed by God or*
> *condemn themselves to be governed by tyrants.*

Penn's statement was clearly made in the context of the charter of that province:

> *Whereas the glory of Almighty God, and ye good of mankind, is the reason and end of government, and therefore government in itself is a venerable ordinance of God; and forasmuch as it is principally desired and intended by the proprietary and governor, and the freedom of the province of Pennsylvania, and territories thereunto belonging, to make and establish such laws as shall best preserve true Christian and civil liberty, in opposition to any unchristian, licentious, and unjust practices, whereby God may have His due, Caesar his due,*

*and the people their due, and insolvency and
licentiousness on the other, so that the best and
firmest foundation may be laid for the present and
future happiness both of the governor and people
of this province and territories aforesaid and their
posterity.*

As former Georgia Senator Zell Miller writes,

It's not who's team you're on, its whose side you're on. [16]

Miller's point is critically important. There are some good
Christian legislators on both sides of the isle, but whether
they are Democrats, Republicans or Independents should be
of secondary importance. Of primary concern to voters is
whether a candidate is a Christocrat! Whether a Christian
legislator refuses to factor in biblical principles to his decision-
making because he is ashamed of his Lord, Savior, and King,
Jesus Christ, or because he has never
been trained to, he should realize that
in both instances he is apostatizing from
the Christian faith. Put another way, he
is denying God! The first commandment
admonishes us to, "Have no other gods
before Me." [17] In complete contradiction
to this, non-Christians encourage us
to be pluralists, by saying, "This isn't
a 'religious' matter, it's a 'real world'
matter." But what they are asking us to
do is to worship their god, the state, not
our God, the triune God of the Bible.

*Polytheism leads to
relativism (all moral
codes are equal);
relativism leads to
humanism (man
makes his own laws);
and humanism leads
to statism (the State
best represents
mankind as the
pinnacle of power).*

We must understand that political
pluralism is a process of public moral
deception and judicial deferral. So, what

13

should Christians do in the face of such an ugly political picture? Should we wash our hands of the system because it attracts arrogant, self-serving, unethical people who view themselves as mini-gods? Certainly not! They're simply being consistent with the tenets of their non-Christian worldview. Were it not for our negligence and lethargy, indeed our apostasy from God in cultural matters, these politicians could easily be replaced by Christian statesman. Instead of cleaning our hands of any involvement in politics, we should clean up the current political scene by raising its ethics to conform to biblical principles. George Washington provides this excellent advice:

> *If to please the people we offer what we ourselves*
> *disapprove, how can we afterward defend our work?*
> *Let us raise a standard to which the wise and honest*
> *can repair. The event is in the hand of God.* [18]

Eleven hundred years before the birth of Christ the prophet Samuel proclaimed,

> *He who rules over men righteously, who rules in the*
> *fear of God, is as the light of the morning when the*
> *sun rises, a morning without clouds, when the tender*
> *grass springs out of the earth, through sunshine after*
> *rain.* 2 SAMUEL 23.3-4

I doubt very seriously whether anyone would metaphorically describe their local, state or federal legislators as "a morning without clouds." The more likely description would be "we're having a very overcast day, with a threat of a tornado!" How, then, do we follow Jethro's advice to Moses to:

*...select from all the people able men, such as fear
God, men of truth, hating covetousness; and place
such over them to be rulers of thousands, rulers of
hundreds, rulers of fifties, and rulers of tens.*

EXODUS 18.21-22

The first step in doing this is to have a proactive plan, and
not wait for the parties to give us their choices for candidates.
This may be an unsettling thought, but in the event we can't
convince Christians with developed worldviews to run for
office, we may have to run for the office ourselves! The
following checklist offers some suggestions for qualifications
to look for in potential candidates.

CHECKLIST FOR EVALUATING A CANDIDATE

- He has a regenerated heart and therefore seeks truth
  rather than prestige or personal profit and power.
  DEUTERONOMY 1.17; 2 CHRONICLES 19.6-7
- He has a humble attitude and will not succumb to
  flattery or be bought by favors or bribery. DEUTERONOMY
  16.19
- He trusts in Christ's sovereign control of His Kingdom
  and puts the best interests of the people (God's interests)
  above the pressures of private and special interests.
  DEUTERONOMY 17.17; LEVITICUS 19.15; PSALM 118.9
- He demonstrates a godly lifestyle, governing himself and
  his household well. (The personal habits of conduct of
  those who seek office are rightly matters of concern).
  1 TIMOTHY 3.4-5; PROVERBS 25.28
- He exercises sound judgment; he upholds God's
  principles of self and civil government. 1 TIMOTHY 3.6-7;
  MARK 12.16-17
- He "loves righteousness and hates iniquity." EXODUS 18.21

15

When it comes to civil government, what, then, is the basis of our difference from non-Christians? As philosophers like to say, "What is our epistemology?" In other words, how do we know what we know? America was founded when the collective worldview of our country was Christian. As a result, the U.S. Constitution, as well as state constitutions and our civil law codes, reflect Christian principles. So in this regard, if we said, "America needs to return to traditional values," we would be correct. However, every culture has traditional values, (many of which are abhorrent to biblical ethics) so it would be a good idea to forgo the euphemism and say what we mean: "America needs to return to the Christian values which caused God to bless us abundantly."

Those holding the prevailing non-Christian worldview today become very intolerant when we say that Christianity is the only true religious view. "You Christians are just a bunch of narrow-minded fanatics," we are likely to hear. Yet, isn't this exactly what each of us has been called to do regarding the way we live? Jesus commands us to pray that His Father's will "will be done on earth as it is in heaven," [19] and how do we expect to carry out that command if we don't demonstrate to our non-Christian neighbors in our daily walk that we are living exclusively according to biblical principles?

Non-Christians tell us to feel free to believe whatever we want, as long as we leave those "religious" beliefs inside our homes and churches, so they can set the cultural agenda for the "real world." But shouldn't we be telling them to keep their non-Christian beliefs to themselves! The 26th President of the United States, Theodore Roosevelt, says it well:

> *There are those who believe that a new modernity*
> *demands a new morality. What they fail to consider*
> *is the harsh reality that there is no such thing as*
> *a new morality. There is only one morality. All else is*

*immorality. There is only true Christian ethics over
against which stands the whole of paganism.
If we are to fulfill our great destiny as a people, then
we must return to the old morality, the sole morality.*
THEODORE ROOSEVELT, 1858-1919

Instead of turning to the Bible to guide
us in the operations of civil government,
we've turned to the Greek idea that all
being and all reality is the same, with no
distinction being made between created
reality (us) and uncreated reality (God).
Pastor Joe Morecraft explains:

*Contrary to the wishes
of America's founders,
and of Theodore
Roosevelt, pluralism is
the rule of the day.*

*According to this philosophy the ultimate order for
human society is the state. Everything else, including
the church and religion, must be subservient to it.
The citizen belongs to the state, body and soul. The
state must embrace and regulate all of life, including
worship. Plato, the Greek philosopher, taught that
children belong less to their parents than they do to
the city (state). The state is the manifestation of the
divine order of things. In its head, the human and
the divine meet. Therefore man must yield to the
central governmental total allegiance, give up all
thoughts of independence or meaning outside of its
totalitarian authority, and be unquestioningly
devoted to its defense. It is beyond criticism, as it
regulates, plans and orders every facet of human
society.* [20]

Later chapters will discuss worldviews, and the authority
behind them, but in setting the stage for that we should
recognize that by refusing to take a stand for God's absolute
truths during the last 150 years, our republican form of civil

government has degenerated into the form of governing that our Founders feared the most: democracy, or as some refer to it, "government by collective ignorance." 20th century theologian R.J. Rushdoony comments on how the "solution" of democracy has only compounded our cultural problems:

> *Democracy only aggravates the centralization of power into institutional hands, because democracy has no solution to the problem of human depravity and often fails even to admit the problem. The doctrine of the priesthood of all believers, when properly developed, gives a Christian answer to the problem. The centralization of institutional power cannot flourish where priesthood flourishes.* [21]

Now let us contrast Machiavelli's 500-year-old governing principles with Christ's 2,000-year-old principles. We begin by looking at three tactics in common use today:

- Creating Emergencies
- Buying Votes
- Governing According to Smoke & Mirrors

IS IT MACHIAVELL*IAN* OR CHRIST*IAN*
To Create Emergencies?
Machiavelli Principles 7, 17 & 20

7   *Of New Dominions Acquired by the Power of Others, or by Fortune.*

#17   *Of Cruelty and Clemency, and Whether It Is Better to be Loved or Feared*

20   *Whether Fortresses and Other Things Which Princes Often Contrive Are Useful or Injurious*

18

*For you are all sons of God through faith in Christ
Jesus. For as many of you as were baptized into
Christ have put on Christ. There is neither Jew nor
Greek, there is neither slave nor free, there is neither
male nor female; for you are all one in Christ Jesus.
And if you are Christ's, then you are Abraham's seed,
and heirs according to the promise.*

GALATIANS 3.26-29

According to the Christian worldview, the only dividing line among humans is whether or not a person is a Christian. It doesn't matter which side of the tracks you're from, or what ethnic group you're in, or who your daddy is, but only whether you have placed your life in the hands of Jesus Christ.

Non-Christians approach the world from an opposite perspective. They see humans divided along the lines of the "elite," and the "worker bees." The "elite" include civil rulers, media executives, entertainers and superstar athletes, professors, and business executives. They look to themselves to set culture's agenda, while the masses are destined to simply follow along and be happy that they are employed and have various civil government services provided.

Christians know that Christ calls everyone into His Kingdom to perform certain things and equips us accordingly. Therefore no one is "elite." Indeed, those who have been given more abilities are expected to produce greater results.[22] This means that if a person is called to be a civil ruler, generally speaking, Christ will keep him in that position as long as he is faithful to conform his legislation to biblical principles.

According to Machiavelli, who dismisses Christ's sovereign rule over His Kingdom, non-Christian civil rulers can't depend upon God's faithfulness to keep them in office because the masses are "ungrateful, wicked and fickle:"

19

For it may be said of men in general that they are
ungrateful, voluble, dissemblers, anxious to avoid
danger, and covetous of gain; as long as you benefit
them, they are entirely yours; they offer you their
blood, their goods, their life, and their children,
as I have before said, when the necessity is remote;
but when it approaches they revolt. And the prince
who has relied solely on their words, without
making other preparations, is ruined; for the
friendship which is gained by purchase and not
through grandeur and nobility of spirit is bought
but not secured, and at a pinch is not to be
expended in your service. ...Men love at their own
free will, but fear at the will of the prince, and ...a
wise prince must rely on what is in his power and
not on what is in the power of others, and he must
only continue to avoid incurring hatred..."

PRINCIPLE 17

Machiavelli's advice to civil rulers in light of such an untrustworthy constituent is to take matters into their own hands. This is why non-Christian civil rulers live in constant fear of two "arch-enemies:"

1. The ambition of the masses, and
2. The boredom among the masses.

Unless a civil ruler can keep the populace happy some ambitious person will rise up to challenge and possibly defeat him in the next election. On the other hand, if events and circumstances go too well for too long, the populace may get bored and demand a change "for the sake of change," thinking, "Anyone can govern us." In the face of this constant two-pronged fear, non-Christian civil rulers have come up with three antidotes:

1. Keeping the citizenry too busy to think about their deteriorating cultural conditions (through sporting events, work and entertainment).
2. Creating emergencies (and then successfully solving them) to enhance their value in the eyes of the voters.
3. Making citizens dependent upon civil government services so they are less dependent on their own self-government and personal responsibility.

Christian civil rulers see no need to create phony emergencies in order to manipulate voters to keep them in office. Since God tells us He is concerned about the fall of a sparrow and has numbered the very hairs on our heads, [23] we know that He is well aware of what is going on in American politics, and will reward us for our faithful service for Him. In addition, we also have full confidence that:

> God "removes kings, and sets up kings," [24] and is therefore perfectly capable of controlling the results of the ballot box.

Are You a Practical Atheist?

Practical atheists are those who would never dream of saying, "There is no God," yet they live and make daily decisions as though He doesn't exist.

> If God were to accuse you of being a practical atheist would you have enough evidence to clear yourself?

As creatures, we often attempt to act as if we were the Creator (with the ability to determine results), rather than acting as obedient creatures, then resting in the assurance

21

that our Creator will bring about His desired results in His perfect timing as we live and make decisions that conform to biblical principles.

There is a great temptation to trust in ourselves rather than in the Holy Spirit. We too often are prone to measure our faith by our eyes, imagining the only things that can be accomplished are those that seem practical. But, as Paul said to Agrippa, "Why should it be thought a thing incredible with you, that God should raise the dead?" [25]

Whether we can imagine it or not does not diminish God's ability to accomplish His purpose. All we are doing by living according to our limited knowledge is limiting our effectiveness for Him. It is only by following God's revealed instructions that civil rulers will be able to set society's moral tone.

> The difference between God's rules and man's rules is that God's rules always work because He makes them work.

The certainty about God's providence helps us cope with current circumstances, because we know they are just a small part of His overall plan. This is a tremendous advantage over non-Christians who are slaves to current situations, and can only cry out at such times with a frustrated, "Why me?" As Christians, we must incorporate the following seven guidelines into our daily walk:

- Relate our Biblical knowledge to situations and circumstances.
- Center our thoughts upon God, not man.
- Govern our life according to the Word of God.
- Base our faith only upon what God's Word says is possible; not what we may imagine is possible.

- Teach others to observe "all things whatsoever I command you." MATTHEW 28.20
- Base church government and worship upon the principles in God's Word.
- Do what we've been commanded to do, and refrain from doing those things God forbids. [26]

Machiavelli writes,

> *Without doubt princes become great when they overcome difficulties and opposition, and therefore fortune, especially when it wants to render a new prince great. He who has a greater need of gaining a great reputation ...raises up enemies ... o that he may have cause to overcome them ...so that by suppressing them he will augment his greatness.*
>
> PRINCIPLE 20

Is It Machiavell*ian*, or Christ*ian*?

It's Machiavell*ian*
to create emergencies in order to get citizens to support your programs (i.e. The Patriot Act) and to allow you to take personal liberties from them that, under normal (peaceful) circumstances, they would never willingly give up.

It's Christ*ian*
for the civil government to fulfill only those responsibilities that God has assigned it and to not usurp the self-governing spheres of the individual, family and/ or church that are commanded by God to provide education and social programs.

23

He adds,

> *It was, therefore, necessary to disturb the existing condition and bring about disorders in the states of Italy in order to gain secure mastery over a part of them.*   PRINCIPLE 7

The 19th Century Russian philosopher, Karl Marx, takes a page from Machiavelli's book by teaching that the best way for civil rulers to sustain their administrations and to progress toward a utopia is to fight "preventative wars." In other words, to "strike the first blow" against an enemy before he can attack you.

Is It Machiavell*ian*, or Christ*ian*?

It's Machiavell*ian*
to start wars in order to conquer territories so the civil ruler can enlarge his power, and also for him to build confidence among the citizens for his exploits.

It's Christ*ian*
to only fight defensive wars. (See Case Study Five – A Christian Perspective on Just War)

As has been mentioned, non-Christian civil government is all about power—obtaining it as well as retaining it. The question for every scheming non-Christian civil ruler is: "What 'emergency conflict' can I create and promote that the voters will be willing to "fight and die for?" Conversely, the question voters should be asking is:

24

> *Are our civil rulers promoting and advocating policies that are consistent with, or conflicting with, what our fathers "fought and died for?"*

The irony in Machiavelli's non-Christian approach to civil government is that he correctly observes that humans can't be trusted, [27] but then he contradicts himself by instructing throughout *The Prince* that civil rulers can effectively lead their constituents. Is he not including civil rulers among the (fallen and sinful) human race? Just how does the "elite" acquire their "smart gene" that the masses have been unable to obtain? It's difficult to imagine what is sillier: The pompous arrogance on the part of non-Christian civil rulers, or the willingness on the part of Christian voters to actually believe such representatives are looking out for their constituents' best interests.

While non-Christians are busily separating their thoughts and actions from God, we (should be) busily conforming our thoughts and actions to biblical principles. Both Moses and Peter express Jesus' admonition to "Be holy for I am holy," [28] and the only way to do that is to "keep His commandments."[29] Our choice in electing civil rulers is to either elect people who hate God's way of doing things and want to distance themselves farther and farther from His rules, or to elect those who love God's rules and want to conform their decisions to His principles with every passing day. One has a goal to become more corrupt, the other to become more holy. It shouldn't be such a difficult choice for us to make! Pastor Paul McDade contrasts the ultimate motives of Christians and non-Christians:

25

Unregenerate man, however, is an unstable ally. Ultimately, the thing which he seeks to expedite is his own sin and rebellion against God. Therefore to place either the form of civil polity, or the law of the civil state itself upon the foundation of man's reason or nature is to surrender them to unregenerate man. Every appeal to natural law or traditional values in modern Christian circles is a surrender of the gospel.[30]

IS IT MACHIAVELL*IAN* OR CHRIST*IAN* ▚▚▚▚▚▚▚▚▚▚▚▚▚▚▚
To Buy Votes Through Social Services, Roads, Schools & Healthcare?
Machiavelli Principle 9

9   Of Civic Principality

> *The wise prince will seek means by which his subjects will always and in every possible [situation] have need of his government, and then they will always be faithful to him.*

First, consider the Christian principle of obeying the Lord:

> *Now it shall come to pass, if you diligently obey the voice of the LORD your God, to observe carefully all His commandments which I command you today, that the LORD your God will set you high above all nations of the earth.*   DEUTERONOMY 28.1

> *Hear, O Israel: The LORD our God, the LORD is one, You shall love the LORD your God with all your heart, with all your soul, and with all your strength. And these words which I command you*

26

*today shall be in your heart. You shall teach
them diligently to your children, and shall talk of
them when you sit in your house, when you walk by
the way, when you lie down, and when you rise up.
You shall bind them as a sign on your hand, and they
shall be as frontlets between your eyes. You shall
write them on the doorposts of your house and on
your gates.* DEUTERONOMY 6.4-9

Without an absolute standard to which to conform their legislation, political parties focus on partisan issues. As the decibels of demagoguery rise with each piece of proposed legislation, the debates ultimately come down to, "It's us vs. them." Instead of being driven by whether the proposed legislation is constitutional, or ethically the right thing to do, the consideration among both parties is whether or not the proposed legislation will attract enough votes to keep them in office.

Statesmen have been replaced by politicians, and the few remaining statesmen deserve our support, because certainly they must see themselves as being on an island surrounded by sharks.

Sadly, in too many cases, the issue comes down to ethnic voting blocks, instead of Christian ethics.

As mentioned, the tactics of a non-Christian civil ruler boils down to finding a way to make the voters think they can't do without his governance. One way of doing this is to break the Eighth Commandment by "stealing" taxpayer money from another district and using it to build roads, hospitals, and/or to provide a wide array of social services in his district. Congressmen, particularly, like to brag, "For every dollar you sent to Washington, I was able to return $2 for community programs." Apparently no one seems to mind that their representative has just robbed the tax revenues from another state. Perhaps the moral (no pun intended) to this is, "Keep me in office because I am a very effective thief." Notice, again, how Machiavelli puts it:

> *The wise prince will seek means by which his*
> *subjects will always and in every possible condition*
> *of things have need of his government, and then*
> *they will always be faithful to him.* PRINCIPLE 9

Machiavelli's portrayal of civil rulers is drastically different from the one Paul describes in Romans, where he says they are "appointed by God" to be "His ministers" to us "to benefit us," not take advantage of us. Hear his inspired words.

> *Let every soul be subject to the governing author-*
> *ities. For there is no authority except from God,*
> *and the authorities that exist are appointed by God.*
> *... For rulers are not a terror to good works, but to*
> *evil. Do you want to be unafraid of the authority?*
> *Do what is good, and you will have praise from the*
> *same. For he is God's minister to you for good. But*
> *if you do evil, be afraid; for he does not bear the*
> *sword in vain; for he is God's minister, an avenger*
> *to execute wrath on him who practices evil. ...For*
> *because of this you also pay taxes, for they are God's*
> *ministers attending continually to this very thing.*
> ROMANS 13.1,3-4,6

How different God's view of civil rulers is from Machiavelli's view, which encourages legislators and judges to be, in Ezekiel's words, "like wolves," as they go after "dishonest gain." [31] Zephaniah, a contemporary of Ezekiel, 600 hundred years before the birth of Christ, also likened the southern kingdom of Judah's civil rulers to "ravening wolves" because they were not conforming their governance to biblical principles.

Her princes in her midst are roaring lions; her judges are evening wolves that leave not a bone till morning. Her prophets are insolent, treacherous people; her priests have polluted the sanctuary, they have done violence to the law.   ZEPHANIAH 3.3-4

Is It Machiavell*ian*, or Christ*ian*?

It's Machiavell*ian*
for today's civil rulers to "bribe" the electorate by showering them with social services and building roads in their communities, and to exercise long-term control through their most effective long-term weapon, state-mandated government schools. The schools are providing indoctrination into dependence upon state-provided benefits and services, and are, in effect raising "wards of the state" who are incapable of governing themselves or thinking for themselves.

It's Christ*ian*
for parents to be in charge of, and to directly control, the education of their children. In contrast to the false education provided by government schools, true education instructs children in the meaning of life and how to become consistent servants of Christ by incorporating biblical principles into their everyday lifestyle. True education fosters self-governing capital-istic principles instead of dependence upon either socialist or fascist state-provided services.

Occasionally, the voters will become so fed up with a political party that the political party will turn to a relatively unknown candidate and position him as a free-thinking independent who will not carry out the policies of the party, and who will instead be more concerned with the voters' priorities. Of course this is a lie, because the party would never support someone who would not agree to further their legislative interests. Still, it makes a compelling story line, and only proves that both parties realize how self-serving they are and that they have no interest in serving those who put them in office.

The counsel of Machiavelli in these instances is this:

> *When the nobility see they are unable to resist the people, they unite in exalting one of their number and creating him prince, so as to be able to carry out their own designs under the shadow of his authority. The populace, on the other hand, when unable to resist the nobility, endeavor to exalt and create a prince in order to be protected by his authority. He who becomes prince by help of the nobility has greater difficulty in maintaining his power than he who is raised by the populace, for he is surrounded by those who think themselves his equals, and is thus unable to direct or command as he pleases. But one who is raised to leadership by popular favor finds himself alone, and has no one, or very few, who are not ready to obey him.*
>
> PRINCIPLE 9

Is It Machiavell*ian*, or Christ*ian*?

It's Machiavell*ian*
to stress pragmatism by urging voters to vote only
for the candidates of major parties, because "the
independent party candidate probably won't win, and
even if he does, he will have no support in Congress (or
the State house)." In other words, "Choose the lesser of
two evils."

It's Christ*ian*
to vote for the candidate that most closely conforms
his platform to biblical principles and to trust in God's
sovereignty to place in office the civil ruler we deserve.
As Stonewall Jackson said, "The duty is ours, the results
are God's."

IS IT MACHIAVELL*IAN* OR CHRIST*IAN* ▆▆▆▆▆▆▆▆▆▆▆
To Govern According to Smoke & Mirrors?
Machiavelli Principle 18

#18   *In What Way Princes Must Keep Faith*

> *The princes of Judah are like those who remove a
> landmark; I will pour out My wrath on them like
> water. Ephraim is oppressed and broken in
> judgment, because he willingly walked by human
> precept.*   HOSEA 5.10-11

As has been established, Machiavelli sees it as impossible
to be an effective civil ruler by applying Christian principles
to one's governance. However, that does not mean that he
doesn't recognize the need on the part of voters for their

31

leaders to be honorable and trustworthy persons. While Machiavelli cites the need for the legislator to "have a mind disposed to adapt itself according to the wind ... not deviating from good, if possible, but be able to do evil if constrained," he nevertheless is adamant that the civil ruler should "seem" like he is full of integrity.

> *A prince ...should seem to be all mercy, faith, integrity, humanity, and religion. And nothing is more necessary than to seem to have this last quality, for men in general judge more by the eyes than by the hands, for everyone can see, but very few can feel.*   PRINCIPLE 18

Machiavelli explains his reasoning:

> *Everybody sees what you appear to be, but few feel what you are, and those few will not dare to oppose themselves to the many, who have the majesty of the state to defend them.*   PRINCIPLE 18

This Machiavellian Principle is the epitome of approaching the world with a non-Christian worldview and lifestyle which is not confined by any absolute ethical standards. Machiavelli has no qualms about urging civil rulers to be a "skillful pretender and dissembler," who "seem" to have the virtues of good faith, charity, humanity and religion. The reason for his counsel is that he believes that the masses "are so simple and so subject to present needs that he who deceives in this way will always find those who will let themselves be deceived."

> *And if all men were good, this precept would not be good; but since they are wicked ...*
>   PRINCIPLE 18

It would be hoped that Christian civil rulers would see the fallacy of such hypocrisy.

This is to view the world as though it were a *bi*verse (with many co-equal ethical views), not a *uni*verse (with one absolutely true set of ethics). Are we a simply a "force of nature," as Machiavelli suggests, or a "force of God?" Are we an evolved "animal," or a "creature of God?" Can cultural salvation come only through the state? We should hope that Christian civil rulers would be on their guard to not become caught in the trap of governing by "smoke and mirrors" –presenting themselves as something they are not, and that they would not resort to using "cruelty and fraud to secure themselves" in their political offices (Principle 18).

> To attempt to live by Christian ethics on Sundays and Political ethics Monday through Saturday is to approach life with one foot in God's camp and one foot in man's camp.

Christian civil government is based upon biblical principles, not political expediencies. To opt for political expediency is to opt out of trusting in and relying upon God's sovereign control of His creation. It is to show our true colors as to just which god we believe, and to demonstrate to all who are observing us (including the triune God of Scripture) exactly to whom it is that we trust our soul.

Whether we're a legislator or not, we can all rest in full confidence that it takes only three votes to be a winner in life: Those of the Father, Son and Holy Spirit. May we never be ashamed to contrast the best advice that man has to offer with the best advice God has to offer!

Is It Machiavell*ian*, or Christ*ian*?

It's Machiavell*ian*
to approach life with no absolute ethical standard (easy, since non-Christians don't believe in absolutes!). Therefore, since most people realize that it is better to treat others "fairly" and "honestly," and to behave in a "moralistic" manner, non-Christian civil rulers find it expedient to talk as though they are moralistic and have the interests of their constituents at heart.

It's Christ*ian*
to incorporate biblical principles into our approach to life. Since we believe in absolutes and absolute truth, we have no doubt that the best way to treat others is according to what God says, not according to the latest opinion poll. Instead of treating others in a moralistic manner, we treat others in a Christian manner, because that is the only true way to live and govern ourselves.

Christian Legislative Building Blocks

In order to turn our culture around, we must frame the debate in terms of God's ideas vs. man's ideas.

Sadly, in too many cases, the issue comes down to ethnic voting blocks, instead of Christian ethics.

The issue for non-Christian politicians is not to improve our culture, but rather to get an advantage over their political opponents.

The difference between God's rules and man's rules is that God's rules always work because He makes them work.

Are our civil rulers promoting and advocating policies that are consistent with, or conflicting with, what our fathers "fought and died for?"

Contrary to the wishes of America's founders, pluralism is now the rule of the day.

God "removes kings, and sets up kings," [32] and is therefore perfectly capable of controlling the results of the ballot box.

To attempt to live by Christian ethics on Sundays and Political ethics Monday through Saturday is to approach life with one foot in God's camp and one foot in man's camp.

Polytheism leads to relativism ("all moral codes are equal"); relativism leads to humanism ("man makes his own laws"); and humanism leads to statism ("the State best represents mankind as the pinnacle of power").

35

NOTES

1   1 Corinthians 3.19-20
2   McDade, Rev. Paul R., *Study Guide for Wines*, Rev. E.C., *The Roots of the American Republic*, (The Plymouth Rock Foundation, 1977),
3   Matthew 6.10
4   Calvin, John, *Commentary on Samuel* (Baker Book House, 1981)
5   See The Barna Group, www.barna. org
6   *Choose This Day: God's Instructions on How to Select Leaders*, and *The Christian Civil Ruler's Handbook* by Buddy Hanson, (Hanson Group), www.graceandlaw. com, not to mention *The Christian Prince*.
7   Bastiat, Frederic, *The Law*, (Foundation for Economic Education, [1850], 1990) p. 35

8   *ibid.*, p.39
9   *ibid.*, p.43
10   *ibid.*, pp.51-52
11   *ibid.*, p.25
12   *ibid.*, p.8
13   *ibid.*, p.21
14   Psalm 82; Romans 13
15   Federer, William J., *America's God and Country: Encyclopedia of Quotations* (Amerisearch, Inc., 2000) p. 18. Federer provides a date for the quotation (July 4, 1821), and gives the source as follows: John Wingate Thornton, *The Pulpit of the American Revolution* 1860 (reprinted NY: Burt Franklin, 1860; 1970), p. XXIX.
16   Miller, Sen. Zell, *A National Party No More: The Conscience of a Conservative Democrat* (Stroud & Hall, 2004)
17   Exodus 20.3
18   George Wash-

ington, 1787 Constitutional Convention, in Federer, *op.cit.*
19   Matthew 6.10
20   Morecraft, Joe, *Fundamentals of Christianity*, Vol. II, (to be announced), pp. 144-45
21   Rushdoony, R.J., *Institutes of Biblical Law*, (P & R Publishing, 1973), p.764
22   Luke 12.48
23   Matthew 10.29-30
24   Daniel 2.21
25   Acts 26.8
26   Hanson, *The Christian Civil Ruler's Handbook* (Hanson Group), p. 14
27   Genesis 8.21; Isaiah 53.6; Jeremiah 17.9; Matthew 15.19
28   Leviticus 11.44-45; 1 Peter 1.16
29   John 14.21,23
30   McDade, *op. cit.*, p. i
31   Ezekiel 22.27
32   Daniel 2.21

THE
CITIZEN'S ROLE

2

OUR CALLING & MISSION

*Then Jesus came to them and said, «All authority in
heaven and on earth has been given to me. Therefore
go and make disciples of all nations, baptizing them
in the name of the Father and of the Son and of the
Holy Spirit, and teaching them to obey everything
I have commanded you. And surely I am with you
always, to the very end of the age.»*

MATTHEW 28.18-20

*HELP WANTED: Someone to represent Me. You don't
have to give your best effort, just be nice, polite and
don't be particularly dedicated or passionate about
performing your duties.*

It's safe to say that none of us would want such a milque-
toast individual to represent us, so why should we imagine
that the Creator of the universe would be satisfied with such a
person? Before reading further, pause and reflect on this very
basic question. Think about why it is that so many sincere,
well-meaning Christians attempt to fulfill their calling to
Christ with such a blasé attitude. Why is it that only one in
seven Christians relies on the Bible as his moral compass? [1]
Doesn't Jesus warn us that attempting to serve Him inside
our homes and churches and to serve the state outside of
them will result in our "loving one and hating the other?" [2]

Was Jesus mistaken in giving this warning? Should we ask Him to correct His "mistake," or does the fault lie with us—which means it is we who need to repent? As silly as this line of questioning seems, it's high time we realized how ridiculous our attitude toward serving our Lord, Savior and King must look to Jesus as He observes our every thought, word and decision. After all, it is only by His mercy and grace that we have been called into His Kingdom. With that calling we have received a clear-cut and objective mission for our lives, which is to bring about God's will on earth as it is in heaven. We accomplish this mission by evangelism: telling others how they can join Christ's team in carrying out this mission, and by clarifying to our brothers and sisters who are already on the team how they can use their God-given skills to be better servants (disciples) in Christ's Kingdom.

Each of us is expected to incorporate this purpose and message into every phase of our lifestyle, so that those who observe us can tell that we live according to an explicit and uncompromising set of ethics. For most of us this means that during our working hours our actions must speak louder than our words, because to take time away from our assigned work to talk about Christ would be to steal time from our employer (breaking the eighth commandment).

Christian legislators, however, can and should express biblical reasons for supporting or opposing proposed legislation. This will not only serve to clarify how a Christian civil ruler should act, but will also cast a light on the hypocrisy of those who profess to be Christians, but who rule as though they are merely non-Christian conservatives.

The words of Jesus at the beginning of this chapter are as familiar as they are misunderstood. Many Christians would say that Jesus is giving Marching Orders to His disciples and to all Christians afterwards to take the gospel message to all nations. He is certainly telling us to be evangelistic, but He is also commanding us to make disciples. When He commands us to "teach them to obey everything I have commanded you," He is asking for a lot more on our part than handing out gospel tracts or giving a copy of the New Testament to graduates of a new membership class at church. Teaching "everything" clearly means everything, in both the Old and New Testaments.

Our calling, then, not only includes evangelizing, but discipling. Discipling is hard. It takes time. It includes answering questions, which forces us to stay on our toes regarding Bible study and even saying, "That's a good question, let me do a little research and get back with you." Again, this requires time and a real dedication to our Christian faith. Nevertheless, this is what Jesus commands.

Notice also that He assures us He is not only alive and well on planet earth, but that He is in complete control of all situations and circumstances. "All authority" in heaven and earth has been given to Him. So when Jesus commands us to go and make disciples (not just converts) of all nations—and not just of a few converts in each nation, that's a tall order! But we can have confidence that we will be successful in our endeavors because He never asks us to do anything which He can't enable us to handle! [3] In addition, we not only have the King of kings and Lord of lords in our corner, but also His Father and the Holy Spirit. If knowing this doesn't make you want to attempt to "leap tall buildings in a single bound," you might want to check your pulse!

Our Lord, Savior and King works this perfect and unchanging plan in four self-governing spheres: individual, family, church, and state. As mentioned in the first chapter, each sphere has its particular responsibilities and is directly accountable to God. These spheres, which are discussed in chapter five, are designed to work together to completely transform culture.

Regardless of our vocation, whether we be a legislator, judge, home schooling mom, a student or a CEO, we can be confident that God has given us specific gifts and abilities which we can use to bring honor and glory to Him as we go about our daily duties. I started to write "daily routine," but when we realize that we have been called to turn the world rightside up, it should be very apparent that there is nothing "routine" about our purpose, calling and mission.

The former Prime Minister of the Netherlands, Dr. Abraham Kuyper, explains:

> *There is not a square inch of ground in heaven or on earth or under the earth in which there is peace between Christ and Satan. ...No one can stand back, refusing to become involved. He is involved from the day of his birth and even from before his birth. Jesus said, "He who is not with Me is against Me, and he that gathers not with Me, scatters."* [4] *If you say that you are "not involved" you are in fact involved on Satan's side.* [5]

Sometimes when adults become Christians they think that they should look for a "Christian" occupation; but as Dr. Kuyper points out, we don't have to be concerned about working for a business that has "Christian" in its name. Every legitimate and ethical vocation is perfectly suitable for fulfilling our calling to be "salt and light" in our community by demonstrating God's will in our situation and circumstances.[6]

19th Century philosopher and social activist Henry David Thoreau remarks on the unique significance of being able to "affect the quality of each day":

*It is something to be able to paint a particular
picture, or to carve a statue, and do so to make a few
objects beautiful; but it is far more glorious to carve
and paint the very atmosphere and medium through
which we look. To affect the quality of the day—that
is the highest of the arts.* "WHERE I LIVE"

The palette which Christ has given us with which to
"paint" each day is made up of a narrowly defined ethical
standard that accepts no additions or deletions. If the
thought of being "narrow-minded" toward behavior (ours
and others') is unsettling to you it is only because non-
Christians have been more successful in conforming us to
their "ever-changing, anything goes, subjective ethics" than
we have been in conforming them to Christ's "non-changing,
objective" ethics. They attempt to heap guilt on us by telling
us to be "tolerant," but don't seem concerned about their
intolerance in preventing us from praying publicly before
sporting events, having Christian displays at Christmas, or
even using the word Christmas, or the color green! Of course,
the list of their intolerant acts could go on—which emphasizes
how dishonest non-Christians are in their accusations of
"intolerance" against us.

We must get over the attitude that it is not right to impose
our beliefs on others. Had earlier Christians acted as we have
for the last few generations, we would still be sacrificing children
(instead of baptizing them), and rather than having someone
over to supper, we likely would be having them for supper.

The reason we should not feel guilty nor be hesitant
about promoting God's laws is that all law is "religious."
Someone may object: "Wait a minute, law is law, and religion
is religion." But it should be remembered that a religion is
nothing more than a system of beliefs and values, and that a
society's laws simply reflect that system of beliefs. For example,

43

if law is based upon man's reason, then man's reason is the god of that society. In regard to this point, we should not be hesitant to remind our non-Christian neighbors that the 7th Circuit Court of Appeals has ruled, "Atheism is religion ..." The court ruled an inmate's First Amendment rights were violated because the prison refused to allow him to create a study group. In 1961 (in "Torasco v. Watkins") the Supreme Court described "secular humanism" as a religion, and said that a religion need not be based on a belief in the existence of a supreme being.

When we say we believe in God, but conform our daily decisions to another god (e.g., man, science, the state, etc.), we're breaking the first commandment by worshiping multiple gods and being blasphemous toward the one, true, triune God of the Bible. Our duty and calling from God is to "... continue in the things [we] have learned and become convinced of." [7] This optimistic long-range outlook of Paul reminds us of his words to the Galatians: "And let us not lose heart in doing good, for in due time we shall reap if we do not grow weary." [8] In other words, there is absolutely no need to compromise with a "movable" kingdom, [9] when ours is the Kingdom that cannot be moved." [10]

> By not "imposing" Christian beliefs on others, we allow them to "impose" their beliefs on us.

Pastor Morecraft relates our calling and purpose in life to Christ's three-fold office as prophet, priest and king, and indicates that we are to image Him by resuming the task of fulfilling the original calling of Adam:

> *Adam was created in the image of God to exercise dominion over the earth, as a prophet, interpreting life in terms of God's Word, as a priest, dedicating all of life to the glory of God, and as a king, subduing all of life under God. Jesus Christ came to*

earth to reveal the true image of God, to restore
that image in His people, and to put man-in-Christ
back in the right position to carry out his original
Creation Mandate. [11]

When we consider what a magnificent and meaningful
calling we have, we, like David, should humbly exclaim to
Christ,

When I consider Your heavens, the work of
Your fingers, the moon and the stars, which
You have ordained, what is man that You
are mindful of him, and the son of man that
You visit him? For You have made him a
little lower than the angels, and You have
crowned him with glory and honor. You
have made him to have dominion over the
works of Your hands; You have put all things
under his feet.   PSALM 8.3-6

> *We are living in God's world and we must live by His rules.*

IT'S TIME SOMEBODY READ THE DIRECTIONS!

19th Century Scottish writer and historian Thomas
Carlyle admonishes us with this wise counsel: "Our grand
business is not to see what lies dimly in the distance, but to
do what clearly lies at hand." [12] We must stop blowing an
"uncertain trumpet," for

If the trumpet makes an uncertain sound,
who will prepare for battle?   1 CORINTHIANS 14.8

When we realize that our salvation is not a nightcap, but
a helmet," [13] we should be motivated to "walk in a manner
worthy of God who calls us into His kingdom and glory," [14]
by "being fruitful in every good work, and increasing in the

45

knowledge of God; strengthening with all might, according to His glorious power, unto all patience and long suffering with joyfulness." [15] A psalmist provides the contrast between the worldview and lifestyle of Christians and non-Christians:

> *Blessed is the man who does not walk in the counsel*
> *of the wicked or stand in the way of sinners or*
> *sit in the seat of mockers. But his delight is in the*
> *law of the Lord, and on His law he meditates day*
> *and night. He is like a tree planted by streams of*
> *water, which yields its fruit in season and whose*
> *leaf does not wither. Whatever he does prospers.*
> *Not so the wicked! They are like chaff that the wind*
> *blows away. Therefore the wicked will not stand*
> *in the judgment, not sinners in the assembly of the*
> *righteous. For the Lord watches over the way of the*
> *righteous, but the way of the wicked will perish.*
>
> PSALM 1

When the Pilgrims stepped off the Mayflower and onto the shore of Plymouth, Massachusetts, they proclaimed that the reason they had made the perilous journey across the ocean to America was

> *...for the glory of God and advancement of the*
> *Christian faith* [16]

As we go about confronting and changing the momentum of our current ungodly cultural agenda by stepping out boldly for Christ's Kingdom,

Let us not fear how men will respond to the truth, but fear how God will respond if we compromise.

Commentator John Lofton counsels,

> *Christians should stop worrying about what "the world" thinks about them—the world, after all, crucified our Lord—and start obeying what God commands them to do!*

Great opportunities for meaningful service surround us, and while Christ will bring about His will, with or without us, why would we want to be excluded!

> *For if you remain silent at this time, relief and deliverance will arise for the Jews from another place, and you and your father's house will perish. And who knows whether you have come to the kingdom for such a time as this?* ESTHER 4.14

What about Persecution?

Will we meet resistance and persecution as we go about our efforts to "un-quo the status?"[17] Sure, we will! God promises that very thing immediately after the sin of Adam and Eve. Satan is told that God will place enmity between Eve's seed (Christians) and his seed (non-Christians) and that his seed will "bruise us on the heel" (a non-lethal injury), but that Eve's seed will "bruise him on the head (a killing blow). [18] This promise is as exhilarating for Christians as it is devastating for non-Christians. Satan is told from the get-go that he is a defeated foe. All he has is smoke and mirrors as he tries to convince us that he is in control of events on earth. So, if you didn't know it before, the cat is now out of the bag, and you can

> *Begin making Satan's worst nightmare come true by basing your daily decisions upon the biblical principles you already profess to believe.*

47

Exactly how our obedience will be used by Christ to accomplish His purposes is something we will have to discuss in heaven. Thankfully, He has called us to be in the obedience business, while He takes care of and controls the results. What we do know is that

> Living and governing ourselves according to biblical principles brings order out of the chaotic "law of the jungle" that our evolutionary non-Christians believe in and according to which they legislate.

Since we're all living in the midst of it, we don't have to be reminded of the diabolical differences between a non-Christian's purpose for life and that of a Christian. Non-Christians, with their self-centered interests, are motivated to amass power and control while bringing honor and esteem to themselves. This was the self-expressed motivation behind the building of the Tower of Babel: "Let us make a name for ourselves."[19] The four examples in the chart on the following page should more than suffice.

While non-Christians are striving to build a name for themselves by serving their interests, we should be striving to build a name for God by serving His interests.

God has "written His laws on our hearts and promises to be our God," so instead of being concerned about the negative consequences that may or may not result by obediently following Him, our focus should be on the sure and certain blessings that He promises to us and to our children and their children.[20] Non-Christians, who scoff at our absolute ethics as being archaic, will one day be destroyed by their own wisdom!

Man's Ideology Determines His Purpose

✔ Everybody does his own thing (anarchy)
✔ Man is an economic unit to fund the state's priorities (communism/fascism/socialism)
✔ The more central government expands, the more bureaucrats usurp the liberties of citizens, forcing them to conform to their regulations, instead of being self-governing.
✔ Law becomes an instrument of social reform, as courts usurp the responsibilities of elected representatives by imposing their ethical agenda upon the populace. Lawmakers outwardly complain, but inwardly refuse to impose constitutional restraints upon the courts, by using rhetoric that the court system is "running away" with our constitutional rights, when the truth is that the legislators are "running away" from their responsibilities to police the courts because they agree with the courts' rulings and are complicit with them in their unconstitutional and anti-American decrees.

Do not be deceived, God is not mocked; for whatever a man sows, that he will also reap.

GALATIANS 6.7

Their attempt to remove Christ from His throne is similar to attempting to remove the law of gravity from physics. It simply cannot be done. The Creator of the earth may allow a country, or several countries, to live in darkness for a time in order to suit His eternally perfect purposes, but sooner or later Christ will raise His scepter, through the obedient members of His kingdom, and "crush our enemies under our feet." [21]

As people who have been rescued from eternal separation from our Creator, we are no longer compelled to have selfish ambition, but now have the will of Christ imbedded in our hearts. [22] So let us join in taking part in Christ's victory on earth by making Satan's worst nightmare come true!

May we "Stand firm, letting nothing deter us from giving ourselves fully to the work of the Lord, because we have been promised that our labor in the Lord is not in vain!"[23] As we refuse to be conformed to the non-Christian agenda of the current collective worldview, [24] we will be able to say with Joseph,

> *How then could I do this great evil and sin against*
> *the Lord?*   GENESIS 39.9

MAKING A POSITIVE DIFFERENCE

We are creatures of the triune God of Scripture, who communicates to us through His Word about how to live and govern ourselves. We have been called into Christ's Kingdom to make a positive difference in the world! Christ promises to bless us and future generations if we obey His objective rules of behavior, and to discipline us if we disobey them. Christ has given us an easy-to-understand, black and white ethical code through which we can filter our daily decision-making. Since we are able to correctly determine good and evil, and since God's counsel has no "shades of grey," we know without doubt how we should live and what consequences to expect from life.

Therefore, if we attempt to live and govern ourselves in any other way than by conforming our actions to Scripture, we are living a non-Christian lifestyle.

Who's Noticing Whom?

As you go about your daily divine duties (non-Christians would refer to these as their daily "routine,") do your lifestyle and worldview reflect the biblical principles which you profess to be absolutely true, or do they reflect the relative ethics of whatever is currently in vogue in the collective non-Christian culture? Non-Christians have a very routine existence: all ethics are up for grabs and are awaiting the next politically correct fad that exalts personal autonomy and deifies individual reasoning. Such mindless ethical relativity makes non-Christians unable to prove that the behavior of Mother Teresa is better or worse than that of a suicide bomber. This is not to say that they don't have opinions about whose behavior it would be better to copy, but that's all they have. So, regardless of how strongly they may hold a particular belief, they cannot definitively say that someone with a different belief (opinion) is wrong. The futility and utter foolishness of basing one's life upon a relative ethical code, is proven by their attempt to proclaim value judgments from their list of politically-correct mantras. If they were consistent with their ungodly beliefs, they would make no such proclamations. However, even though they are stupid when it comes to approaching life, they aren't crazy. They know that somebody has to issue rules of behavior, or else we would all live in chaos and anarchy. This relegates them to a life of insisting on the one hand that "you can't tell me how to live," and insisting on the other hand, "this is the way you should live!" In the double-speak of George Orwell, "Some things are so stupid, only intellectuals can believe them." [25] So the next time you hear a non-Christian make a biblically correct proclamation, you should inform him that he is borrowing from our ethical standard. And, if you really want to get under his skin, you could say, "Welcome to Christianity!"

Our daily divine duties have been given to us with a personal guarantee (from our Creator) that they will lead to a successful overthrow of the non-Christian cultural agenda.

It should not be surprising that God's ethical standards have a proven track record. Throughout history, civilizations that have based their civil government and personal lifestyles upon biblical principles have achieved peace and personal liberty as a direct result of their self-government. Those that have based their civil government upon a centralized, top-down system see their citizens being tyrannized by dictators.

Now that we've clarified the distinction between living according to God's terms and living by our terms, we should ask ourselves: "Who's leading whom?" If the non-Christians with whom you come in contact each day are not upset with your lifestyle, you're not leading them, but are following them. Instead of presenting a lifestyle based upon biblical principles which will lead them to successfully govern their actions, and demonstrating to them why they should conform to God's ways, you are following their ungodly principles by conforming your ethical behavior to their standard. Since God promises that His servants will be persecuted in some form or other as a result of following His will, the fact that a Christian is not persecuted is a good indication that he is living according to man's will.

When we fail to understand that non-Christians have a "take no prisoners" attitude toward life's agenda, we make the critical mistake of thinking we can lead them to Christ by not rocking the boat with biblical principles and impressing them with our "niceness." We imagine that our good manners will either cause them to want to stop their pushy way of living and convert to Christianity, or else, that they will simply appreciate our "niceness" and leave us alone. Even if we didn't have Jesus' instructions to the contrary, such reasoning on our part would be a stretch, since non-Christians can't definitively define "niceness" (or anything else). Jesus tells us that such non-confrontation on our part will cause us to be "trampled under their feet." [26]

What would you rather be: A member of Christ's army who is "knocking down the gates of hell," [27] or a "doormat for Jesus?" [28] This doesn't mean that we should carry our Bibles around saying, "Thus says the Lord!" It simply means that we should live each day as well as we are able in conforming to biblical principles. A Christian lifestyle is the most effective sermon a non-Christian will hear because it works! People are attracted to success. They will ask you for your secret to success, whether that be with your spouse, your children or your vocation.

This is also not to say that Christian legislators should be rigid and inflexible in their efforts to pass God-honoring legislation. In today's situation, in which many legislators are not Christians and a sizeable number of the Christians don't have a developed Christian worldview, compromise will be the only way to get some good legislation passed. As long as such compromise is confined to the methods and means of passing legislation, but not to the absolute biblical principles, the Christian legislator will be on solid ground.

It is true that we're swimming upstream by going against the flow of culture, but because of the Christian principles upon which America was founded, at least we have a skeletal framework within which to operate. When the Israelites went into the Promised Land they didn't have this luxury. There were no churches. There were not even any hypocrites. Everyone was a heathen and didn't know any other way to live. Yet, what did God instruct Moses to tell them? Let's take a listen.

> *Surely I have taught you statutes and judgments,*
> *just as the LORD my God commanded me, that you*
> *should act according to them in the land which you*
> *go to possess. Therefore be careful to observe them;*
> *for this is your wisdom and your understanding*

> *in the sight of the peoples who will hear all these*
> *statutes, and say, "Surely this great nation is a wise*
> *and understanding people. For what great nation is*
> *there that has God so near to it, as the LORD our*
> *God is to us, for whatever reason we may call upon*
> *Him? And what great nation is there that has such*
> *statutes and righteous judgments as are in all this*
> *law which I set before you this day?"*
>
> DEUTERONOMY 4.5-8

"If you will stick to your knitting," Moses instructs them, "they will notice your lifestyle and ask you to explain your worldview to them." Are your neighbors noticing your worldview and taking cues on how to live, or are you noticing their worldview and taking cues from them on how to live? It's one way or the other. Every day, in every way, in everything we do, we are either imaging Christ or Satan. We should never forget this. To go through life on cruise control, is to go through life in a non-Christian manner, with an end result of bringing honor and glory to Satan, not Christ. Indeed, Jesus makes a promise in Genesis (to Abraham) and in Matthew's gospel that our obedience to Him in our everyday decision-making will knock down the gates of hell." [29] He also tells us in Luke's gospel to "occupy until He returns." [30] Neither of these admonitions from Jesus provides the slightest indication that we should live lives of quiet desperation, while not rocking culture's ethical boat.

The renowned sports writer Grantland Rice provides a fitting conclusion for this section:

> *To have your name inscribed up there is greater yet by far,*
> *than all the halls of fame down here & every man-made star.*
> *This crowd on earth, they soon forget the heroes of the past,*
> *they cheer like mad until you fall & that's how long you last.*

I tell you, friend, I would not trade my name, however small,
if written there beyond the stars in that celestial hall
for any famous name on earth, or glory that they share.
I'd rather be an unknown here and have my name up there.

IS IT MACHIAVELLIAN OR CHRISTIAN ▓▓▓▓▓▓▓▓▓▓▓▓▓▓
Introducing a "New Order" Of Things
Machiavelli Principle 6

#6   *Of New Dominions Which have Been Acquired*
By One's Own Arms and Ability

> *And do not be conformed to the world, but be trans-*
> *formed by the renewing of your mind, that you may*
> *prove what is that good and acceptable and perfect*
> *will of God.*   ROMANS 12.2

> *How then could I do this great wickedness and sin*
> *against God?*   GENESIS 39.9

> **It must be considered that there is nothing more**
> **difficult to carry out, nor more doubtful of success,**
> **nor more dangerous to handle, than to initiate a**
> **new order of things. For the reformer has enemies**
> **in all those who profit by the old order, and only**
> **lukewarm defenders in all those who would profit**
> **by the new order, this lukewarmness arising partly**
> **from fear of their adversaries, who have the laws**
> **in their favor; and partly from the incredulity of**
> **mankind, who do not truly believe in anything new**
> **until they have had actual experience of it.**
>   PRINCIPLE 6

At some point in our lives each of us has experienced utter
failure at introducing something new. It might have been a

new product or service, a new meal, or hairstyle, or just a new way to do a familiar activity. The significant thing is not that our project or idea failed, but that what Machiavelli says is true: We're all creatures of habit, and even though we may admit that something is not producing the level of results we would hope, we stay with it because "the devil we know is better than the devil we don't know." Political parties have been known to use this human character trait in an effort to turn a negative opinion of an incumbent into a positive by saying, "At least you know where Bill stands on the issues. Who knows where Joe (the unknown challenger) stands!"

In politics this "fear of the unknown" is compounded by bureaucrats and legislators who are benefiting from the present order of things and will do practically anything to resist a new order, even if they know it might do a better job of serving the public. So, from man's perspective, Machiavelli's counsel is very practical. By now, you know I'm going to ask this, but I'm still going to ask it: "What if the 'new order' of things represents a closer conformity to God's will?"

At this particular time, when we're living in the midst of a collective non-Christian worldview, it is difficult to find any way of doing business, legislating, or anything else that does not conform to Satan's will. But if we turn this present reality on its head (as Paul commands us!), we find unlimited opportunities to "enlarge the place of our tent."[31] The winning edge we have over non-Christians is that they have only themselves and their own faulty wisdom and reasoning ability. At best, they can figure out a "truism" based upon observing human nature, but they cannot arrive at a "truthful" solution. Indeed, many non-Christians don't even believe "truth" exists.

> A Christian legislator cannot "make up" for his sinful disobedience of supporting ungodly legislation by doing extra activities in his church.

On the other hand, we know that truth exists, and we know what it is! In addition, Jesus promises throughout Scripture to bless our obedient decisions and actions and curse our disobedience.[32] In other words, we do not live in a random universe where "good" and "evil" happen for no apparent reason. God created an orderly universe and promises to reward us with consequences based upon our behavior. His repeated assurances of victory for Christians on earth, along with some most remarkable object lessons, serve to cement our faith with confidence.

It is impossible for non-Christians to "renew their minds" because they are still in the same natural state in which each of us came into the world. We, however, have been graciously and mercifully given a supernatural heart transplant, which means that we not only can, but are expected to renew our minds away from our former unholy method of thinking that produced nothing but unholy decisions and actions. We have been called to present a holy lifestyle in every situation and circumstance, and there is no biblical basis for being intimidated at doing what we can to usher in a new order of things in our communities.

This does not mean that we should not expect to feel uncomfortable in setting out to swim upstream in an ungodly culture. That's only natural. But may we never forget that we have been called to live according to the supernatural and perfect will that God has for the earth, not man's natural and imperfect will.

- ✔ Was Noah uncomfortable in beginning to build a boat to protect himself and his family from a flood, when there had never even been a thunderstorm? [33] Very probably.
- ✔ Was the wealthy Abram uncomfortable when he was asked to leave his hometown to go to an unknown destination? [34] Very probably.

✔ Was the prophet Ezra uncomfortable in making the dangerous trip from Babylon to Jerusalem without a military escort? [35] Very Probably.

✔ Was Esther uncomfortable in appearing before the king without an appointment (which could have resulted in her immediate execution) to appeal for the safety of the Jews?[36] Very probably.

✔ Was Gideon uncomfortable when Jehovah asked him to reduce the size of his army from 10,000 men to 300 before engaging 15,000 Midianites in battle? [37] Very probably.

Non-Christians are fearful of change because to their way of thinking, reasoning and logic there is no supernatural God to intervene on their behalf, which means they have to do what they can to control the results. So when a situation looks improbable to them, they have no other logical course of action but to shy away from it. They don't have historical examples like Noah, Abraham and Gideon to look back on. In fact, if they are consistent with their worldview, once they rule out absolute truth, history becomes meaningless! Why do we allow these people to intimidate us! Not only can they not see the end from the beginning, they don't even know how the "beginning" began, and are even more clueless about how the "end" will end. If the blind want to lead the blind, fine, but we have no reason to let them lead us. [38] The Holy Spirit has liberated us from such sightless living by enlightening us to the truth that we are in the obedience business, and that God is in the results business. We know that His eternally perfect plan for the earth calls for us to work toward bringing about His desired results, but we don't know how our obedience will cause His will to be done on earth as it is in heaven.[39] The good news is that we don't have to know how Christ uses our obedience to expand His

Kingdom. What a liberating relief it is not to have to try to figure out how all the obedience of all Christians can result in a redeemed world!

No wonder King Solomon could write, "The wicked flee when no man pursues, but the righteous are bold as a lion."[40] No wonder that Paul could confidently encourage his contemporary, Timothy, with, "For God has not given us a spirit of fear, but of power and love and of a sound mind."[41]

We can turn once again to Paul for his admonition to the Christians in Phillipi, because it applies equally well to us:

> *Only let your conduct be worthy of the gospel of*
> *Christ, so that whether I come and see you or am*
> *absent, I may hear of your affairs, that you stand fast*
> *in one spirit, with one mind striving together for the*
> *faith of the gospel.*   PHILIPPIANS 1.27-28

Is It Machiavellian, or Christian?

It's Machiavellian

to be fearful of change, because to their way of thinking, reasoning and logic there is no supernatural God to intervene on their behalf. This means they have to do what they can to control the results.

It's Christian

to focus our attention on consistently obeying God in every situation and circumstance, then resting in His sovereign control of His creation to bless our obedience so that, ultimately, His exact desired results will take place.

59

The following questions will reveal whether you perform your legislative duties as a Conservative, or as a Christian. While similar in many regards, the ultimate difference is huge. Conservatives base their legislation and governance on lower taxes and smaller government than do the Liberals. Conservative social policies and programs are generally moralistic and mirror the 5th through the 10th Commandments (honor those in authority, don't kill, cheat, steal, lie or covet). As has been stated, Christians should base their legislation and governance on all Ten Commandments (the first four providing the only sure and certain foundation for so acting) and the Old Testament Case Laws, which explain how God intends for us to apply His Laws. Without basing one's actions and legislation upon the foundation of the first four commandments, a person (a civil ruler) has only "his reasons" for so acting (instead of God's reasons... Hebrews 12.16).

Should the results of this self-evaluation not be what you would prefer, you can use these questions to implement a strategy to bring your score more in line with your priorities.

Christian Civil Ruler's Self-Evaluation*

1.   I agree with King Solomon that, "The fear of the Lord is the beginning of knowledge," (PROVERBS 1.7) and regularly stop to consider God's Word before making a policy decision, a vote, or a judicial decision.

_____YES (Christian)   _____NO (Conservative)

2.   God is a living reality to my soul, and I know more about Him through personal Bible study than through what others write and say of Him.

_____YES (Christian)   _____NO (Conservative)

Christian Civil Ruler's Self-Evaluation *(cont.)*

3.   I am pleasing God with my lifestyle by daily presenting biblical alternatives to those with whom I come in contact (i.e. being "salt and light" MATTHEW 5.13-16..."That servant which knew his Lord's will, and prepared not himself, neither did according to His will, shall be beaten with many stripes." Luke 12.47; "They that despise Me shall be lightly esteemed."1 SAMUEL 2.30)

_____YES (Christian)   _____NO (Conservative)

4.   The top priority in my life is to serve God.

_____YES (Christian)   _____NO (Conservative)

5.   I have a daily Quiet Time that not only includes Bible Study, but time to reflectively think about God's Word.

_____YES (Christian)   _____NO (Conservative)

6.   I am walking by faith, in the fear of God, diligently attending to His commandments, and I trust in and rely on the promises and assurances in His Word.

_____YES (Christian)   _____NO (Conservative)

7.   I recognize that thinking and acting "neutrally" (or "tolerantly" toward all religions) represents an attempt to reject God's wisdom and replace it with my own.

_____YES (Christian)   _____NO (Conservative)

8.   The civil government is only one of the four self-governing realms that God uses to transform His creation so that it operates by His rules. Each realm (Self, Family, Church, and State) is important, and is directly accountable to God.

_____YES (Christian)   _____NO (Conservative)

9. I submit to constructive criticism from fellow Christians, as well as to any biblical principle I've just learned that I either didn't know or had previously misunderstood, and I repent from my previous behavior.

_____YES (Christian)   _____NO (Conservative)

(continued)

Christian Civil Ruler's Self-Evaluation *(cont.)*

10. I refuse to send my children to public schools or to private non-Christian schools because I know that they hate everything about my Lord and Savior. Besides, since their curriculum is not based upon God's Word, what they are teaching, by definition, is error (Psalm 119.142,151; John 17.17).

_____YES (Christian)   _____NO (Conservative)

11. I honor God's Sabbath by not purchasing any products or services and generally spend the day with my family and friends and/or in visitation and Bible study.

_____YES (Christian)   _____NO (Conservative)

12. I realize that any proposed legislation that does not conform to God's Word is a part of culture's problem, not its solution. The only way to solve culture's problems is by conforming new legislation (and judicial decisions) to biblical principles. Current legislation that doesn't conform to Scripture should either be taken off the books or defunded.

_____YES (Christian)   _____NO (Conservative)

TOTAL SCORE   _____YES (Christian)   _____NO (Conservative)

* This self-Check comes from the *Christian Civil Ruler's Handbook*. For a detailed analysis of these questions. see bhanson@graceandlaw.com and Buddy Hanson, *God's Ten Words: Practical Applications from the Ten Commandments* (Hanson Group, 2002).

Christian Legislative Building Blocks

By not "imposing" Christian beliefs on others, we allow them to "impose" their beliefs on us.

We are living in God's world And we must live by His rules.

Living and governing ourselves according to biblical principles brings order out of the chaotic "law of the jungle" that our evolutionary non-Christians believe in and according to which they live and legislate.

While non-Christians are striving to build a name for themselves by serving their own interests, we should be striving to build a name for God by serving His interests.

A Christian legislator cannot "make up" for his sinful disobedience of supporting ungodly legislation by doing extra activities in his church.

Let us not fear how men will respond to the truth, but fear how God will respond if we compromise

NOTES

1 The Barna Group, www.barna.org
2 Luke 16.13
3 Hebrews 2.18
4 Matthew 12.30
5 Kuyper, Abraham, "Address at the Free University of Amsterdam," 1880, in Bacote, Vincent E., *The Spirit in Public Theology: Appropriating the Legacy of Abraham Kuyper* (Baker Academic, 2005)
6 Matthew 5.13-16
7 2 Timothy 3.14
8 Galatians 6.9
9 Daniel 2.21; Job 12.23
10 Hebrews 12.28

11 Morecraft, *op.cit., Fundamentals*, pp.153-54
12 Carlyle, Thomas, 19th century Scottish writer and historian
13 Baptist Pastor and writer, Dr. Vance Havner
14 1 Thess. 2.12
15 Col. 1.10-11
16 The Mayflower Compact
17 For a full discussion see Buddy Hanson, *It's Time to Un-Quo the Status* (Hanson Group, 2006)
18 Genesis 3.15
19 Genesis 11.4
20 Exodus 20.5-6
21 Romans 16.20
22 Philippians 2.3-5

23 1 Corinthians 15.58
24 Ephesians 5.7-11
25 Orwell, George, *1984* (Signet Classics, 1950)
26 Matt. 5.13; 7.6
27 Matthew 16.18
28 Matthew 5.13
29 Genesis 22.17; Matthew 16.18
30 Luke 19.13
31 Isaiah 54.2
32 Leviticus 26; Deuteronomy 28
33 Genesis 6.14-22
34 Genesis 12.1-4
35 Ezra 8.22
36 Esther 4.14
37 Judges 7
38 Matthew 15.14
39 Matthew 6.10
40 Proverbs 28.1
41 2 Timothy 1.7

LIVING LARGE

(WITH A CHRISTIAN WORLDVIEW)

ULTIMATE AUTHORITY:
WHY DO WE DO THE THINGS WE DO?

AS CREATURES, WE ARE CONSTANTLY IN "MENTAL" MOTION. FROM the moment of our physical birth we begin plotting how we can convince those around us to "be reasonable and do things our way." [1] We are repelled by the very idea of conforming our self-focused and subjective worldview and lifestyle to the triune God's others-focused and objective ethical standard. We dismiss the idea of there being such a thing as absolute truth, because that would give us no choice but to admit how rebellious we are. Instead, we decide on one of the following tactics:

✔ Proclaim that there is no such thing as "truth," or
✔ Imagine that each person is the determiner of "truth."

Either of these alternatives provides a rationalization for living according to a non-Christian worldview, but neither really solves anything because, sooner or later, both views of the world will manifest their utter failure in addressing the concerns of life. Since both worldviews are based upon false presuppositions, they will be unable to help a person determine "good and evil." [2] As non-Christians continue to "suppress the truth in unrighteousness," [3] one of two things will happen:

- It will become obvious to them that their lifestyle is built upon the unreliable fictional fables of their own imaginations. As they continue to experience these epiphanies, they will be driven to repent of their self-centered ways and turn to Jesus, or
- They will be become more disillusioned, "living lives of quiet desperation." [4] as God "sends them strong delusion" so they will continue to believe the lie and be condemned to eternal destruction. [5]

> Only a Christian worldview and lifestyle provide meaningful answers to the various situations and circumstances with which we are faced, because only such a lifestyle is built upon the solid foundation of the absolute instructions of Christ.

Since we were created to be "complete in Christ" [6] all attempts to run away from Him will lead to increased frustration. This is because a lifestyle built upon the ever-changing and subjective sand that flows through the hour glass of sinful man's imagination will not provide a purpose, direction or hope that can be substantiated. This is why it is necessary to humble ourselves by making it clear to everyone that we depend upon the guidance and blessings of our Lord, Savior and King. He is "the Rewarder of those who diligently seek Him." [7] His divine providence has given us the perfect instruction book on how to govern ourselves.

WILL SUCCESS SPOIL ROCK HUNTER?

The 1950s hit Broadway play turned movie was a romantic comedy in which ad-man Rockwell Hunter (Tony Randall) strived for success, but when he attained it he discovered that he couldn't handle it. The movie's conclusion is, "There's no success like *no* success!"

Comedy aside, achieving success can result in unpleasant consequences. Probably every football fan has seen his favorite team be upset by a much less talented opponent the week after achieving one of their best-ever victories, because they were so busy celebrating their victory that they failed to give proper attention to the next game. Non-Christians also have a problem with success. Viewing themselves as "the master of their fate and the captain of their soul," they find that the successes for which they work so hard and which they put so much time and effort into achieving, only provide hollow victories. It's as though the pursuit is more worthwhile than the prize. For them, the logical next step is to re-adjust their goals to a bigger challenge, only to find that, once the new challenge is mastered, the lasting satisfaction they hoped for is, again, missing. Sooner or later even the most driven and success-oriented non-Christian must question the self-centered optimism of William Ernest Henley's "Invictus":

> ...In the fell clutch of circumstance I have not winced
> nor cried aloud, under the bludgeonings of chance
> my head is bloody, but unbowed.
> ... It matters not how strait the gate, how charged
> with punishments the scroll, I am the master of my
> fate: I am the captain of my soul.

In the crevices of their minds, non-Christians must certainly ask, "What difference does it make if I am the captain of my fate, if all of my time and effort leads to no meaningful satisfaction?" No amount of man-centered logic or pragmatism will result in a satisfactory answer to such a question. Only the "peace of God, which surpasses all understanding" will provide satisfaction to our life's endeavors.[8] Only as we let the "peace of God rule in our hearts" will we find meaning and purpose in our vocation, our family, and our relationships with others. [9]

69

GOD AS THE SOURCE OF AUTHORITY

I am the way, the truth, and the life. No one comes
to the Father except through Me.

JOHN 14.6

To look at this verse only from a salvation perspective is to rob ourselves of our Savior's counsel on how to live and govern our lives. Jesus is the only way and the only life that is true, and He has given both of those to us. Praise God for that. If this were all Jesus did for us it would still be far more than any of us deserves. But He has done even more by giving us an inerrant guidebook (the Bible) on how to live our lives and govern ourselves! He has given us truth!

• Truth to use in improving our relationships with others
• Truth to use in our homes for our families
• Truth to use in our vocation, and yes
• Truth to use in legislating and for judicial decisions

All day, every day, with every decision we make we are "determining good and evil." Of course, this is how Eve got us all in trouble. [10] So, how do we avoid making the mistake Adam allowed Eve to make? I'm tempted to say, "By simply conforming our thoughts and decisions to the biblical principles we profess to believe." However, we all know too well that such a course of action is not "simple." But may we never forget that we have the assistance of the Holy Spirit and the entire Trinity as we go forth each day to bring glory and honor to God by imaging Christ instead of Satan. Again, as we can all affirm, the more ways in which we make decisions without relying on the biblical principles in which we profess to believe, the sillier and more unholy our decisions become.

Isaiah, David and Paul provide us with a compelling case for submitting our lives and our governance to God's authority.

For the LORD is our Judge, the LORD is our Lawgiver, the LORD is our King; He will save us.
ISAIAH 33.22

For the kingdom is the LORD's, and He rules over the nations. PSALM 22.28

Let every soul be subject to the governing authorities. For there is no authority except from God, and the authorities that exist are appointed by God. Therefore whoever resists the authority resists the ordinance of God, and those who resist will bring judgment on themselves. For rulers are not a terror to good works, but to evil. Do you want to be unafraid of the authority? Do what is good, and you will have praise from the same. For he is God's minister to you for good. But if you do evil, be afraid; for he does not bear the sword in vain; for he is God's minister, an avenger to execute wrath on him who practices evil. Therefore you must be subject, not only because of wrath but also for conscience' sake. For because of this you also pay taxes, for they are God's ministers attending continually to this very thing. Render therefore to all their due: taxes to whom taxes are due, customs to whom customs, fear to whom fear, honor to whom honor. ROMANS 13.1-7

George Washington's 1789 Thanksgiving Proclamation makes it clear that he and other early Americans had no problem in attributing sovereignty to the triune God of Scripture:

71

It is the duty of all nations to acknowledge the providence of Almighty God, to obey His will, to be grateful for His benefits, and humbly to implore His protection and favor.

MAN AS THE SOURCE OF AUTHORITY

There is a way that seems right to a man, but its end is the way of death.   PROVERBS 16.25

When the triune God of Scripture is not recognized as the governor of our actions, we are left with four options:

✔ Self (anarchy)
✔ State (communism)
✔ Elites (fascism)
✔ The masses (i.e., a democratic majority...socialism)

Each of these choices results in "man" being the source of authority. Whether it is an individual, an inner circle of rulers, a group of educated "elites" or the "collective ignorance" of an entire community, "creatures" are attempting to make life's decisions instead of turning to and trusting in their Creator. The celebrated English novelist, G.K. Chesterton, once astutely remarked, "When men stop believing in God, they don't believe in nothing; they believe in anything."

As Christians, we should know well the outcome of such man-centered civil governments. It was Shakespeare who remarked, "There's small choice in rotten apples," [11] and even though he wasn't directly describing man's fallen condition, the description certainly fits. After all, Paul says of himself: "For I know that in me nothing good dwells," [12] and Jehovah tells Noah after the flood: "I will never again curse the ground for man's sake, although the imagination of man's heart is evil from his youth," [13] Someone once quipped that a self-made man "has no one to blame but himself," and the same goes for Christians in regards to our culture which continues to unravel right before our eyes. Of all the people on the face of the earth, only we "who have had the veil lifted" are able to understand the truth, [14] for "the message of the cross is foolishness to those who are perishing." [15] And since the triune God of the Bible is perfect, so is His eternal plan for His creation. Therefore,

> *If we don't like the direction in which our culture is going, we have no one to blame but ourselves for failing to trust in God enough to follow His instructions.*

Adolph Hitler told German pastors,

> *I will protect the German people. You take care of the church. You pastors should worry about getting people to heaven and leave this world to me.*

Upon hearing this, the vast majority of the German pastors should not have become accomplices to his deeds by not educating their congregations on the ungodly nature of his plans. The same applies to American pastors in our generation for not speaking out on the gross evils of such things as the god-opposing public (government) school system which systematically and intentionally instructs our children that we are biological accidents of nature and that there is no such thing as absolute truth. As members of Christ's Kingdom, we have an obligation to obey the commands of our Lord, Savior and King exclusively. To worship more than one God, (the God of the Bible inside our homes and churches, and the god of the state outside of our homes and churches in our vocations and relationships) breaks the first commandment. [16] Listen carefully to Jehovah's words to the Israelites.

> Now it shall come to pass, if you diligently obey the
> voice of the LORD your God, to observe carefully
> all His commandments which I command you today,
> that the LORD your God will set you high above all
> nations of the earth. ...But it shall come to pass, if
> you do not obey the voice of the LORD your God,
> to observe carefully all His commandments and His
> statutes which I command you today, that all these
> curses will come upon you and overtake you...
>
> DEUTERONOMY 28.1, 15

The Jews knew the right words to say, and they vowed to obey God in the Promised Land, but their actions didn't measure up and we all know the rest of that story.

> We, too, should know the rest of America's story if
> we do not repent from conforming our worldview
> and lifestyles to that of non-Christians.

WHICH "GOD" DEFINES THE FAMILY?

- If it is the civil government (Caesar), then what's to prevent it from also defining how many children, and which genders each "family" can have? That's the way China does it.
- If Caesar is defining the family, what's to keep the civil government from also defining how we should raise our children. For example, is spanking "child abuse?" Or, how about raising them according to Christian principles?

A judge in Colorado recently ordered a Christian mother not to teach her child that homosexuality is wrong.

- If Caesar is defining the family, is incest acceptable behavior?
- If Caesar is defining the family, how many "spouses" (husbands and/or wives) make up the "family unit?"

The overarching issue facing America is "Which god defines our ethics?" If our god is the triune God of Scripture, then our ethics are carved in stone (and on our heart!) [17] and are the same today as they were for our grandparents and will be for our grandchildren. [18] If, however, they are the ethics from any other god (i.e. man or the state) they will change as rapidly as the latest opinion poll.

Ethics are everything. They manifest themselves in one's decisions: legislation, if you are a legislator, judgments, if you are a judge, company policies, if you are a CEO, raising and educating children, if you are a parent. Here's the rub: Christians, and even non-Christian conservatives, want judges to uphold the Constitution by judging the cases in terms of the clear words in the Constitution. Non-Christians neither like nor believe in absolutes, so they don't like the absolute Christian principles upon which the Constitution is based and want judges to "amend" it by making unconstitutional decisions.

Non-Christians have us in a box and it is a box that we constructed with our own apathy (by not providing solid Christian judicial nominees, and for our Churches refusing to discipline legislators who are church members for acting according to unbiblical ethics). In addition, we are shamelessly living according to the non-Christian myth that certain aspects of our culture are "secular" and therefore off-limits to Christian ethics. Once non-Christians got us to agree with this mythical dichotomy all they had to do was gradually classify more and more aspects of culture as "secular" until all we were left with is what goes on inside our Churches and homes.

In answering the question, "Which 'god' defines the family," we need to be aware that upon our answer hang all the other cultural issues. The oft-quoted John 3.16 begins with "For God so loved the world ..." and Jesus reminds us that He came "to destroy the works of the devil." [19] Somewhere between these two verses too many Christians have imagined that Christianity is a private and personal internal matter, and that Satan has unlimited reign in the external areas of our life (those areas outside our homes and churches). Non-Christian civil rulers (legislators and judges) would be more than happy to encourage us to continue believing this. God's truth, however, presents a 180-degree different meaning. Simply put, Jesus came to pay our sin debt and the Holy Spirit changes our heart so we can change the world by conforming it to biblical principles. Any definition of Christianity less than this robs God of the honor due Him and relegates us to being mere "fruit inspectors," (of various cultural issues), instead of properly being "root extractors (of ungodly social issues)."

ARE YOUR DAILY DECISIONS BASED UPON "WHAT COMES NATURALLY?" OR UPON "WHAT COMES SUPERNATURALLY?"

Inside our homes and churches we have no problem with understanding and agreeing that it is critical to make decisions based upon biblical principles, since only God's Word is true. However, an unfortunate metamorphosis happens to far too many of us when we step out of our doors and into Christ's Kingdom. It's as if our worldview undergoes an instant transformation as we imagine ourselves stepping into a jungle, and we begin living according to its various "laws." But, as we know, it's not a "jungle" out there, but a "kingdom." Indeed, it's The Kingdom. [20] We also know that Jesus is very serious about us living according to the "things of God, and not the things of man." As familiar as we are with His rebuke of Peter to "get behind Me," we apparently have forgotten the sentence that follows the rebuke:

> *Get behind Me, Satan! You are an offense to Me for you are not mindful of the things of God, but the things of man.*   MATTHEW 16.18

David, in praying to Jehovah, specifically mentions that he "has not hidden" His righteousness within his heart, but has "declared" it:

> *I have proclaimed the good news of righteousness in the great assembly; indeed, I do not restrain my lips, O LORD, You Yourself know. I have not hidden Your righteousness within my heart; I have declared Your faithfulness and Your salvation; I have not concealed Your loving kindness and Your truth from the great assembly.*   PSALM 40.9-10

Paul sounds as though he is addressing some brothers and sisters with non-developed Christian worldviews, as he quotes the words the 6th century prophet Habakkuk spoke to Judah soon before the Chaldean armies of Nebuchadnezzar captured Jerusalem and sent them into captivity:

> *For I am not ashamed of the gospel of Christ, for it is the power of God for salvation ... the just shall live by faith.*   ROMANS 1.16-17

Certainly no Christian civil ruler or citizen has any reason to be "ashamed" of God's Word, so the question must be asked, "Why do we live as though we are?"

77

Is anyone ready to say that Jesus really didn't mean it when he commanded us to "go and bear fruit?" [21] I can't imagine any Christian seriously coming to such a conclusion.

> *If we live in the Spirit, let us also walk (and legislate!) in the Spirit.*

While we're saved by faith in Christ alone, [22] the Bible assures us that saving faith is accompanied by works, or as Paul terms it, "the fruit of the Spirit."

> *But the fruit of the Spirit is love, joy, peace,*
> *longsuffering, kindness, goodness, faithfulness,*
> *gentleness, self-control. ... And those who are*
> *Christ's have crucified the flesh with its passions and*
> *desires. If we live in the Spirit, let us also walk in*
> *the Spirit.* GALATIANS 5.22-25

Saving faith is a "living" faith, not a "hidden," "secret," or "private" faith, and certainly not one that is meant to be confined to the inside of our homes and churches. It is Jesus, Himself, who says,"He who has My commandments and keeps them, is he who loves Me," [23] and "If you know these things, blessed are you if you do them." [24] As mentioned, Scripture is equally clear that we should expect to be cursed if we don't incorporate them into our worldview and lifestyle.

The foolishness of non-Christian civil rulers is that they use some very persuasive arguments in an effort to attract votes. As people who don't believe in absolute truth, nor, therefore, in absolute meanings for their words, why do they do that? And further, why do the non-Christian voters believe them? The answer is that even though they dislike Christianity, they have to "borrow" our principles in order to communicate with each other, even though the legislator doing the speaking and the voter doing the listening don't believe words have absolute meanings! About the best rebuttal non-Christians can muster is: "Our words may not be true tomorrow, but they are today." Talk about a worldview built upon sand!

Aristotle provides an excellent example of this type of rhetoric. He advocated legislation that was "just and noble." That sounds very good, and who would disagree with that? However, when we hear a legislator or a political candidate make a statement like this we should ask them to explain what criteria they are using to determine what is "just and noble" and what is "unjust and ignoble." In other words, what is their ethical standard? If they are a pluralist and believe that all gods are equally irrelevant to real life, they will likely support:

Every Christian's greatest privilege is to know and follow God's will because only biblical principles mirror reality and only biblical principles provide us with the true way to live and govern ourselves. This is why no form of civil government will last long that is not based upon biblical principles.

- government schools, and propose tax increases to help fund them, saying, "It's for the children," when they cannot prove that the curriculum on which they plan to spend the tax revenues is any better (or worse!) than any other curriculum.
- property taxes, and even invoking "eminent domain" to steal a person's property
- marriages between persons of the same sex
- life sentences, instead of the death sentence for murder
- abortion
- women in combat roles

- judges who render rulings in order to "improve society," rather than based upon the clear words of the written law code.

> *The key question for legislators and judges for which voters must demand an answer is: "Does the civil government's authority originate in our imagination, or in the pages of the Bible?"*

Christian voters cannot afford to neglect to ask this question, and Christian civil rulers cannot afford to sincerely and honestly deal with the answer, with every decision they make. Pastor Morecraft summarizes:

> *Neither the state nor the church is the ultimate authority controlling all of life, for neither the church nor the state is God. But Jesus is God incarnate, and therefore His authority is ultimate and totalitarian," and all human authorities are limited and accountable to Him.* [25]

Typical Excuses From Non-Christian Legislators

- "I respect your views, but I have to represent all the people."

Such a statement reflects a pluralistic view, where all religions are seen as being essentially the same, in which case the will of the majority of the voters takes precedence over principle.

- "I'm personally opposed to the issue, but it's not my place to impose my views on others."

It is the legislator's duty to "impose God's view" on others, because they are "ministers of God for our good." (ROMANS 13.3-4)

Typical Excuses From Non-Christian Legislators *(cont.)*

• "Let's agree to disagree."

Christians disagree over several things. For example: whom, when and how to baptize, how often to observe the Lord's Supper and whether to serve grape juice or wine, whether to sing psalms exclusively or to also sing hymns and/or praise songs. However, when it comes to doctrine on how to live and govern ourselves, God has laid out some very specific responsibilities for the individual, family, church and state, and each self-governing sphere should be careful to stay within its God-appointed boundaries and not usurp the responsibilities of other spheres. A flippant "let's agree to disagree" attitude reflects a lack of respect for our Lord, Savior and King, Jesus Christ.

• "My office doesn't get involved in moral issues."

This excuse reflects the legislator's belief in the myth of life's being composed of two realms: "real life," and "religion." This gives you an excellent opportunity to ask the Christian legislator* what portion of Scripture teaches such a view of life. Of course, he won't be able to cite Scriptural support, and if you handle this in an empathetic instead of a confrontational manner you could go a long way in helping him develop his Christian worldview. His answer to this question (as well as to any issue before him) will boil down to either public opinion or God's opinion. If you can succeed in getting him to recognize this, you will have done a great service for Christ's Kingdom.

Abortion Excuses

• "The government should not be involved in such a personal issue."

The only civil rulers you should spend your time with are those who profess to be Christians. Non-Christians will think you are foolish, so leave them to their own wisdom and do what you can to vote them out of office in the next election.

(continued)

Typical Excuses From Non-Christian Legislators *(cont.)*

You're exactly correct, but the problem is that the civil government did become involved when it allowed the Roe v. Wade decision to stand. Our Declaration of Independence reflects God's Word by stating that our rights come from our Creator, not from the civil government. Therefore you should do what is necessary to take this decision off of the law books.

- "Legislators should not be practicing medicine."

I agree, but neither should legislators be allowing the abuse of medicine, which is exactly what taking the life of an unborn child amounts to.

- "Abortion is the law of the land."

Abortion is not a "law," but a judicial ruling, and even if it were a law, that wouldn't necessarily make it right. Unconstitutional laws can be changed, just as slavery and segregation laws were. According to the fifth amendment to the U.S. Constitution, "No person...shall be deprived of life, liberty, or property, without due process of law." How can an infant have "due process of law" when he can't even talk? Besides, in the 1812 Marbury v. Madison case, Chief Justice John Marshall commented that "any law that was repugnant to the constitution was unconstitutional."

IS IT MACHIAVELL*IAN* OR CHRIST*IAN*
To Conform Legislative Policies to "The World?"
Machiavelli Principle 15

#15 *Of the Things for Which Men, and Especially Princes, Are Praised or Blamed*

For whom He foreknew, He also predestined to be conformed to the image of His Son... ROMANS 8.29

*Also it shall be, when he sits on the throne of his
kingdom, that he shall write for himself a copy of
this law in a book, from the one before the priests,
the Levites. And it shall be with him, and he shall
read it all the days of his life, that he may learn to
fear the LORD his God and be careful to observe
all the words of this law and these statutes, that his
heart may not be lifted above his brethren, that he
may not turn aside from the commandment to the
right hand or to the left, and that he may prolong his
days in his kingdom, he and his children in the midst
of Israel.*   DEUTERONOMY 17.18-20

*For I am not ashamed of the gospel of Christ, for it
is the power of God to salvation for everyone who
believes, for the Jew first and also for the Greek.*
        ROMANS 1.16

Machiavelli admits that the world we live in is not the
world we would prefer, but that it is useless to "fight city
hall" by attempting to live according to how we ought to
live.

*For how we live is so far removed from how we
ought to live, that he who abandons what is done
for what ought to be done, will rather learn to
bring about his own ruin than his preservation. ...
Therefore it is necessary for a prince, who wished to
maintain himself, to learn how not to be good, and
to use this knowledge and not use it, according to
the necessity of the case.*   PRINCIPLE 15

Such common sense pragmatism flies in the face of the
Apostle Paul's instructions to "image God, not the world,"
and to "conform the world to God's successful principles,"

83

not ourselves to the world's unsuccessful principles. Machiavelli's attitude is symptomatic of the worldview of all non-Christians. The only "truth" he knew was what he could observe. This is the fault of non-Christians, because to their way of thinking, if they can see, feel, smell and taste something, it must be real. Christians don't argue that such things are not "real," but that in and of themselves, they may be "real bad." Listen to Paul:

> *For we walk by faith, not by sight.*
>
> 2 CORINTHIANS 5.7

> *Now faith is the substance of things hoped for, the evidence of things not seen. ... without faith it is impossible to please Him.*   HEBREWS 11.1

Each Christian's calling includes making the invisible "visible" to our non-Christian neighbors. We do that by confidently living according to God's rules in all of our situations and circumstances. Think about it for a minute. How else are we supposed to testify to non-Christians about how life (and civil government) is supposed to be if we don't live out our faith. Non-Christians are certainly not hesitating to live out their faith, but try as they might, they're failing miserably to find a meaningful existence. They are looking for answers, but they are looking in all the wrong places. We, of all the people on the earth, have

Any piece of legislation, any school curriculum, any advice we may come across for our family...anything that does not conform to God's Word is, by our own definition, false, and will not work, regardless of how much time, effort or money we throw at it.

84

been mercifully and graciously given the correct answers on how to live and govern ourselves, and there is no biblical precedent that encourages us to keep them locked up inside our homes and churches.

We say that God's Word is "truth," and get upset if someone who professes to be a Christian says, "Well, I believe that God's Word may be 99 percent true, but there are one or two verses with which I have a problem." We get upset with such a statement because if God's Word is not entirely true, then nothing is necessarily true and all ideas are "up for grabs." Yet, far too many of our Christian brothers and sisters don't carry out the full implications of God's Word being "true."

Is It Machiavell*ian*, or Christ*ian*?

It's Machiavell*ian*
to believe that everybody has "evolved" from some lower form of life and therefore has no intrinsic value. The only option of such a worldview is to miss no opportunity to rule by intimidation.

It's Christ*ian*
to recognize that everyone has been created by God and therefore has enormous "value." This provides Christians with the option of treating others according the principles in commandments five through ten, and basing the authority for our actions upon the first four commandments. Since non-Christians cannot arrive at how we "ought" to live, we should take the lead by demonstrating in our everyday lifestyle how God would have us to treat others.

If a person wants to maintain his rule he must learn how not to be virtuous, and to make use of this or not, according to need.   PRINCIPLE 15

IS IT MACHIAVELL*IAN* OR CHRIST*IAN* ▓▓▓▓▓▓▓▓▓▓
To Legislate According to Public Opinion Polls?
Machiavelli Principle 19

19   *That We Must Avoid Being Despised and Hated*

This is love, that we walk according to His commandments. This is the commandment, that as you have heard from the beginning, you should walk in it.
2 JOHN 6

Therefore you shall be careful to do as the LORD your God has commanded you; you shall not turn aside to the right hand or to the left. You shall walk in all the ways which the LORD your God has commanded you, that you may live and that it may be well with you, and that you may prolong your days in the land which you shall possess.
DEUTERONOMY 5.32-33

You, through Your commandments, make me wiser than my enemies; for they are ever with me. I have more understanding than all my teachers, for Your testimonies are my meditation. I understand more than the ancients, because I keep Your precepts.
PSALM 119.97-100

86

As a Christian you are probably as irritated by public opinion polls as I am. After all,

Who needs Public Opinion Polls to determine how to live, when we have God's inerrant Word?

In addition, whose opinion counts, a random sample of fallen sinners, or the triune God of Scripture?! Yet, in a time way before such "polls," Machiavelli strongly suggests that legislators and judges make their decisions in accordance not with what they prefer, but with what their constituents prefer. To act in this way is to blaspheme God's counsel and place our trust completely in man.

He will chiefly become hated by being rapacious, and usurping the property...of his subjects, which he must abstain from doing, and whenever one does not attack the property or honor of the generality of men, they will live contented. ...

He is rendered despicable by being thought changeable, frivolous, effeminate, timid, and irresolute. ... Whence it may be seen that hatred is gained as much by good works as by evil, and therefore, as I said before, a prince who wishes to maintain the state is often forced to do evil, for when that party, whether populace, soldiery, or nobles, whichever it be that you consider necessary to you for keeping your position, is corrupt, you must follow its humor and satisfy it, and in that case good works will be inimical to you.

PRINCIPLE 19

87

Is It Machiavell*ian*, or Christ*ian*?

It's Machiavell*ian*
to seek out coalitions with other legislators to get your bills passed, even if you have to add compromises to your bill with which you are uncomfortable, or which will weaken it. After all, it's not what's in the legislation that counts, but how you can "spin" the passage of it to your constituents when you get back to your district.

It's Christ*ian*
to stay abreast of how your constituents feel about certain issues and address them in a way that conforms to biblical principles. However, if a sizeable portion of the voters in your district are in favor of a piece of legislation that goes against Scripture, you should find a way to keep it from coming up for vote. Then, even though you have opposed it in committee, you won't have to go on record of having voted against it.

IS IT MACHIAVELL*IAN* OR CHRIST*IAN*
To "Flip-Flop" on Policy Issues?
Machiavelli Principle 21

#21 *How a Prince Must Act in Order to Gain Reputation*

If the foundations are destroyed, what can the righteous do?   PSALM 11.3

The instant I speak concerning a nation and concerning a kingdom, to pluck up, to pull down, and to destroy it, if that nation against whom I have spoken turns from its evil, I will relent of the disaster that I thought to bring upon it. And the instant I speak concerning a nation and concerning a kingdom, to build and to plant it, if it does evil in My sight so that it does not obey My voice, then I will relent concerning the good with which I said I would benefit it.　　　　JEREMIAH 18.7-10

Let us hear the conclusion of the whole matter: fear God and keep His commandments, for this is man's all.　　　　ECCLESIASTES 12.13

We've discussed how civil rulers resort to creating dangerous straw men (either a foreign dictator, or a social problem), then hope that by knocking them down, they will be esteemed in the eyes of voters. Here, Machiavelli suggests another way to win esteem:

Be consistent with your policies, and don't "flip-flop."

It is interesting that even a non-Christian recognizes that people don't like to be lied to, so Machiavelli says to would-be princes, "If you're going to lie about something, stick with the lie and people will be more forgiving than if you adapt the lie as time goes by."

Nothing causes a prince to be so much esteemed as great enterprises and giving proof of prowess. ...A prince is further esteemed when he is a true friend, or a true enemy, when ...he declares himself without reserve in favor of some one or against another. This policy is always more useful than remaining neutral.　　　　PRINCIPLE 21

Is It Machiavellian, or Christian?

It's Machiavellian
to appear to be a civil ruler who keeps his word and doesn't waffle on issues.

It's Christian
to be the kind of civil ruler that the non-Christian only appears to be. Even when the non-Christian legislator succeeds in deceiving his constituents in the short term, you can be confident that he is not deceiving our Lord, Savior and King, Jesus Christ.

Christian Legislative Building Blocks

Only a Christian worldview and lifestyle provide meaningful answers to the various situations and circumstances with which we are faced, because only such a lifestyle is built upon the solid foundation of the absolute instructions of Christ.

If we don't like the direction in which our culture is going, we have no one to blame but ourselves for failing to trust in God enough to follow His instructions.

Every Christian's greatest privilege is to know and follow God's will, because only biblical principles mirror reality and only biblical principles provide us with the true way to live and govern ourselves. This is why no form of civil government will last long that is not based upon biblical principles.

The key question for legislators and judges for which voters must demand an answer is this: "Does the civil government's authority originate in our imagination, or in the pages of the Bible?"

Any piece of legislation, any school curriculum, any advice we may come across for our family ...anything that does not conform to God's Word is, by our own definition, false and will not work, regardless of how much time, effort or money we throw at it.

If we live in the Spirit, let us also walk (and legislate!) in the Spirit.

Who needs Public Opinion Polls to determine how to live, when we have God's inerrant Word?

Be consistent with your policies, and don't "flip-flop."

NOTES

1 Genesis 6.5
2 Genesis 3.5
3 Romans 1.18
4 Thoreau, Henry, philosopher and naturalist, *Walden*, 1854, in 150th Anniversary Illustrated Edition of the American Classic (Houghton Mifflin Co., 2004)
5 2 Thessalonians 2.11-12
6 Colossians 2.8-10
7 Hebrews 11.6
8 Philippians 4.7
9 Colossians 3.15
10 Genesis 3.5
11 Shakespeare, William, "The Taming of the Shrew" in *The Complete Works* (Clarendon Press, Oxford, 1988)
12 Romans 7.18
13 Genesis 8.21
14 1 Corinthians 4.3-4
15 1 Corinthians 1.18
16 Exodus 20.3
17 Jeremiah 31.33
18 Hebrews 13.8
19 1 John 3.8
20 Matthew 12.18; 3.2; 4.17; 10.7
21 John 15.16
22 James 2.20
23 John 14.21
24 John 13.17
25 Morecraft, *ibid.*, *Fundamentals*, p.146

How Do You View The World?

A POPULAR SAYING AMONG SALES MANAGERS TO THEIR SALES force is, "Your attitude will determine your altitude." [1] As Christians, our "altitude" has already been determined, but our "attitude" about how we view the world will greatly affect how we approach each day of service in Christ's Kingdom. The following chart provides a light-hearted look at the final result of each worldview. I'm certain you will find yourself described by one of the views. Hopefully it's the "Capitalism/ Christianity" one. If not, What's Scripture Got To Do With It? would be a good place to begin thinking through how you can "connect your Spiritual Dots" to your feet and begin "walking your talk." [2]

Worldviews Contrasted	
Socialism	You have two cows, the government takes one cow and gives it to your neighbor.
Communism	You have two cows, the government takes both and gives you part of the milk.
Fascism	You have two cows, the government takes both and sells you the milk.
Bureaucracy	You have two cows, the government takes both of them, shoots one, milks the other and pours the milk down the drain.
Capitalism/ Christianity	You have two cows, you sell one and buy a bull.

Worldviews Contrasted *(cont.)*	
Nazism	The government shoots you and seizes both cows.
Politically Correct	Since either eating a cow, or drinking the milk of a cow might hurt the feelings of other cows, let's admire them for what they are and starve to death.
Postmodernism	I have definite ideas about cows, and you have no right to attempt to alter them; however, I also know that I have no right to attempt to alter your ideas about cows, so let's just "agree to disagree" about what we should do with them.

Now that you've sharpened your view of the world, let's see if that affects the way you have interpreted some very familiar words of Scripture. Jesus' last words on the cross were not, "Tag, you're it" to Satan. He did not leave Satan in control of the earth until He returns in judgment, but rather He said, "It is finished"—meaning that He had successfully completed the mission for which His Father had sent him, which was, in part, to "defeat the works of the devil." [3]

Sadly, the message of many Bible teachers on the radio and TV, and from pulpits, is quite the opposite of what Jesus says. All too often the message we hear is, "Satan is in control, we're second class citizens, and there is nothing we can do to positively impact our culture, so don't waste your time trying to improve it because when Jesus returns He will straighten everything out." To these so-called Bible teachers, we have only one suggestion. Admittedly, it's a controversial one, but nevertheless, here goes: "Stop listening to each other's radio and TV programs, and read your Bible!"

By following this advice they would discover that it is we, not Satan, who have been given the ability to set the agenda for the earth. God promised Adam and Eve (and the rest of us) that Eve's seed would be successful in "crushing" the head of Satan and his seed, and all that Satan would be able to do in the meantime is wound us on the foot. [4] Paul repeated this promise to the Christians in Rome by stating, "The God of peace will crush Satan under your feet shortly." [5] Either the majority of today's pastors are lying, or God lied when He promised to Abraham that it would be his seed (not Satan's!) through whom "all the families of the earth would be blessed." [6] I don't know about you, but I'm going with God on that promise. It is also worthy of note that when Isaiah compiled the list of names he ascribed to Jesus (Wonderful Counselor, Mighty God, Everlasting Father) he concluded with "Prince of Peace." [7] To listen to the pessimistic message gushing forth from many in the church today, one would think Jehovah would have instructed Isaiah to conclude with "Prince of Retreat," or "Prince of Cultural Irrelevance." But He didn't, and we can praise God for that! Indeed, King David tells us in no uncertain terms,

> For the kingdom is the Lord's: and He is the
> governor among the nations.   PSALM 22.28

Another psalmist adds,

> The Lord nullifies the counsel of the nations; He
> frustrates the plans of the peoples. The counsel of the
> Lord stands forever, the plans of His heart from
> generation to generation.   PSALM 33.10-11

We are obliged to "occupy until He comes," [8] "make disciples of all the nations," [9] "be the salt and light of the earth," [10] and "bring every thought captive to the obedience of Christ." [11] We must be content with laboring for the long term and not putting all of our hope in the upcoming elections—or even in politics alone. If Jesus is our King, we must proceed according to His marching orders—which involve a gradualist principle.

> *The Kingdom of God ...First the blade, then the head, after that the full grain in the head.*
>
> MARK 4.26-28

> *For who has despised the day of small things?*
>
> ZECHARIAH 4.10

> *The kingdom of heaven is like a mustard seed, which a man took and sowed in his field, which indeed is the least of all the seeds; but when it is grown it is greater than the herbs and becomes a tree, so that the birds of the air come and nest in its branches.*
>
> MATTHEW 13.31-21

> *The kingdom of heaven is like leaven, which a woman took and hid in three measures of meal till it was all leavened.* MATTHEW 13.33

Like Israel of old, we have been given the land of promise, but for us "the Promised Land" is the entire earth. [12] Christ, our commander, has promised us victory, but there are no victories without battles. Let us therefore arm ourselves for conflict through Bible study and reflection on how to incorporate into our worldview and lifestyle the biblical principles we hold so dear. The following chart lists Spiritual Building Blocks upon which we can erect our view of the world. As can be seen, we have more than enough ammunition to take back our culture!

Spiritual Building Blocks

CHRIST

- Christ is in sovereign control of the earth.
- His eternally perfect plan always has been, is now and always will be on schedule and will succeed with or without America.
- Christ lived a perfect life, died and overcame death to redeem us and to defeat the works of the devil.
- Christ gave us absolute truths to instruct us in how to live and govern ourselves.
- We live in an Open (personal) universe where we can communicate to God through our prayers, and He to us through His Word.
- God's Word is true, which means that any idea or decision that does not conform to His Word is false.

MAN

- We can know for certain that we are saved.
- We have "peace of mind" as a result of believing in and acting on God's truths.
- We know that when we die we will go to heaven.
- We should filter all of our decisions and actions through the biblical principles in which we profess to believe, as we think His thoughts after Him.

DUTY

- Our worldview and lifestyle should reflect that we
  - fear the Lord
  - live according to His will
  - worship Him with all our heart and soul
  - obey His commands and laws
- We must have a "take no prisoners" attitude in our daily battle for the control of our culture, as we share the gospel and disciple our brothers and sisters.
- Parents have the responsibility for educating their children; and if they send their children to Christian schools instead of home-schooling them, they should be careful that the curriculum is a God-fearing one.
- We live in an orderly universe where our decisions have consequences.

97

A CHRISTIAN NATION

Non-Christian revisionist textbook writers and their media elite counterparts spin lies about our country's having been founded upon pluralistic religious principles. The truth is exactly the opposite, as the following citations prove:

- "We are a Christian people, and the morality of the country is deeply engrafted upon Christianity." (1892 Supreme Court Justice David Brewer in US vs. Church of the Holy Trinity)
- "A Christian people." (1931 Supreme Court Justice George Sutherland, in a review of the 1892 decision)
- Americans "are a religious people and our institutions presuppose a Supreme Being." (1952 Justice William O. Douglas, Zorach vs. Clausen)

While we may find it comforting that our founders created a Christian governance, we will lose that precious heritage if we don't live and rule in a Christian manner.

The Bible is not a "dead letter," but history proves that that is exactly what America will be if we don't repent and begin living and governing ourselves as God commands us. Hear the words of Isaiah, Asaph, Hosea and Habakkuk:

For the nation and kingdom that will not serve thee shall perish; yea, those nations shall be utterly wasted ... and thou shall know that I the Lord am thy Savior and thy Redeemer, the mighty One of Jacob.

ISAIAH 60.12,16

If My people would but listen to Me; if Israel would follow My ways, how quickly would I subdue their enemies and turn My hand against their foes!

PSALM 81.13-14

98

My people are destroyed for a lack of knowledge.
Because you have rejected knowledge, I will also
reject you from being priest for Me; because you
have forgotten the law of your God, I will also forget
your children.   Hosea 4.6

They will be held guilty, they whose strength is their
god.   Habakkuk 1.11

Each of us has been called to "seek first Christ's Kingdom and righteousness," [13] to "display strength and take action,"[14] and to "not keep quiet" [15] until Christ's righteousness shines like the dawn.

Who Are You?

It is said that the secret of life is to know who you are and where you are going.Nazi concentration camp survivor Corrie Ten Boom says, "The first step on the way to victory is to recognize the enemy," and as Pogo tells us, "We have met the enemy and he is us!"

So the first step to take in developing your Christian worldview is to be certain you have an accurate understanding of who you are, which is a nice way to say, "how bad you are." That's correct; in the eyes of our completely holy God we are completely unholy on our own merits. This is why we make our prayers, praises, petitions and intercessions through Jesus' name. Otherwise they would never be heard, much less accepted and acted upon by God the Father. So if you are tempted to compare yourself with the weirdoes on the evening news, stop. God judges us by *His* ethical standard, not *our* ethical standard.

Edward J. Young, the former Professor of Old Testament at Westminster Theological Seminary, notes that fallen Adam (including us) "needs above all else a complete reversal of all his values." [16]

> We must learn to hate what formerly we loved, and learn to love what formerly we hated.

With his fall into sin, Adam became allied to Satan and alienated from God. But now, through God's gracious and sovereign promises in the Adamic Covenant, all Christians are separated from the serpent by an enmity and hostility toward him which God places in our heart, making it possible to love God with all our heart. 17

In far too many cases, we have been aiding and abetting non-Christians in destroying our culture. As the 16th century English poet Edmond Spencer writes in his Faerie Queen, "The shaft of the arrow had been feathered with one of the eagle's own plumes." Some of the ways we have "feathered the arrow" that non-Christians shoot at us are these:

- ✔ Imitating non-Christian thoughts instead of imitating God's will.
- ✔ Imagining that God created a biverse, instead of a universe, and that, as a consequence there are two divergent realms: a real life realm and a religious life realm. This myth has caused us to let non-Christians set culture's agenda by default!
- ✔ Believing the lie that Jesus failed in His earthly mission and did not "defeat the works of the devil."
- ✔ Failing to challenge the false definitions of the words non-Christians use. Even the heathen 4th century Chinese philosopher Confucius recognized that when "words lose their meaning, people lose their liberty." Lenin gives further proof that our non-Christian neighbors are "more shrewd than we are" [18] when it comes to fighting the culture war: "He who controls the word, controls the thought."

✔ Approaching each day as though we were human
sailboats cast upon the sea of life, destined to go in
whichever direction the prevailing winds take us. One
day Christians will once again be directing the winds of
culture, but in the meantime we must adjust its sails in
order to get it heading back in the right direction.

✔ Thinking that the collective non-Christian worldview
that is prevalent in our lifetime is "normal." Any serious
reading of the way God commands us to live in His
inerrant Word should easily convince us that our times
are abnormal, and that it is time for us to "un-quo the
status!" Even Shakespeare's Hamlet recognizes this:

> *The time is out of joint. O cursed spite that ever I*
> *was born to set it right.*   HAMLET 1.5

Unlike Shakespeare's fictional character who felt over-
burdened, and even cursed with the responsibility to "set it
right," we are God's real characters who have His promises
and assurances that we can successfully bring about His will
on the earth as it is in heaven.

> *Our Lord, Savior and King has given us supernatural eyes*
> *and supernatural ears by which we can correctly see and*
> *hear His directions for living and governing ourselves.*

Yet, many of us continue to live as though He hadn't
made those changes in our heart. This was Jehovah's message
to the Jews in Judah:

> *O foolish people, and without understanding, which*
> *have eyes and see not; which have ears, and hear not.*
>   JEREMIAH 5.21

101

As we develop our worldview and begin to legislate and live according to biblical principles we will no longer be hypnotized by the familiar, and we will also realize that God has not called us to be "the bug," but "the windshield." [19]

The second step to take in developing our Christian worldview is to recognize that before we can expect to change our culture we must change our faith! This brings up this uncomfortable question:

Do we really have faith in Christ's Word, or are we simply giving mental assent to it, while trusting in our own wisdom to shape our daily decision-making?

King Solomon and the prophet Isaiah remind us that God really is smarter that we are:

> *There is a way that seems right to a man, but its end is the way of death.*   PROVERBS 14.12

> *Woe to those who call evil good and good evil, who put darkness for light and light for darkness, who put bitter for sweet and sweet for bitter.*
>   ISAIAH 5.20

> *... as the heavens are higher than the earth, so are My ways higher than your ways, and My thoughts than your thoughts.*   ISAIAH 55.9

Culturally speaking, we're in a hole, and the first thing we need to do is stop digging by refusing to conform ourselves any further to the non-Christian culture that is currently in vogue. Yes, tares have been sown in our wheat field while we have been sleeping, [20] but the good news is that the field still belongs to us and there is no better time to begin reclaiming it than now! As mentioned, we can overcome the ideological hallucinations of man with the truth of God's Word. Those who live by the sword may be shot by a bullet by those who don't, but God has empowered us through His Word to overcome both the sword and the gun. Economist John Kenneth Galbraith writes,

> Faced with the choice of changing one's mind
> or proving that there is no need to do so, almost
> everyone gets busy on the proof.

This attitude, however prevalent, is not Christian. Unlike non-Christians, our pride is not at stake, but rather God's honor. And it is at this point that we need to educate ourselves in developing an all-encompassing Christian worldview and in assisting our brothers and sisters to do so. Ideally, churches would offer such training, but in a day when the condition of most pulpits is deplorable, the emphasis is most likely going to have to come from the pews. We must first educate our brothers and sisters that we are indeed living in the Promised Land, and that they are betraying the God of their faith by remaining in "Egypt."

Remember the childhood chant, "One for the money, two for the show, three to get ready, and four to go!" The "Four to Go" chart gets you ready to "go" in your service to God by asking four key questions to assist you in identifying exactly where you are in your walk with Christ. Think your answers through carefully and honestly, and then ask your church officers and/or other Christian brothers and sisters to help you work through and improve those areas that need repenting of and strengthening. None of us is perfect and each of us should have a passion for becoming the best servant we can be for Christ in His Kingdom.

"Four to Go!"

1. In what ways is your lifestyle as a Christian different from that of your non-Christian neighbors?

2. Where do you draw the line in regard to God's sovereignty? (No one disputes that God is sovereign in the "religious" world inside our homes and churches, but what about out in the "real world?" Is there a point at which you "draw the line" and make decisions on the basis of your own wisdom, or do you continue to trust in and rely on God's wisdom and guidance?)

3. Is there a point beyond which you hesitate to defend the faith? (If so, what is it, and is there anything you could do to move that point further back so you will not be ashamed to take a stand for Christ's Kingdom in all situations and in all circumstances?

4. How does not having a developed Christian worldview cause sincere, well-meaning Christians to severely limit their effectiveness for Christ in His Kingdom?

TRUE EDUCATION

The number one factor contributing to a person's worldview is the education he receives. This is why the Bible stresses the importance of the role of parents in the education of their children. Not every Christian family can home school, but no family can avoid God's direct command to be responsible for the education of their children. This means that if you send your children to a Christian day school, you must be very familiar with its curriculum, because on Judgment Day, Jesus is going to hold you directly responsible for it.

If you are among the 95 percent of adult Christians who don't have a developed Christian worldview, think back to where you picked up your erroneous view of the world. You will probably have to go no further than, "Oh, I learned that in fourth grade (in a public school!)." Pastor Morecraft tells how critical it is to obtain a godly education:

> *Paul makes clear that Christ is the source of all*
> *truth, wisdom and knowledge. In his letter to the*
> *Colossians, he writes, "In Christ is gathered up all*
> *the treasures of wisdom and knowledge."* [21] *In his*
> *second letter to the Corinthian Christians, he adds,*
> *"you have been made complete in Him."* [22]
> *Education becomes the invigorating task of inter-*
> *preting life, history and every other aspect of*
> *creation from the viewpoint of the written revelation*
> *of Christ, which is the truth.* [23]

As newspaper columnist Bob Talbert writes, "Teaching kids to count is fine, but teaching them what counts is better." When King Solomon gave the following advice he did not have America's public schools in mind.

> *Train up a child in the way he should go, and when*
> *he is old he will not depart from it.*
>
> PROVERBS 22.6

Neither did the apostle Paul:

> *And you, fathers, do not provoke your children*
> *to wrath, but bring them up in the training and*
> *admonition of the Lord.* EPHESIANS 6.4

105

> *We must recognize that America's public (government) schools are the state's churches as they attempt to proselytize our children away from the values we teach in the home and to make them wards of the state who will have to depend upon state-provided services, instead of being responsible self-governing members of the community.*

The core doctrine of the public (government) schools is to systematically implant ideas like the following from some of the most scurrilous leaders of all time. This is an explosive statement and I'm certain it will cause some double-takes, but my reply is "Show me the curriculum." Or, better yet, examine the curriculum yourself.

- The State incarnates the Divine Idea upon earth (Hegel).
- The State is the supreme power, ultimate and beyond repeal, absolutely independent (Fichte).
- Everything for the State; nothing outside the State; nothing against the State (Mussolini).
- The State dominates the nation because it alone represents it (Hitler).
- The State embraces everything, and nothing has value outside the State. The State creates the right (Franklin Delano Roosevelt).

Morecraft concludes,

> *Our primary goal is to glorify God. To reach that goal we educate ourselves and our children so that a Christian mind will be developed in us, by which we can look at every area of life from the revealed perspective of Christ in the Bible. On that basis, through Christian education, a Christian culture*

and heritage will be transmitted to our children. As we learn how to build on that heritage in our own time, in our homes, schools, churches, businesses, and communities, we will guarantee for coming generations the prosperity, strength and peace that God promises to His faithful people. [24]

"DO" DILIGENCE

Who will rise up for Me against the wicked? Who will take a stand for Me against evildoers?

PSALM 94.16

This is the question Jesus asks each of us, and there is no justifiable way we can avoid answering it. In addition, our answer will prove whether we are for Him or against Him.[25] We all know this, and we all know that we should have an overwhelming desire to live for God, yet for many there is a problem in connecting their Spiritual Dots to their feet and "walking their talk." It's not easy advancing from a mental agreement of a biblical truth to a physical achievement of it. But advance we must! And since Jesus has guaranteed to bless our obedience, we will find that taking the first step will be the hardest, and that we will be comforted and gain confidence with each succeeding step. Tristan Emmanuel, Director of Canada's Equipping Christians for the Public Square, describes the process in three steps:

- *Understanding is knowing what to do;*
- *Wisdom is knowing what to do next;*
- *Virtue is actually doing it.*

As we set about to "repair the breaches of the house, wherever any breach shall be found," [26] we must understand with the American patriot and politician Samuel Adams:

> *It does not require a majority to prevail, but rather an irate, tireless minority keen to set brush fires in people's minds.*

A contemporary of his, the great American patriot Patrick Henry provides a model for all Christian civil rulers to follow:

> *Should I keep back my opinion at this time I should consider myself guilty of treason toward my country and treason toward the majesty of Heaven, which I revere above all earthly kings. I have no doubt that God, who in former years had hardened Pharoah's heart that He might show forth His power and glory in the redemption of His chosen people, has, for similar purposes permitted the flagrant outrages which have occurred ...Therefore, we have only to trust in the never-changing, all-powerful God of Hosts who ultimately defines holiness for our lifestyle!*

Our bravery comes from our fear of the Lord. We must recognize that the motivation for our actions stems from whether we fear the Lord (and are obedient to His will), or whether we fear men (and are obedient to their will).

The reason people fear their peers so much is that they fear God so little. The answer to how we can begin to improve our culture is to simply give our best efforts to living a life of consistent obedience to biblical principles in all situations and circumstances. God's Word is the only antidote against the collective non-Christian virus that is infecting our culture. And it begins with taking that first step.

Sow a thought and you reap an act;
Sow an act and you reap a habit;
Sow a habit and you reap a character;
Sow a character and you reap a destiny.

ANONYMOUS

The rousing words from Pastor Samuel Langdon's sermon are as inspiring today as they were in 1775:

If God be for us, who can be against us? The enemy has reproached us for calling on his name, and professing our trust in him. They have made a mock of our solemn fasts, and of every appearance of serious Christianity in the land. On this account, by way of contempt, they call us saints: and that they themselves may keep at the greatest distance from this character, their mouths are full of horrid blasphemies, cursing, and bitterness, and vent all the rage of malice and barbarity. And may we not be confident that the Most High, who regards these things, will vindicate his own honor and plead our righteous cause against such enemies to his government, as well as our liberties? O, may our camp be free from every accursed thing! May our land be purged from all its sins! May we be truly a holy people and all our towns—cities of righteousness!

The next chapter examines the vision that is guiding your approach to not only your lifestyle, but also to your legislation. The following "Worldview Check-Up From The Heart Up" will help get your mind in gear for that. Take the test and see what your score is. Each question is worth four points. And relax, only you and God will know the score!

Worldview Check-Up From The Heart Up

	GOD (Yes)	MAN (No)
1. Do you agree that the Bible is totally accurate and is truth? (If your answer is "No," it's OK to stop taking the test, because you're worshiping a non-Christian god)	____	____
2. Since God's Word is true, do you agree that this means any decision (i.e., a piece of legislation, a school curriculum, or anything) that does not conform to God's Word is false and can't be expected to produce positive results?	____	____
3. Do your daily decisions (including your legislation) demonstrate that you trust in God's wisdom, instead of man's wisdom? (1 Corinthians 15.58)	____	____
4. Does your lifestyle demonstrate your belief that "God is not mocked; for whatever a man sows, that he will reap?" (Galatians 6.7)	____	____
5. Do your trust your career to "what was written in earlier times," (Romans 15.4) or to the latest public opinion polls?	____	____
6. Before each legislative vote do you ask yourself, "Does this vote reflect the will of Christ?"	____	____
7. Do your words reflect agreement with Paul's statement: "For I know that in me nothing good dwells?" (Romans 7.18), which leads you to give God the credit for any successes you may have?	____	____
8. Does your lifestyle testify that you are created in the image of God (and therefore have as your primary passion to serve Christ in His Kingdom), or does it testify that you are created in the image of carbon-dioxide (and that you are primarily interested in serving yourself and bringing glory and honor to yourself)?	____	____
9. Do you consider your Christian ethical values to be superior to all other ethical values?	____	____

Worldview Check-Up From The Heart Up *(cont.)*

	GOD (Yes)	MAN (No)

10. The Lord's prayer commands us to use our God-given abilities to bring about God's will on earth. Do you agree with Jesus that that is man's purpose in life? ____ ____

11. Do you view the Bible as being God's "Owner's Manual" to instruct Christians in how to live and govern ourselves, instead of being merely a devotional guide? ____ ____

12. Is it true that there is not even one verse of Scripture that justifies Christian parents' sending their children to (or being employees in) the God-opposed public (government) schools? ____ ____

13. Does your lifestyle reflect that you are commanded to be ready "in season and out" to defend the faith by giving a reason why you are a Christian? (2 Timothy 4.2) ____ ____

14. Have you been so busy living that you have neglected a serious Bible study on how to live and incorporate into your daily lifestyle the biblical principles in which you believe? ____ ____

15. Do you agree that Christians should "give their all" to serving in Christ's Kingdom, instead of giving what is "left over?" ____ ____

16. Do you believe that Christ is in sovereign control of His Kingdom, instead of the popular myth that Satan is "alive and well" on the earth? (Psalm 2) ____ ____

17. Do you strive to make all of your moral choices on the basis of their conformity to Scripture? ____ ____

Worldview Check-Up From The Heart Up *(cont.)*

	GOD (Yes)	MAN (No)
18. In times of trouble and/or personal crisis do you turn exclusively to fellow Christians (and God) for counsel and guidance?	____	____
19. Do you have a spiritual dialogue with your children and spouse at least three times a week? (prayer, Bible study, discussing a sermon, etc.)	____	____
20. Do you agree that if a man doesn't "manage his household" he shouldn't be a legislator?	____	____
21. Would you rather lose in a cause that will someday "win," or disobey God through compromise in a cause that will win today, but will someday "lose?"	____	____
22. People who "believe" in God, yet trust in man's wisdom, are good, moral, law-abiding citizens, but are not Christians. Do you agree?	____	____
23. Do you study the Bible at least three times a week?	____	____
24. Jesus came to save us from having to keep the Law perfectly, but He didn't come to abolish the demands to live according to His Law, because it is by conforming our actions and decisions to the Law that we become holy. Do you agree?	____	____
25. Do you believe that salvation is a gift of God and cannot be earned?	____	____

TOTAL SCORE*   _____

* DETERMING YOUR GRADE – Each question is worth four points. The numerical score is not as important as what you decide to do about it. NONE of us has "arrived" in our Christian walk and we never will. The important thing is whether we're continuing to grow in God's grace and knowledge and whether we incorporate biblical principles into our daily walk. In other words, are we putting off the "old man" and putting on the "new man?" In order to be successful as members in Christ's Kingdom we have to put aside our agenda and put on Christ's agenda. This requires continuous prayer and much humility.

Christian Legislative Building Blocks

While we may find it comforting that our founders created a Christian governance, that won't amount to a hill of beans if we don't live and rule in a Christian manner.

Each of us has been called to "seek first Christ's Kingdom and righteousness," [27] to "display strength and take action," [28] and to "not keep quiet" [29] until Christ's righteousness shines like the dawn.

We must learn to hate what formerly we loved, and learn to love what formerly we hated.

Do we really have faith in Christ's Word, or are we simply giving mental assent to it, while trusting in our own wisdom to shape our daily decision-making?

We must recognize that America's public (government) schools are the state's churches as they attempt to proselytize our children away from the values we teach in the home and to make them wards of the state who will have to depend upon state-provided services, instead of being responsible self-governing members of the community.

Our bravery comes from our fear of the Lord. We must recognize that the motivation for our actions stem from whether we fear the Lord (and are obedient to His will) or whether we fear men (and are obedient to their will).

NOTES

1 See the various books and tapes by sales motivation guru Zig Ziegler.

2 Hanson, Buddy, *What's Scripture Got To Do With It?* (Hanson Group, 2005), www.bhanson@ graceandlaw.com

3 1 John 3.8

4 Genesis 3.15

5 Romans 16.3

6 Genesis 12.3

7 Isaiah 9.6

8 Luke 19.13

9 Matthew 28.19

10 Matthew 5.13-16

11 2 Corinthians 10.5

12 Romans 4.13

13 Matthew 6.33

14 Daniel 11.32

15 Isaiah 62.1

16 E.J. Young, *Genesis Three* (Banner of Truth Trust, 1984)

17 Morecraft, *op.cit., Fundamentals*, p.47

18 Luke 16.8

19 Dire Straits, "The Bug"

20 Matthew 13.24-30

21 Colossians 2.3

22 2 Corinthians 13.9

23 Morecraft, *op.cit., Fundamentals*, Vol. II, p. 162

24 Morecraft, *op.cit., Fundamentals*, Vol. II, p. 163

25 Matthew 12.30

26 2 Kings 12.5

27 Matthew 6.33

28 Daniel 11.32

29 Isaiah 62.1

CAN CULTURE BE CHANGED?

WHICH VISION IS GUIDING YOUR LIFESTYLE AND LEGISLATION

*Those who have caused trouble all over the world
have now come here. They are all defying Caesar's
decrees saying that there is another king, one called
Jesus.*   ACTS 17.6-7

*It will be necessary to adjust the Christian dogma to
the ideas which we National Socialists represent.*
                                            ADOLPH HITLER

SCROLL THROUGH THE ANNALS OF HISTORY, AND AS YOU STOP ALONG
the way to look at a particular society's culture, you will see
that if they were living according to God's rules things were
probably going well, and if they were living according to their
rules, things probably weren't going well. The reason the
word "probably" is used in the preceding sentence is because
God doesn't usually reward or punish us immediately for our
decisions and actions. This means that sometimes a society
that is living according to non-Christian principles, may not
be cursed immediately because of the blessings that have
accrued from the obedience of previous generations. Sooner
or later, however, disobedient societies will fill up God's cup
of wrath and will receive His perfect justice.

One constant throughout all societies and all generations
is the all-out war (either ideological or physical) over whether

God's will or man's will sets the cultural agenda. Statists strive to eliminate Christianity because they see themselves as god. In Mussolini's words: "The state is God walking on earth." Mussolini's contemporary, Adolph Hitler, stated his contempt for the triune God of the Bible by telling the uncompromising and internationally renowned Pastor Martin Niemoeller,

> *The religions are all alike, no matter what they call themselves. They have no future—certainly none for the Germans.* [1]

Those who believe that man, apart from God, is fully capable of bringing about a heaven on earth are called utopians, and history proves that while utopians always fail to bring about "heaven on earth," they succeed in bringing about hell on earth.

Machiavelli's *The Prince* is the most famous book on civil government, but it is neither the best, nor the first, since the Bible holds those distinctions.

God invented civil government and it is only as we govern ourselves according to God's inerrant Word that we will be governed in a "civil" manner.

Just as the Bible provides specific guidelines on how to carry out the functions of the God-appointed self-governing spheres (individual, family and church), so does the Bible provide specific guidelines on how we should govern ourselves. It should come as no surprise that the methods of our perfectly holy God are a great deal different from the methods of perfectly unholy and non-redeemed man. Paul puts it like this:

> *For though we live in the world, we do not wage war as the world does. The weapons we fight with are not the weapons of the world. On the contrary,*

*they have divine power to demolish strongholds. We
demolish arguments and every pretension that sets
itself up against the knowledge of God, and we take
captive every thought to make it obedient to Christ.*

2 CORINTHIANS 10.4-5

Each of God's four appointed self-governing spheres
is assigned specific duties, and no sphere should usurp the
responsibilities of another. The chart below illustrates four
areas that today are being governed very unsuccessfully by
the state. Man, "the state," wants to predestine all outcomes
for life on earth, but that is not God's plan, so the result is
that man's plans are frustrated. The only way we can turn the
world "rightside up" is to follow God's instructions.

The Purposes of "Government"

The Issue	The Responsibility MAN SAYS	GOD SAYS
To protect citizens from invasion, and to keep communities safe for people to live, work and play	Civil Government	Civil Government
To take care of people who can't take care of themselves	Civil Government	Church
To educate the children	Civil Government	Family
To protect the environment	Civil Government	Individual

Pastor Morecraft explains why we are commanded to declare Christ's lordship in the political arena:

> *Christ's comprehensive and unlimited lordship is of particular importance for the political realm. Since He is the unrivaled Monarch of the political process of the United States, Christians have the duty to declare His lordship in the American political arena; and we should not rest until His divine rights and absolute authority are recognized and voluntarily submitted to in the executive, legislative and judicial branches of our civil government at the national, state, county, municipal and individual levels. For a Christian to seek anything less is to act as if Christ is something less than what He is in fact: "King of kings and Lord of lords."* [2]

God's vision of civil government is contrasted with man's vision in the following chart. While not intended to be a complete compilation of the two opposing views, it nevertheless shows the uncompromising nature of both forms of governing. Ultimately, both have a "take no prisoners" attitude, since Christ will not lower the standards of His Kingdom, and man will not elevate his.

The Bible is not difficult to understand, and indeed was written in a manner so it could be understood by the general population. However,

Once God's clear Word is cast aside, ethics become very murky as we begin to look for rationalizations to justify our sinful behavior.

The most direct route would be to declare that there is no such thing as absolute truth, thereby making the principles in

Identifying Your Legislative Approach

GOVERNMENT ACCORDING TO GOD

So speak and so do as those who will be judged by the law of liberty.
                                                                JAMES 2.12

Righteousness exalts a nation, but sin is a reproach to any people.
                                                            PROVERBS 14.34

And He said to them, "Render therefore to Caesar the things that are Caesar's, and to God the things that are God's."   MATTHEW 22.21

GOVERNMENT ACCORDING TO MAN

✔ There is no transcendent standard of government outside of man.
✔ Whatever serves the state is "moral" and is considered "truth."
✔ The state gains its "mandate to govern" either by popular vote, or, failing that, by court rulings that imaginatively interpret the plain written words of the law according to subjective "penumbras formed by emanations"* Instead of an objective reading of the U.S. Constitution.

See the explanation on next page.

our Constitution "relative" to the times in which we live. For example, non-Christians may present this argument:

> *Our founders were living in the midst of an agrarian culture, and we are living in a sophisticated high-tech culture, so surely our ethics have to be looked at in a manner different from theirs.*

Some judges and justices shy away from making such an obviously unbiblical statement and resort to playing word games, since they consider themselves as our intellectual superiors and can't imagine that we will be able to see through their ethical shell game. The height of this arrogance was reached when Supreme Court Justice William O. Douglas proclaimed that "prenumbras formed by emanations" justified his decision to overlook some specific guarantees of the Bill of Rights. A penumbra is a partial shadow between regions of complete darkness and complete illumination, as in an eclipse, and whatever "illumination" Justice Douglas received was very clearly not from God.

Other justices, not liking the clear intentions of the absolute principles contained in our Constitution, suggest turning to the laws of other countries. When they come to a particular case with their decision in mind, and can't find specific words, or even, "prenumbras formed by emanations" they search the laws of other countries until they find one, then cite that as justification for their ruling! For Christians, this is absolutely insane behavior, but for a person who doesn't believe that Christ is the incarnation of God's Word, they have no respect for His clear Word. They would probably repeat Pontius Pilate's query to Jesus: "What is truth?" [3] So instead of viewing words as clear means of communicating our intents, they distort and abuse them in order to change culture according to their self-centered agenda. In other words, they view themselves as gods!

In the 18th century the second President of America, John Adams, remarked,

> *Our Constitution was made only for a moral and religious people. It is wholly inadequate for the government of any other.*

When President Adams made this statement the word "religion" was synonymous with "Christianity." His meaning was that without a people who believed in absolute truths, a constitution wasn't worth the paper it was written on, because judges and legislators would attach their personal meanings to it. The U.S. Constitution (and each of the original State Constitutions) was written to provide personal liberty for self-governing citizens and protection from a tyrannical civil government. In Patrick Henry's words,

> *The Constitution is not an instrument for the*
> *government to restrain the people, it is an instrument*
> *for the people to restrain the government—lest it*
> *come to dominate our lives and interests.*

It is all too obvious that today's judicial branch has turned Patrick Henry's words on their ear by refusing to attach absolute meanings to the words we use. Even Confucius, the 6th century B.C. non-Christian Chinese philosopher, recognized the importance of the absolute meaning of words.

> *If language is not correct, then what is said is not*
> *what is meant; if what is said is not what is meant,*
> *then what ought to be done remains undone; if*
> *this remains undone, morals and art deteriorate; if*
> *morals and art deteriorate, justice will go astray;*
> *if justice goes astray, the people will stand about*
> *in helpless confusion. Hence there must be no*
> *arbitrariness in what is said.*   Confucius

If judges can read into the Constitution "rights" that are not there they can also read out of the Constitution rights that are there.

This points up the critical importance of not only electing Christian civil rulers (legislators and judges), but doing what we can to make certain they know how to "connect their Spiritual Dots" to their legislative and judicial decisions. Otherwise, we will have what we have now: Christians civil rulers who behave as though they are merely "conservative" in their approach to governing. It has been said that a conservative is a person who has grown fond of the order which liberals have forced on him. Such a person is obviously not the kind of ally we need in order to help turn our culture around.

> *He that rules over men must be just, ruling in the*
> *fear of God.*   2 SAMUEL 23.3

Researcher George Barna admonishes each of us to get serious about serving in Christ's Kingdom. Living as though we are capable of determining truth on our own is wholly incompatible with repeatedly affirming that "God's Word" is truth.

> *Is God's moral truth an obsession with you? It*
> *ought to be, for every follower of Christ. After all,*
> *our decisions are influenced by the accuracy of the*
> *perspectives we bring to every point of decision; we*
> *cannot make great choices if we are working with*
> *faulty information. And if our purpose is to love*
> *God, and we do so by honoring Him and respecting*
> *His laws and principles, then we must gracefully and*
> *gratefully bow to His revelation of truth in order to*
> *do what is right and appropriate in His eyes.* [4]

Paul instructs us that God gave us His inerrant Word in order that we may "be complete, thoroughly equipped for every good work." [5]

CHRISTIAN, CONSERVATIVE OR DEIST ...
WHICH DOES YOUR LIFESTYLE SAY YOU ARE?

As the saying goes, "Actions speak louder than words." So the question each of us needs to answer is: "Does our lifestyle reflect that we are a Christian, or a non-Christian?" Since this book is aimed at Christians, a more useful question might be: "Do our daily decisions (whether in the legislature, in the courthouse, the home, or another vocation) testify to those around us that we are a Christian or a Deist?

Were I not, by God's grace, a Christian, I probably would be a deist. From a non-Christian viewpoint, there are a couple of good reasons to be a deist. First, this explains the orderliness in creation that cannot be explained by a totally chance and random "Big Bang" theory. Second, imagining that God created the universe (and us) and is now sitting idly by watching us "do our thing" is compatible with the non-Christians' self-centered point of view because it doesn't hold them accountable for their actions. Since Deists don't allow for any on-going communications with God, we could make up ways to worship Him one day a week, then push Him completely out of our minds during the rest of the week, while we attend to our "real world" obligations. The separation of the church and state takes on a completely new meaning for Deists.

According to Christianity, as we have seen, God assigns both of these spheres specific responsibilities, and the state should not usurp the responsibilities of the church, nor vice-versa. Both, however, are accountable to operate according to biblical principles. On the other hand, Deists have no such guidelines, so they can live like hell on earth and imagine that they will go to heaven when they die. Talk about the best of both worlds!

While deists can't see that theirs is a false religion, the scales from our eyes have mercifully been removed so we can correctly see the truth.[6] We know that God is actively involved in His Creation, and we know that we have been called to transform our culture into one that reflects His will.[7] And

> We know that before we begin our godly attack on culture, we need to attack ourselves, and get our worldview and lifestyle squared away.

We also have confidence our godly walk will help transform our culture because God gives us His Word that evil will eventually perish. [8]

The Difference between Conservative and Christian Civil Rulers

At any moment we are either imaging Christ (keeping His laws), or Satan (breaking Christ's laws by living according to a different set of rules). Approaching your legislative duties from an exclusively Christian perspective (imaging Christ) may seem an overwhelming task. And well it would be without the Creator God's help. The thought of having the Creator God in your corner, watching over you and directing your every move through His revealed Word should more than offset any "peer pressure" to image Satan. The difference being a Christian makes is that we have God guiding us, blessing our obedience!

- How can we expect to improve on God's will by living according to our ideas?
- Since the Triune God has brought us out of darkness and into light, why are we more concerned about how people will respond to His truth, than we are about how He will respond to our compromising His truth?

The ultimate question is, "Under which ideas shall we live: true or false ones?" To compromise with the proponents of false ideas is to agree that society's problems are not inside us (a sinful heart), but are outside us (bad family or social environment, bad education). Such a position leads to dealing only with the symptoms of what ails society. The results are:

> *There is no biblical warrant for religiouse pluralism.*

- more civil government programs
- higher taxes, and
- the continuation of the problems

Scripture teaches that God is primarily concerned with a society's ethics. We live in an orderly universe where predictable results follow our actions (including legislative decisions). This means that good (or godly) legislation will produce good results. Why, then, leave God out of your strategy to govern? Your duty is to be Biblically correct, not politically correct.

> *Do your best to present yourself to God as one approved, a workman who does not need to be ashamed and who correctly handles the word of truth.*   2 TIMOTHY 2.15

TEN QUESTIONS THAT ONLY THE BIBLE CORRECTLY ANSWERS

Jesus does not command us to transform the culture of the world to His Father's principles and then leave us on our own to figure out how to do it. He knows too well that if He did, we would, with the best of intentions, mess things up royally. The purpose of *The Christian Prince* is to describe the biblical frame of mind from which civil rulers should approach their vocation. In-depth explanations to the following questions can be found in such works as my books *Choose This Day: God's Instructions on How to Select Leaders,* and *The Christian Civil Ruler's Handbook.*[9] For our purposes, the following questions will help solidify your thinking:

1. How should we govern ourselves?
2. Are there any limits to civil government?
3. What criteria should civil rulers use for legislating, and governing?
4. Should political knowledge rest on experience and man's reason, or upon the instructions our Creator has given to us?
5. Does the Bible give any support for the state's educating our children?
6. What kinds of services are we currently paying for, through our taxes, that should be handled by the individual, the family, or the church?
7. What kinds of civil laws are "good," and which are "evil" and should be overturned?
8. What kinds of wars are "just?"
9. What's more important: peer acceptance, or God's acceptance? Staying in office, or staying in the good graces of our Lord, Savior and King?
10. Is our political goal to bring down the other party's principles, or to honor Christ's principles by governing ourselves according to His will? Your stance for Godly principles will automatically "bring down" your opposition's principles; but if your priority is to merely contrast your "conservative' principles with their "liberal" principles, you will sooner or later lose esteem not only with voters, but with God.

A Christian legislator's biggest mistake is to believe he is representing someone other than Jesus Christ. It is true that our constituents vote us into office and we owe them our best representation, but such representation must be based upon biblical principles, not just the latest public opinion poll. We must guard against Christianity becoming just another religious alternative, or simply a custom from by-gone days. As Christians, we know that Christianity is the one, true religion, but knowing that does not fulfill our commitment to God. It is incumbent upon us to provide a daily demonstration of its superiority over all false religious views, including the religious view of the state! As a Christian legislator, you must be like Issachar "who understood the times with the knowledge of what [you] should do." [10]

The following statement from Martin Luther is as familiar as it is famous. Until now you may have never considered its applications to civil government. Luther, after all, was a theologian, but the underlying premise of *The Christian Prince* is that all vocations are godly and to be successful, must incorporate biblical principles into their daily duties. To see how explicitly Luther's admonitions apply to civil rulers, read his words as though they were yours.

> *If I profess with the loudest voice and clearest exposition every portion of the truth of God except precisely that little point which the world and the devil are at the moment attacking, I am not confessing Christ, however boldly I may be professing Christ. Where the battle rages, there the loyalty of the soldier is proved. He is disgraced if he flinches at that point.* MARTIN LUTHER

As a legislator or a judge, you are always going to be dealing with "hot button" cultural issues. When you do, will you be hesitant to present the biblical reasons for supporting or opposing certain issues? As a judge will you make your rulings based strictly upon the written words of the law? Luther tells us that we find out the worth of the soldier in the heat of the battle. As a legislator are you flinching at that point because a biblical stand may be too controversial? Or, as a judge, if public sentiment opposes a decision based upon the law, will you be faithful to stand on the law instead of public opinion? If not, how do you plan to present your reasons for "bailing out" on your Lord, Savior and King, Jesus Christ when you see Him on Judgment Day?

IS GOD'S RULE LIMITED TO THE COZY CONFINES OF OUR CHURCHES AND HOMES?

We are commanded not to serve two masters. This means that it is not enough to "love" Christ inside our Churches and homes, while we "hate (or "despise") Him by obeying ungodly laws in the workplace, the State House, the school, and in our day-to-day activities. The purpose of God's Word is to show us how to live and govern ourselves. It gives us direction. When God's laws are taken away, so is the true meaning of life.

> *Any law that violates the law of God is no law at all.*
> WILLIAM BLACKSTONE
> COMMENTARIES, VOLUME 1, 1765

To keep God's truths on the sidelines of life and to not advocate and promote His principles, is to live as if His Word is irrelevant to day-to-day activities, and to imply that man's will is superior to God's. The following verses testify that God's will is superior to ours, and that He is in complete control of His creation and doesn't need any help from our "wisdom."

> *For the kingdom is the Lord's and He rules over the nations.* PSALM 22.28

By Me kings reign, and rulers decree justice.

PROVERBS 8.15

The king's heart is in the hand of the Lord, like the rivers of water; He turns it wherever He wishes.

PROVERBS 21.2

For a society to succeed it must follow God's instructions, for "God is not mocked." [11] Our goal, as Christians, and your goal as a Christian civil ruler, is to live according to "every word that proceeds from the mouth of God." [12] These words, as revealed in Scripture, reflect God's will for our life, and in order to effect His will "on earth as it is in heaven,"[13] we have no other option but to conduct our personal and public actions according to His Word. Nowhere in Scripture does God instruct us that His laws are no longer the best way to conduct our civil affairs. This means that for a society to imagine it is smarter than God is to insult its Creator, Lord, Savior and King!

As king Solomon proclaims, "Righteousness exalts a nation, but sin is a disgrace to any people." [14] It should not be forgotten that the non-Jewish city of Sodom was destroyed for breaking an Old Testament case law,[15] and the non-Jewish city of Nineveh was spared destruction because it repented and began living in obedience to God's Word. [16] Any nation can be assured that unless it does its best to follow God's laws, it will perish. [17]

Old habits do die hard, but as the 14th Century Catholic writer Thomas Kempis notes, "Habit is overcome by habit," and the Biblical Legislative Checklist is presented to help you replace any non-Christian approaches to your legislative duties with Christian ones.

Nowhere does Scripture teach that God's principles for living are intended to be applied exclusively to the private aspects of our lives.

131

Biblical Legislative Checklist [18]

		YES	NO
1.	Does the proposed legislation limit its regulations to the jurisdiction of the Civil Government's realm—its tasks of keeping the peace, pursuing law-breakers, and providing a defense against an invasion?	____	____
2.	In which direction does the proposed legislation take us? Closer to God's will (reducing spending, taxes, and services by eliminating or not funding an ungodly piece of legislation that is currently on the books), or further from God (increasing spending and taxes through increased bureaucracy)?	____	____
3.	Does it promote self-government, or does it promote central government by infringing on one or more of the other three realms of self-governing authority (Self, Family, and Church)?	____	____
4.	Are there any amendments to the legislation that compromise its biblical warrant? This is the classical "You have to 'go along' (with the beliefs [legislation] of others) in order to 'get along' (have some of your beliefs [legislation] accepted by others)." One's beliefs in this ungodly way of legislating are based on who's the most influential, not on an absolute and transcendent standard.	____	____
5.	Since all civil government programs are funded by taxpayers, will this proposed legislation result in an increase or a decrease in the civil government's spending (and taxes)?	____	____
6.	To whom will it bring honor: man (a politician or political party) or God (by helping to bring an area of civil government into compliance with Scripture)?	____	____
7.	Is the genesis of the proposed legislation public opinion, or God's opinion?	____	____

YES   NO

8. Whose ethics does it reflect? The triune God of
Scripture, or a false god (including one's self)? Since
non-Christian Conservatives and Liberals imagine man
to be the ultimate authority in ethics, there will always
be a dispute among them as to which man knows best.
As Christians, we know that "Father knows best."   ____   ____

9. Whose values does it represent? There can be no "good
behavior" rating for any legislation that is not based
on Scripture. At best, there can be only "near-good
behavior" which mirrors Christian principles, (e.g. don't
kill, don't steal, etc.). However, these "near-good"
behaviors will only continue for a while, since sooner
or later the consensus of the people will change, being
based on relative truth which is subject to change at
any time, for any reason.   ____   ____

10. Does the proposed legislation reflect Good Intentions,
or God's Intentions? Even though many in leadership
positions enact policies, laws, and regulations with
good intentions, their plans will fail because one result
of Adam's "fall" is that the unregenerate mind of man
cannot and will not act in a consistently righteous
manner.   ____   ____

11. Will the proposed legislation protect property rights?   ____   ____

12. Will this bill put a bandage over a cultural issue, or
cure it?   ____   ____

13. Does the proposed legislation conflict with our state's
constitution? Or with the U.S. Constitution?   ____   ____

IS IT MACHIAVELL*IAN* OR CHRIST*IAN* ▓▓▓▓▓▓▓▓▓▓▓▓▓▓▓▓▓
To Be Pragmatic?
Machiavelli Principle 21

#21 *Of Mixed Monarchies*

> *Surely I have taught you statutes and judgments,
> just as the LORD my God commanded me, that you
> should act according to them in the land which you
> go to possess. Therefore be careful to observe them;
> for this is your wisdom and your understanding in
> the sight of the peoples who will hear all these
> statutes, and say, "Surely this great nation is a wise
> and understanding people." For what great nation
> is there that has God so near to it, as the LORD our
> God is to us, for whatever reason we may call upon
> Him? And what great nation is there that has such
> statutes and righteous judgments as are in all this
> law which I set before you this day?*
> DEUTERONOMY 4.5-8

> *Trust in the LORD with all your heart, and lean
> not on your own understanding; in all your ways
> acknowledge Him, and He shall direct your paths.
> Do not be wise in your own eyes; fear the LORD
> and depart from evil. It will be health to your flesh,
> and strength to your bones.* PROVERBS 3.5-8

> *There is a way that seems right to a man, but its end
> is the way of death.* PROVERBS 14.12

The socialist philosopher Karl Marx once remarked that "religion is the opiate of the people." The point he was emphasizing is that the state should be careful to always keep certain religious views available to the citizens because they must have somewhere to go to comfort themselves from the heavy hand of the tyrannical socialist state. To Marx's way of thinking any religion would suffice, as long as it didn't hold its adherents accountable to live out their religious beliefs. "Just keep them inside your homes and churches and you will be allowed to continue to worship," was Marx's (and the KGB's) point—and is the prevailing thought of many of today's American legislators and judges, sadly including many who profess to be Christians.

Marx knew that such a religious view would prove harmless to the state's agenda. Unfortunately during the past 150 years, Christianity has become the "opiate" of the vast majority of our Christian brothers and sisters. As a result, it has become culturally irrelevant. It is not uncommon for pastors to teach their congregations that their beliefs are irrelevant to current social and cultural issues. I'm certain you've heard the statements:

- "Religion and politics don't mix," and
- "Politicians are dishonest and can't be trusted."

Such statements raise the question: "If Christians have nothing to do with the public square, who's left but people who are dishonest and untrustworthy!"

Was Marx correct, then, when he claimed that the chief value of religion was to placate citizens? The answer is both No and Yes. As a non-Christian he was wrong in lumping all religions together as though there was no appreciable difference. Except for Christianity, he would be correct, but Christianity is the one true religion. Indeed, without the absolute truths of Scripture, no one would be able to definitively define "good and evil behavior."

On the other hand, and in a much broader sense than Marx intended, religion is the opiate of the people, because everyone has a set of personal ethics by which he makes his daily decisions. Even atheists, who proudly proclaim, "There is no God!" contradict themselves by defining good and evil by their own made-up standards, each acting, in essence, as though he is his own god!

Each of us wants to be successful. Therefore, each of us approaches every day with the set of ethical values in which we trust and rely on to help us succeed. Unfortunately, from Monday through Saturday many of our brothers and sisters trust in a set of ethics different from the ethics they profess to believe in on Sunday. The question to be asked is this:

> As a legislator, what is your "opiate?"—the inerrant and never-changing absolute Word of the triune God of Scripture, or the ever-changing relative word of man?

Attempting to appease God by living according to heaven's rules on Sunday and living according to hell's rules Monday through Saturday should be so ridiculous on its face that we shouldn't need Jesus to tell us we can't "serve two masters."[19]

- Does your ethical standard change when your pleasant circumstances are replaced by unpleasant ones? If you're a Christian, it shouldn't.

- Does it change in emergency situations? If you're a Christian, it shouldn't.

- Does it change when your back is against the wall? Again, if you're a Christian, it shouldn't.

Regardless of what we profess to believe, our true god will be demonstrated by our everyday actions. If we say we are Christians, but walk according to man's ethics during most of the week, we are blaspheming our Lord, Savior and King, Jesus Christ.

Niccolo Machiavelli once stated that he "loved his country more than his soul," [20] which explains why he was such a patriot and supporter of civil government, and why he saw no need to govern according to biblical principles. As Christians, it would be easy to shake our heads in sadness and say, "As street-smart as Machiavelli was, he missed the most important thing!" But before we are tempted to make that response, let us ask ourselves whether or not Machiavelli was being more true to his worldview than we are to ours. He loved the state and was not ashamed to proclaim that love and devotion to anyone who would listen. It consumed his thoughts and desires, and he devoted his life to "evangelizing" future princes to govern according to his well-intended (but misguided) prescriptions. What about us?

> Do we love our Lord, Savior and King more than our country? More than our state? ...More than our community? ...More than our family?

Do we need to be reminded of Jesus' words to His disciples:

> *If anyone comes to Me and does not hate his father and mother, wife and children, brothers and sisters, yes, and his own life also, he cannot be My disciple.*
> LUKE 14.26

Jesus' point was not that we should hate our family, or ourselves, but that we should place His interests and priorities (His standards by which we should live and govern ourselves) above our self-centered desires. If we truly love our soul more than our country or anything else, we can confidently say that we are a member of His Kingdom. If we can't say that, we need to repent and get with His program, before His program gets with us (to paraphrase my drill sergeant).

Is It Machiavellian, or Christian?

It's Machiavellian
to think exclusively in pragmatic terms and to trust no one, because you know how untrustworthy you are (and because you are using yourself or other men as your reference point, instead of Jesus).

It's Christian
to trust in the sovereignty of God in raising up the kind of civil rulers that a community deserves; good ones (as a blessing) for communities who are living according to God's rules, and bad ones (as a judgment) for communities who are living according to man's rules. ROMANS 13

Machiavelli saw the state as being a force intent on bringing about its own will, not a proponent or a maintainer of ethical principles. As we will see in discussing his 18th Principle, he didn't think Christian ethics would work because "all men are wicked, not good." Hence his worldview dictated that people had to be forced to act in certain ways. This pragmatic view is very logical if God is eliminated from the equation, but since God created the equation, there is no way that He can be eliminated from our daily lives without our facing some very unpleasant consequences. Jesus speaks to the distinctive difference it makes to a community to have a civil ruler who governs according to a Christian worldview instead of a non-Christian worldview. *

> *You know that the rulers of the Gentiles lord it over*
> *them, and those who are great exercise authority*
> *over them. Yet it shall not be so among you; but*
> *whoever desires to become great among you, let him*
> *be your servant. And whoever desires to be first*
> *among you, let him be your slave—just as the Son of*
> *Man did not come to be served, but to serve, and to*
> *give His life a ransom for many.* MATTHEW 20.25-28

Machiavelli was being consistent with the viewpoint of philosophies and false religions that say individuals must choose between having a virtuous (religious) private life, or a virtuous (effective) public life. His non-Christian view of the world, however, caused him to conclude some very self-centered, if not outright paranoid outcomes:

- His insistence that it is more important to be "politically correct" than to be "biblically correct" meant that he could not refer to history to learn lessons about different types of civil government. The pages of the Old Testament show that no form of civil government has ever succeeded

---

* *Electing Christians to public office, as important as that is, will only help solve our cultural challenges if they govern according to a Christian worldview. Otherwise the legislator or judge will be a well-intentioned "conservative" who supports the 2nd Table of the Law (commandments 5-10), but who hesitates to proclaim the authority behind his ethics (the 1st Table, commandments 1-4). This denial of God means all political debates come down to conservative man's word against liberal man's word. We cannot expect to improve our culture on the basis of "he said, she said" reasoning. Make no mistake, we must do what we can to elect Christians to public office, but we must also be aware that only one in twenty adult Christians has a developed Christian worldview. [21] This means we have a big-time discipleship job to do to help our Christian brothers understand how to connect their Spiritual Dots from their head to their feet and incorporate biblical truths into their legislative decisions.*

unless it has based its governance upon biblical principles. As the prophet Isaiah exclaims,

> *To the law and to the testimony! If they do not speak according to this word, it is because there is no light in them.* ISAIAH 8.20

Once God's thoughts are tossed to the wind, man is left with his own thoughts:

- "I think the reason all non-Christian civil governments have failed is because they had the wrong kind of leadership." Or "I think the timing wasn't right." Or "I think ..." For a creature to enter a "thinking contest" with his Creator is truly a foolish idea and an un-winnable contest.

- Machiavelli's thoughts mirror the insecurity of never being able to know the outcome of one's actions, once the tenets of absolute truth are dismissed.

> *Whoever is the cause of another becoming powerful, is ruined by himself; for that power is produced by him either through craft or force; and both of these are suspected by the one who has been raised to power.* PRINCIPLE 3

- Machiavelli also demonstrates the meaningless of non-Christian man's words by stating,

> *A prudent ruler cannot, and should not, honor his word when it places him at a disadvantage, and when the reasons for which he made his promise no longer exists.* [22]

In his "The Setting of The Prince," scholar J.R. Hales provides this insight from Machiavelli:

> *Everyone realizes how praiseworthy it is for a prince to honor his word and to be straightforward rather than crafty in his dealings; nonetheless contemporary experience shows that princes who have achieved great things have been those who have given their word lightly.* [23]

- In a world of constant change, absolute ethics don't fit because, without a recognition of God's involvement in ruling and overruling events in His creation, man is left to his own devices in trying to control the outcomes of his decisions. To the non-Christian mindset, absolute ethics are a hindrance to effective policy making, because they rule out the man-centered idea that every ethic is "up for grabs," and in order to "get along in life," we have to "go along with the influence and ideas of non-Christians."
  In Machiavelli's words

> *To act uniformly merely arms one's opponents with a foreknowledge of your probable reactions to a given situation.* PRINCIPLE 3

- Again, when non-Christian civil rulers are left to their own resources in their effort to bring about hoped-for results, they are reduced to appealing to "mass ignorance" in order to get re-elected. Instead of being a statesman and legislating and governing in a manner that conforms to biblical principles, then trusting in God to honor their obedience, they sink to the depths of attempting to "buy votes" by "bringing home the bacon" to their communities in the form of new roads and/or social services.

Without a fixed moral standard, a legislator's reasoning becomes a tentative "Well, I guess it's the right thing to do," instead of a confident, "It's constitutional, and it's biblical and therefore is the right legislation to support."

Christianity frees us from this public/private ethical dichotomy. The truth is that we cannot help exporting our personal ethics into our public actions. If our daily ethics in our vocations are different from our Sunday ethics, this tells us that we view our Sunday ethics as being deficient and/or false! According to this mindset, we'll rely on our Sunday ethics (God's wisdom) as long as they don't conflict with our wisdom and as long as we are in a situation or circumstance where they will be accepted by our associates (or voters).

Ethics, however, cannot be divorced from politics, or any other sphere of life. Non-Christians like to imagine that "the art of politics" boils down to certain skills and/or techniques; that it is a vocation that is beyond good and evil, and is only concerned with expediency and attracting votes and partisan support. But no sphere of life is autonomous—independent of the others—because God created a universe, where all things work together, [24] not a biverse where different ethics apply to different situations. God's creation is designed to be orderly, not chaotic.

Moses' father-in-law, Jethro, gives Moses (and us) the biblical criteria to look for in our leaders:

> *Moreover you shall select from all the people, able men, such as fear God, men of truth, hating covetousness; and place such over them to be rulers of thousands, rulers of hundreds, rulers of fifties, and rulers of tens.* EXODUS 18.21

The idea that there are "religious" (private) and "real life" (public) realms to life is a MYTH. It is completely unbiblical and is put forth by non-Christians who realize that if we live out our faith, their self-centered agendas will be overthrown. The reason for this is that the world was created by God to operate according to His rules, not our rules. Satan and our non-Christian neighbors understand this, but we don't seem to "get it." As Jesus teaches in his parable of the Unjust Steward,

> *The sons of this world are more shrewd in their generation than the sons of light."*   LUKE 16.8

Proponents of this myth, or more accurately, this false religion, say that Christian principles should be kept inside our churches and homes because the absolute dogmas of Christianity will divide the populace and cause dissensions. Their ungodly solution sees relativism and tolerance as bringing unity. [25] All non-Christian worldviews and lifestyles see the means as justifying the ends. Their attitude is, "As long as we achieve our goals, what difference does it make if we have to bend some rules along the way?"

Yes, ethics do begin with the "goal" in mind, but the question is,

> As a civil ruler, whose goals are you setting out each day to accomplish: God's or man's?"

In answering this question we will also answer the question that separates a true profession of Christian faith from false professions. It is this:

> *Who's in control of planet earth: the Creator or the creature?*

143

Machiavelli loved the state more than his soul; other non-Christians love their career, or their children, or their favorite athletic team more than their soul. For us, however, we have admitted that we love God more than anything else and we should be proving this to ourselves and to our neighbors by trusting in and relying upon His word alone to guide and direct us in our daily decision-making.

Non-Christian civil rulers see no God-ordained purpose for the state. Instead of understanding that the purpose of civil government is to defend a community from attack and to provide a safe environment in which the residents can live, work, play and raise their families, [26] they view public office as an opportunity to amass power and personal privileges. They consult other elected officials in other communities in hopes of finding more effective tactics and strategies to use in their governing.

Approximately 700 years before the birth of Jesus, Micah prophesied to the Jews in Jerusalem about God's judgment that would come against them for their failure to live according to His rules. But Micah also told them of a time (our time), when God would restore His people and bless them (us) mightily because of their (our) obedience to His will.

> *Christian civil rulers recognize that they are Christ's cultural Silver Bullets, and it is through their faithful and consistent obedience in incorporating His principles into their worldview and lifestyle that they help bring about His will on earth as it is in heaven.* [27]

Many nations shall come and say, "Come, and let us go up to the mountain of the LORD, to the house of the God of Jacob; He will teach us His ways, and we shall walk in His paths." For out of Zion the law shall go forth, and the word of the LORD from Jesus. MICAH 4.2

While non-Christians are turning to each other and forming coalitions and compromising their values in an attempt to find successful short-term solutions to cultural problems so they can get re-elected, we should be turning to the all-knowing, never-compromising Creator God for His perfect and inerrant answers.

History proves decisively that man's ideas lead to tyranny and heavy-handed central government, while God's ideas lead to liberty and self-government. Non-Christian civil rulers, following Machiavelli's advice, view the words contained in state and federal constitutions as not being worth the paper on which they are written. In a similar fashion, judges (the other God-ordained civil office) usurp the responsibilities of legislators by arrogantly "legislating" from the bench, instead of making rulings based on the absolute written legal code.

Christian civil rulers have the confidence that laws based upon biblical principles will successfully deal with cultural problems, because God's Word (and only those laws that conform to God's Word) is truth! The contrast couldn't be sharper:

Christian civil rulers seek to bring honor and glory to our Lord, Savior and King, Jesus Christ, by faithfully and consistently legislating and judging according to biblical principles. Non-Christian civil rulers seek to bring honor and glory to themselves by legislating and judging according to man's principles.

The POLICY Guide on the next page can be used in a couple of ways. If you are a Christian civil ruler (legislator or judge), sign it, copy it and distribute it in your district. If you are a voter, make a copy of it and give it to incumbents and/or candidates and ask that they sign it. As you read it you will see that the six points that make up the acronym POLICY will quickly separate political demagoguery from Christian doctrine.

POLICY Guide [28]

As a Christian Civil Ruler (legislator or judge) I pledge to conform my actions at the local, state, or federal level to God's will as explained in Scripture. I understand that each Civil Ruler is placed in his position by God, with obedient ones bringing blessings to their constituents, and disobedient ones bringing curses. It is my intention to faithfully serve my Lord, Savior and King and be a fount of blessing to my constituents. The following acronym summarizes the approach to fulfilling my role as a Civil Ruler and by signing it I am merely making public what I have already vowed to God as His servant.

P – To advocate and **promote** God's principles, for by not doing so would be to live as if His Word was meaningless for day-to-day activities, and would also imply that man's wisdom is superior to God's. Jesus cannot be Lord of our individual lives without at the same time being Lord of our culture.

O – My role is to **obey** His revealed instructions; God's role is to bring about the desired results. Therefore I will strive to do the right thing unhesitatingly, even if from my perspective it might appear that I would lose votes, committee assignments, or even election to office. I so act because I firmly place my faith and trust in God's sovereign control of all situations and circumstances.

L – I will **legislate** (and/or make judicial decisions) according to the principles in Scripture, being mindful that no legislation—no action in the civil sphere—should infringe on the other three self-governing spheres of Individual, Family, and Church. Truly, the Lord is "our Judge, our Lawgiver and our King." (Isaiah 33.22) While every American is free to hold his own beliefs, we must never let tolerance toward others interfere with enacting legislation that is founded solely on the truth.

I – The Bible is **inerrant**, infallible, and absolutely true, which means that any legislation or judicial decision that does not conform to its principles is false, and represents society's problems, not its solutions. Since ungodly legislation only deals with the "fruit," and not the "root" of a societal problem, any positive results brought about can only be expected to be temporary.

C – The **Church** and State spheres are both accountable to God and should be in harmony as they carry out God's revealed will. There should neither be a union, nor an absolute separation of these two God-appointed spheres. A Christian civilization does not have anything that is separate from God, for separation from Him is death (Proverbs 8.36; Psalm 10.4).

Y – **You've** called me out of darkness into Your marvelous light so that I can do my part to subdue and rule over Your creation. Christianity is life-transforming and results in a new lifestyle (bringing glory and honor to You). It is not merely a lifeboat (or something we "add on" to our current lifestyle).

Signed _____   Date _____

Christian Legislative Building Blocks

God invented civil government and it is only as we govern ourselves according to God's inerrant Word that we will be governed in a "civil" manner.

Once God's clear Word is cast aside, ethics become very murky as we begin to look for rationalizations to justify our sinful behavior.

As a Legislator, what is your "opiate?" Is it the inerrant and never-changing absolute Word of the triune God of Scripture, or is it the ever-changing relative word of man?

We know that before we begin our godly attack on culture, we need to attack ourselves, and get our worldview and lifestyle squared away.

Nowhere does Scripture teach that God's principles for living are intended to be applied exclusively to the private aspects of our lives.

As a civil ruler, whose goals are you setting out each day to accomplish: God's or man's?

Do we love our Lord, Savior and King more than our country? More than our state? More than our community? More than our family?

Without a fixed moral standard a legislator's reasoning becomes a tentative "Well, I guess it's the right thing to do," instead of a confident, "It's constitutional, and it's biblical and therefore is the right legislation to support."

If judges can read into the Constitution "rights" that are not there they can also read out of the Constitution "rights" that are there.

Christian civil rulers recognize that they are Christ's cultural Silver Bullets, and it is through their faithful and consistent obedience in incorporating His principles into their worldview and lifestyle that they help bring about His will on earth as it is in heaven. (MATTHEW 6.10)

There is no biblical warrant for religious pluralism.

NOTES

1 Stein, Leo, *Hitler Came For Me*, (Pelican, 1942, 2003), p. 241

2 Morecraft, *op.cit.*, *Fundamentals*, Vol. II

3 John 18.38

4 Barna, *op.cit.*, *Think*, pp.160-61

5 2 Timothy 3.16

6 Acts 9.3-19

7 Matthew 6.10

8 Genesis 3.15

9 These can be ordered through your favorite bookstore or through Buddy Hanson's website www.graceandlaw. com, or by emailing bhanson@ graceandlaw.com or calling 205.454.1442

10 1 Chronicles 12.32

11 Galatians 6.7

12 Deuteronomy 8.4; Matthew 4.4

13 Mathew 6.10

14 Proverbs 14.34

15 Homosexuality, Genesis 19.4; cf. Leviticus 18.22; 14.4; 15.12; 22.46; 2 Kings 23.7

16 Jonah 3 all; Luke 11.30,32

17 Deuteronomy 8.20; 30.17-18

18 Hanson, Buddy, *The Christian Civil Ruler's Handbook*, (Hanson Group, 2004), pp. 47-48

19 Matthew 6.24

20 A letter to Guicciardini, cited in Isaiah Berlin's "The Question of Machiavelli" in *The Prince*, (Norton Critical Edition,

1992), p.214, translated and edited by Robert M. Adams

21 George Barna, The Barna Group, www.barna.org

22 Machiavelli, Niccolo, *The Prince* (Norton Critical Edition, 1992). Cited by J.R. Hale, p. 144

23 Hale, *ibid.*, *Setting*, p.144

24 Romans 8.28

25 This is a direct breaking of God's First Commandment, "[Have] no other gods before Me," Exodus 20.3

26 Romans 13.1-7; 1 Peter 2.13-17

27 Matthew 6.10

28 Hanson, *op.cit.*, *Handbook*, p. ix

Becoming the
Change
We Seek

PLAN YOUR WORK,
WORK YOUR PLAN

*Do your best to present yourself to God as one
approved, a workman who does not need to be
ashamed and who correctly handles the Word
of truth.*   2 TIMOTHY 2.15

HOW'S YOUR PLAN PROGRESSING FOR CARRYING OUT GOD'S WILL?
If your response is that you don't have a specific plan, or
that your plan is a little on the fuzzy side, you would do
well to consider what your non-Christian neighbors are up
to. In case you haven't noticed, there is nothing fuzzy or half-
hearted about their plans. In football games, quarterbacks
go through their "progressions" on plays. For example,
on a pass play they will have a primary receiver in mind.
If that receiver is covered, they will go to a second or third
receiver, or as a last resort, pull the ball down and run with
it. The point is that they have a specific plan and according
to the adjustments of the defense, they "progress" through
their various options, and depending upon their decision and
execution, the play will succeed or fail.

As discussed, non-Christians have been "going through
their progressions" for more than a century and a half in
America, meeting little, if any, opposition on the part of
Christians. This has allowed them to make giant strides

toward de-Christianizing our culture. Here are some of the elements of their plans:

- Brainwashing our children by teaching them in their public (government) schools to depend upon civil government services and programs instead of relying upon their personal initiative and self-government. In other words, making them dumbed-down wards of the state.
- Redeeming our personal liberty by taking more and more of our tax dollars to pay for the various social programs that we and our churches should be funding.
- Confiscating our property if they can sell it to someone else to generate more tax revenues.
- Convincing us to segregate "religion" and "real life" into two unrelated mental compartments, thereby making our Christian ethics culturally irrelevant and, in essence, barricading our ethics inside our homes and churches while non-Christians accomplish their politically correct (Marxist) cultural agenda.
- Maintaining an "open border" policy to allow illegal immigrants to flood into our country, then providing them with social services in an effort to build a voting base to keep non-Christian legislators in office.
- Establishing a national religious ethic (Political Correctness) that makes it heretical to incorporate Christian ethics into the cultural discussion and/or one's lifestyle.
- Ignoring the capitalist concepts in state and federal constitutions (which reflect America's collective Christian worldview at the time they were written), and promote socialism (which reflects today's collective non-Christian worldview). [1]

In the face of such a well-thought out and passionately pursued plan, it can be quite intimidating to consider whether legislators, judges, homemakers, policemen, or anyone else can stop the downward spiral of our culture, and even to restore it to being governed according to biblical principles. Yet that is exactly what we have been called into Christ's Kingdom to do. Just because the vast majority of Christians have been negligent in living out a specific plan to redeem our culture, it doesn't follow that such a plan doesn't exist. It most certainly does, and it is revealed on the divinely inspired pages of the Bible. In addition, the fact that non-Christians are currently having their way, doesn't mean that they are thwarting the eternally perfect plans of our triune God. To the contrary, God's plans are exactly on schedule as they always have been and always will be.

When Jesus created the earth, He created an orderly existence. Our actions cause consequences. The success of the plans of non-Christians is proof of that. They are implementing their plans, and we are doing practically nothing to oppose them, so the results we are receiving are ungodly and chaotic (since we are offering no godly and orderly alternatives). Just as God has tested cultures in the past, rewarding those who repented and followed His rules, and disciplining (and even destroying) those who persisted in following man's rules, so is He doing with America. Our calling includes replacing the chaos that results from man-centered civil government with the orderliness that results from a God-centered civil government. The task looks overwhelming, but that's only because we are looking at it from our perspective. So before we throw up our hands in frustration, we should get a glimpse of the earth from God's perspective. David provides words that should not only transform our perspective, but energize our prospects for successfully serving Christ in His Kingdom.

153

*Why do the nations rage, and the people plot a vain
thing? The kings of the earth set themselves, and the
rulers take counsel together, against the LORD
and against His Anointed, saying "Let us break their
bonds in pieces and cast away their cords from us."*
*He who sits in the heavens shall laugh; the LORD
shall hold them in derision. Then He shall speak to
them in His wrath, and distress them in His deep
displeasure: "Yet I have set My King on My holy hill
of Zion."*
*I will declare the decree: the LORD has said to
Me, 'You are My Son, today I have begotten You.
Ask of Me, and I will give You the nations for Your
inheritance, and the ends of the earth for Your
possession. You shall break them with a rod of iron;
You shall dash them to pieces like a potter's vessel.'"*
*Now therefore, be wise, O kings; be instructed,
you judges of the earth. Serve the LORD with fear,
and rejoice with trembling. Kiss the Son, lest He be
angry, and you perish in the way, when His wrath
is kindled but a little. Blessed are all those who put
their trust in Him.* PSALM 2

DON'T WORRY, BE OBEDIENT

Sure, it's easy to get overwhelmed at the prospect of "un-
quoing the status," [2] but remember that there is not just one
non-Christian who is causing all of our cultural turmoil.
There are lots of them doing what they do best. So, instead of
being intimidated by their success, we should be encouraged
by witnessing first-hand that God created a cause-and-effect
universe. The plans and schemes of non-Christians have
been successful because we have not offered any opposition
to them. All that is required for us to begin to take back the
cultural gains they have made is to begin to live by Christ's
rules.

The first step is for each of us to identify an area in our culture that matches our skills and abilities. That's all we have to do, because we know that God promises to bless our obedience in His perfect timing with victory. Think about the pressure non-Christians are constantly under. Since they are their own gods, they bear the full responsibility of not only obeying the dictates of their philosophies and false religions; they also bear the burden for bringing about the desired results. Now that's pressure! Need more encouragement? If so, think for a few moments about the significance of the title, Christian.

• The great privilege that God has bestowed on us in His infinite mercy and grace.
• The great price that was paid so we might bear the name of Christ.

Next ask yourself, "Why we are hesitant to refer to ourselves as Christians at all times?" Whether we're at work, in school, on the playground, on a date, or anywhere, to hesitate to proclaim that we are a Christian is to admit that we fear man more than we fear God!

We are the only people on the face of the earth who have been given the answers to how to live, govern ourselves and get along with our neighbors, yet all too often we ignore the wisdom of our Lord, Savior, and King and turn to fellow sinful creatures in an effort to solve our culture's problems. Then we wonder why things continue to get worse!

America's culture is rapidly declining, not because Christians don't know the answers, but because we haven't "connected our Spiritual Dots" to the problems that face us. This is preventing us from seeing God's complete picture of the way our civil government should operate.

155

Jesus is not interested in how many biblical truths we know, but in how many we incorporate into our lifestyle. Our calling is not to be the smartest person in the Concentration Camp, but to prevent the Concentration Camp from happening. He is not only our personal Savior. He is our Lord (instructing us how to live in all situations and circumstances), and He is our King (instructing civil rulers how to govern).

ENCOUNTERING RESISTANCE

Jesus promises that we will be recipients of some ill treatment as a result of living in obedience to His will. Have you ever wondered why that is? Have you ever wondered whether the cultural situation will be reversed so that it is not us, but them who will be discriminated against? The "Then What Happens" chart illustrates four steps most Christians take and one step that a few take as we go through life. Overall, it's not a very pretty picture:

Then What Happens?

- Everybody is a born sinner and hates the triune God of Scripture, but then what happens?
- The Holy Spirit changes our heart, which enables us to choose Jesus as our Lord, Savior and King, but then what happens?
- When we step outside of our home and church we are swimming upstream against the flow of the collective non-Christian worldview, and then what happens?
- At this point in time non-Christians have captured all of the influential cultural institutions in our culture because they have been more dedicated to living according to their will, than we are to living according to God's will. If their attitude toward us was the same as our attitude toward them, we would not encounter much resistance. Then what happens?
- A few Christians take their beliefs outside of their homes and churches, taking an unashamed stand for Christ's Kingdom in all of the situations and circumstances they encounter, and they are called "heroes of the faith," and their obedience leads to a transformation of their community's culture.

But are these brothers and sisters really heroes, or have they rather realized that to obey God is the only acceptable decision they could make in order to be consistent with their profession of faith? In other words, their actions are not the result of personal bravery so much as a refusal to blaspheme their Lord, Savior and King, Jesus Christ. They have simply seen no alternative but to

✔ conduct their vocational decisions according to the biblical principles they profess to believe
✔ educate their children in the manner in which God says we should "train them up"
✔ cultivate our relationship to our spouse and children according to biblical principles
✔ interact with friends and neighbors according to God's Word

Throughout *The Christian Prince* we have been emphasizing the importance of "Walking in a manner worthy of God who calls us into His own kingdom and glory." [3] Now comes the time when we focus on some of the things you, as a civil ruler, can do to present yourself as an "approved worker" for Christ's Kingdom. It is said that the best preparation for the future is the present duty well seen to and the last duty well done, but by now I hope you are asking, "Who defines duty?" If you are a legislator or a judge, it is not your constituency who defines your duty!

Although you were elected to represent their interests (and should do so, whenever possible), you may have to make a decision to oppose some popular legislation that you know is out of sync with biblical principles. Or you may have to support some unpopular legislation. You certainly won't find either of these tactics in the writings of Machiavelli. However by now it would be hoped that you agree with this:

Any legislation that does not conform to a biblical principle will not prove to be in your constituent's best interests, even though they think that it will and even though it may sound very enticing.

The reason for this, as we have discussed, is that only God's Word is true, which means that any piece of legislation that does not conform to Scripture will not work as we may think it should (no matter how many tax payer dollars are thrown at it!). Pastor Bill Einwechter observes,

> *Reformation always begins when men return to the truths revealed in Holy Scripture (with a return to sound doctrine). This is illustrated in both Scripture and history. The great reformation in the days of Josiah began when the "book of the law of the Lord given by Moses" was found in the Temple. As the law was read to them, the king and people heard the truth of the Word of God and began to act according to its teaching (cf. 2 CHRONICLES 34.14 – 35.27). In the days of Martin Luther, the great doctrines of sola scriptura, sola fide, and sola gratia were rediscovered in the Bible, and the great Protestant Reformation was launched.* [4]

Some civil rulers may be tempted to say, "Such an unflinching stand for Christ's Kingdom presents too big an obstacle in my path." But before you make such a statement, remember whom you are serving. Shouldn't it be thought that the Creator of the Universe can handle whatever obstacle you encounter? "Obstacles" have been defined as "those frightful things you see when you take your eyes off your goals," and your goal, as a Christian civil ruler, is serving our Lord,

Savior and King, Jesus Christ and trusting in Him to "work all things together for good." [5] King Solomon assures us that if we "acknowledge God in all our ways, He shall direct our paths," [6] so what are we waiting for?

We can't plow the field by turning it over in our mind, so let's get busy getting out into the field and becoming the change we seek in the world. The 19th century judge and physician, Oliver Wendell Holmes, writes, "The great thing in this world is not so much where we are, but in what direction we are moving."

Our non-Christian opponents hope that we will be intimidated by their control of all of culture's influential institutions. By default we have allowed them to take over the schools, media and civil government. In each instance they have gained their victories virtually unopposed. But while they hold the upper hand in our culture, they are not invincible. Far from it:

> What man has made, man can change, and everything non-Christians have accomplished has been done without God, and we have God!

Take sportswriters, for example (please, somebody, take them somewhere!), they are the most unreliable sources of information concerning the upcoming season, because to them whoever is winning at the moment will seem to be invincible. So what do they do with their pre-season predictions? They predict last season's winners. Even though repeating championship seasons is rare, sportswriters are so unimaginative and herd-following that they shy away from the hard work of honestly evaluating talent in offering their predictions.

So, to use the sports analogy, non-Christians are in first place in our culture and have a string of impressive victories, but if we examine how they achieved their victories we'll find that they have had a patsy schedule. Since our churches have all but stopped instructing us in how to live out our faith (preferring to focus on evangelism instead of discipleship, and pietism instead of pious living) non-Christians have been able to "run up the score" with no serious opposition. In addition, all they have is their foolish wisdom. This fact should be obvious since their "solutions" for culture's problems don't work. And, as we all know too well, their "solution" for their unsuccessful social policies is to ask us for more tax money to "make it better."

In direct contrast to them, we have the correct answers to culture's problems, and we have the Creator in our corner instructing us in how to go about it.

> *Jesus tells us that we can reclaim culture and have peace and prosperity and personal liberty by governing ourselves through His four appointed spheres, the individual, family, church and civil government.*

Funding such self-governing lifestyles will take no more than nine percent of our money in taxes, plus a ten percent tithe. Sadly, our response to His perfect wisdom is to say, "A ten percent tithe is too much! Let's let the central government provide social services and education." So while the average church member "tithes" less than two percent, he pays close to fifty percent in taxes.

Let's review our situation: Our wisdom costs us 52 percent of our income, while God's wisdom costs us 19 percent. A person doesn't have to be a math wizard to see that not only does our wisdom cost us more money, but the "solutions" we receive from it don't work! Truly, we are paying for our sins of disrespect for and disregard of God's wisdom.

The object lessons of how God dealt with communities and countries that refused to govern themselves according to His Word, should show us that, theologically, we are skating on very thin ice as far as the survival of our country is concerned. Peter warns us:

> *It would have been better for them not to have known the way of righteousness, than to have known it and then to turn their backs on the sacred commandment that was passed on to them.*
> 2 PETER 2.21

Paul adds that the lessons from past civilizations are recorded in Scripture to help us avoid making similar mistakes and suffering similar consequences:

> *Now all these things happened to them as examples, and they were written for our admonition, upon whom the ends of the ages have come.*
> 1 CORINTHIANS 10.11

Do we really need the 19th century Unitarian minister and transcendentalist Ralph Waldo Emerson to tell us:

> *What you do speaks so loudly that I cannot hear what you say.*

Or, for Emerson to counsel:

> *This time, like all times, is a great time, if we but know what to do with it.*

161

Because of his Unitarian beliefs, Emerson didn't know what to do with the times, but we do! Still, even non-Christians understand that it is impossible for any group to win if it doesn't begin. Their problem is that they don't know what the right actions are. So, yes, Mr. Emerson, we do know that

> *Talk is cheap*
> *Words are plentiful, and*
> **Deeds are precious**

We also know that now is the time to get in gear, and that we must become servants of good habits in order to avoid remaining slaves of bad habits. As Christian civil rulers, you accomplish good habits by incorporating the biblical principles you profess to believe into your daily worldview and lifestyle. As the apostle John points out,

> *We know that we have come to know Him, if we*
> *obey His commands. The man who says, "I know*
> *Him," but does not do what He commands is a liar,*
> *and the truth is not in him. By this we know that we*
> *are in Him: the one who says he abides in Him ought*
> *himself to walk in the same manner as He walked.*
>
> 1 JOHN 2.3-6

Hopefully, this book has reminded you that you have been "called out of darkness and into His wonderful light"[7] in order to be "repairers of the breach and restorers of our culture." [8] Whether in your role as legislator or parent, or in your fulltime vocation, may your overriding motivation be not to please men but to please God, who examines your hearts. May you recognize this.

It is futile to attempt to live with one foot in man's camp and the other in God's camp. Neither camp wants only a part of you. Each demands your whole person.

No one can serve two masters; for either he will hate the one, and love the other, or else he will hold to the one and despise the other. You cannot serve God and man. LUKE 16.13; MATTHEW 6.24

IS SERVING THE LORD YOUR TOP PRIORITY?

So that you incline your ear to wisdom, and apply your heart to understanding; yes, if you cry out for discernment, and lift up your voice for understanding, if you seek her as silver, and search for her as for hidden treasures; then you will understand the fear of the LORD, and find the knowledge of God. For the LORD gives wisdom; from His mouth come knowledge and understanding; He stores up sound wisdom for the upright; He is a shield to those who walk uprightly.
PROVERBS 2.2-7

The world will actively seek to turn our minds in a direction different from than which God intends, which is for us to think like Jesus. [9] So we have one of two choices to make:

- To deny and blaspheme God outside of our homes and churches by denying that He knows the correct way for us to live and govern ourselves. *Or*
- To proclaim Him

If we deny Him we will not be persecuted by the world (the non-Christians), but neither will we be living as Christians. While we may not want to admit this, the consequence of living a life that denies God is to be denied by God!

> Many will say to Me in that day, "Lord, Lord, have we not prophesied in Your name, cast out demons in Your name, and done many wonders in Your name?" And then I will declare to them, "I never knew you; depart from Me, you who practice lawlessness!"
> MATTHEW 7.22-23

> Then the King will say to those on His right hand, "Come, you blessed of My Father, inherit the kingdom prepared for you from the foundation of the world: for I was hungry and you gave Me food; I was thirsty and you gave Me drink; I was a stranger and you took Me in; I was naked and you clothed Me; I was sick and you visited Me; I was in prison and you came to Me."
> MATTHEW 25.34-36

As a Christian legislator your ultimate goal is to restore the biblical foundation and original checks and balances between the legislative, judicial, and executive branches. The way to do that is to

- Conform proposed legislation to God's Word, and
- Undo or un-fund existing legislation that does not conform to biblical principles.

Every new law or policy we make should pass the moral scrutiny of the Word of God.

164

Legislators, executives, judges and citizens all have a responsibility to be certain that the laws of the land follow God's Law. Christians are called to "teach" the nations all the laws, ordinances, principles and commands that God has issued. [10]

The "Who Counts The Most?" chart on the next page contrasts the principles for living and governing ourselves as given by God (the Ten Commandments) and those given by man (The Communist Manifesto). As a Christian legislator, compare both lists carefully and see whether you and your fellow legislators are legislating according to God's will or man's will. Once you "count the ways" and compare the totals, you should have the beginnings of a plan of action by which to join with fellow Christian legislators in repenting and turning your state back toward God's principles. In this way you will demonstrate that God's principles "count" for more than man's principles.

Since God holds us accountable for our actions, civil rulers who vote for unbiblical legislation should be called to account by their congregations because we will not see the restoration of civil government until we see the restoration of the Church. [11] One of the marks of the restored Church is a desire to honor God's Word by counseling, then disciplining if necessary, their members who have committed sinful actions (i.e., media executives and business executives who operate their companies according to unbiblical principles, and yes, elected officials who don't enforce biblical principles in their legislation and judicial decisions).

God gave us this advice through Moses' voice, more than 3,000 years ago, and nowhere does the Bible say that this perfect and inerrant counsel has been revoked:

> *Also it shall be, when he sits on the throne of his*
> *kingdom, that he shall write for himself a copy of*

Who Counts The Most?

The Ten Planks of the Communist Manifesto

1. The abolition of personal property ____
2. An income tax ____
3. Abolition of all right of inheritance ____
4. Confiscation of the property of emigrants and rebels ____
5. Centralization of credit by the state by a national bank ____
6. State control of communications and transportation ____
7. State ownership of factories and land management ____
8. Establishment of industrial armies, especially for agriculture ____
9. Abolition of the distinction of town and country, through population re-distribution ____
10. Free education for all children in public schools ____

Man's ways COUNT for ____

The Ten Commandments

1. You shall have no other gods before Me ____
2. You shall not worship idols ____
3. You shall not use the name of the Lord in vain ____
4. Observe the Sabbath day and keep it holy ____
5. Honor your father and your mother ____
6. You shall not murder ____
7. You shall not commit adultery ____
8. You shall not steal ____
9. You shall not lie ____
10. You shall not covet ____

God's ways COUNT for ____

Who COUNTS for more of your time and efforts?

God ____ Man ____

*this law in a book, from the one before the priests,
the Levites. And it shall be with him, and he shall
read it all the days of his life, that he may learn to
fear the LORD his God and be careful to observe
all the words of this law and these statutes, that his
heart may not be lifted above his brethren, that he
may not turn aside from the commandment to the
right hand or to the left, and that he may prolong his
days in his kingdom, he and his children in the midst
of Israel.* DEUTERONOMY 17.18-20

The Governor of the Massachusetts
Bay Colony, John Winthrop, wrote the
following on board the Arbella in 1630.
His words should be just as inspirational
to today's Americans as they were to those
early settlers.

*We cannot expect
to "bear fruit" if we
hide our light for
fear of losing some
friends or votes.*

*For we must consider that we shall be as
a city upon a hill. The eyes of all people
are upon us. So that if we shall deal falsely with our
God in this work we have undertaken, and so cause
Him to withdraw His present help from us, we shall
be made a story and a by-word through the world.
We shall open the mouths of enemies to speak evil of
the ways of God, and all professors for God's sake.
We shall shame the faces of many of God's worthy
servants, and cause their prayers to be turned into
curses upon us till we be consumed out of the good
land whither we are going.*

*And to shut this discourse with that exhortation of
Moses, that faithful servant of the Lord, in his last
farewell to Israel. (DEUTERONOMY 30) "Beloved, there
is now set before us life and death, good and evil, in
that we are commanded this day to love the Lord our*

God, and to love one another, to walk in his ways
and to keep his Commandments and his ordinances
and his laws, and the articles of our Covenant with
Him, that we may live and be multiplied, and that
the Lord our God may bless us in the land whither
we go to possess it. But if our hearts shall turn away,
so that we will not obey, but shall be seduced, and
worship other Gods, our pleasure and profits, and
serve them; it is propounded unto us this day, we
shall surely perish out of the good land whither we
pass over this vast sea to possess it. Therefore let
us choose life, that we and our seed may live, by
obeying His voice and cleaving to Him, for He is our
life and our prosperity."

Christian Legislative Building Blocks

It is futile to attempt to live with one foot in man's camp and the other in God's camp. Neither camp wants only a part of you. Each demands your whole person.

What man has made, man can change, and everything they have accomplished has been done without God, and *we have God!*

Every new law or policy we make should pass the moral scrutiny of the Word of God.

Jesus tells us that we can reclaim culture and have peace and prosperity and personal liberty by governing ourselves through His four appointed spheres: the individual, family, church and civil government.

Any legislation that does not conform to a biblical principle will not prove to be in your constituent's best interests, even though they think that it will and even though it may sound very enticing.

NOTES

1 For a detailed discussion of how to develop a Christian "game plan," see Hanson, Buddy, *EXIT Strategy: How To Exponentially Increase Your Service To God*, (Hanson Group, 2005). bhanson@ graceandlaw.com

2 Hanson, Buddy, *It's Time To Un-Quo The Status*, (Hanson Group, 2006)

3 1 Thessalonians 2.12

4 Einwechter, William, *A Conquering Faith*, (Chalcedon Foundation, 2002), p.1

5 Romans 8.28

6 Proverbs 3.6

7 1 Peter 2.9

8 Isaiah 58.12

9 Barna, *op.cit.*, *Think*, p.9

10 Hanson, *op.cit.*, *Handbook*, pp.26-42; also Old & New Testaments; Matthew 28.20

11 1 Peter 4.17

170

A LOOK BACK AT
MACHIAVELLI'S TOP TEN

In the six chapters of *The Christian Prince* we have discussed what civil government should be, as it conducts itself according to God's truths, instead of according to man's errors. We've also looked at the biblical manner by which we should conduct ourselves as citizens, and why it is critical that we live and govern ourselves with a Christian worldview. And in this chapter we looked at ways to become the positive and God-honoring change that we seek.

Following are six Case Studies that reinforce some of the principles in the six chapters to assist you and civil rulers to clarify your duties and responsibilities. However, before you dig into the Case Studies, it might be helpful to refresh your memory of ten of Machiavelli's favorite tactics that have had such a profound influence on civil rulers, business executives and military commanders during the past five centuries.

Are your legislators and judges ruling and judging according to biblical principles, or merely according to non-Christian conservative principles? In other words, are they Machiavell*ian* or Christ*ian* in carrying out their day-to-day responsibilities? Reviewing Machiavelli's Top Ten will undoubtedly give you some excellent conversation starters with them. Better yet, take a copy of *The Christian Prince* with you to begin your conversation and ask them to read it and get back with you for more conversation!

Also, don't forget to compare your daily behavior in your vocation to these ten principles, because God's absolute and unchanging truths apply to all situations and circumstances.

It's Machiavell*ian*	It's Christ*ian*
1. To create emergencies to get voter support for new programs.	1. To undertake *only* those responsibilities outlined in Scripture (i.e., Romans 13).
2. To start wars to conquer territories.	2. To only fight defensive wars.
3. To "buy" votes by offering services such as public education.	3. For parents to directly control the education of their children.
4. To stress pragmatism by urging voters to vote for a candidate from one of the major parties.	4. To vote for the candidate who conforms his platform to biblical principles, even if he runs as an independent.
5. To "go with the flow" of the latest opinion poll.	5. To incorporate biblical principles into their legislation.
6. To try to control the results of their legislation and judicial rulings.	6. To obey God and trust-in and rely-upon Him to bring about His results in His perfect timing.
7. To rule by intimidation, since you believe that everyone is a biological "accident."	7. To treat everyone with respect and dignity, since they are special creations of God.
8. To seek coalitions and compromises in order to get legislation passed.	8. To support legislation that conforms to biblical principles and oppose it if it doesn't.
9. To *appear* to be a civil ruler who doesn't say one thing and do another.	9. To *be* a civil ruler who says what he means, and means what he says.
10. To trust no one.	10. To trust in the sovereignty of God.

CASE STUDY I

The Importance of Keeping *Who* You Are In Biblical Perspective

Nebuchadnezzar's Nefarious Narcissism

Why study the leadership lessons of a civil ruler who lived more than 2,500 years ago? What can a civil leader in the 21st century gain by an up-close look at someone who ruled in antiquity? These are perfectly natural questions, and should be the expected response from non-Christian civil rulers who are still going about their lifestyle in the original and sinful condition in which they came into this world. However, they are not the ones reading this book, because for them God's wisdom and counsel is utter "foolishness." [1]

On the other hand, you are reading this because you are a Christian, which means that you do not go through your life attempting to "suppress the truth." [2] As a Christian, you also believe in absolute truth, which means that truth is truth, no matter when it is given.

King Nebuchadnezzar ruled Babylon for four decades, and during his reign Babylon defeated her enemies and brought peace and prosperity throughout the Middle East. From man's perspective, Nebuchadnezzar's lengthy reign was arguably one of the most successful of any civil ruler. Christian civil rulers can, therefore learn valuable lessons from his rule, and hopefully avoid the critical mistakes that led to his dramatic downfall.

Nebuchadnezzar's problem was that he saw his military, economic and political successes as being directly attributable to himself, his ingenuity, his people skills, his wisdom, his cunning. His self-worshiping and self-loving attitude is summed up in the following words:

> *Is not this great Babylon, that I have built for a royal*
> *dwelling by my mighty power and for the honor of*
> *my majesty?* DANIEL 4.30

The unfolding episode of Nebuchadnezzar shows how easy it is for self-centered civil rulers to believe that they are self-made and self-sufficient. Not only do the bureaucrats on their staff cater to their every whim, but in times of prosperity and peace, the adulation from the public can be very intoxicating. Personal characteristics of such nefarious narcissism include:

- ✔ Having no high regard for words, since the speakers don't believe in Jesus, "the Word who is God." [3] This means that they will say whatever they think their constituents want to hear, and while they may sound like they mean what they are saying, sincerity is the farthest thing from their mind.
- ✔ Viewing God's rule as being confined to heaven and to our spiritual thoughts.
- ✔ Putting their priorities ahead of God's.
- ✔ Thinking of themselves as being "elite" and superior to the general population.
- ✔ Attributing all of their successes to themselves and their own efforts, skills and intelligence.
- ✔ Thinking they are above the law and beyond punishment, and that they can talk their way out of unpleasant consequences.

Every Christian civil ruler would do well to learn the lessons of king Nebuchadnezzar. It is always better to learn from someone else's mistakes than from our own. Perhaps no ruler in history had a more glorious ascent and a more degrading descent than this king. The events leading to his downfall are described in the fourth chapter of the Book of Daniel. The account of Nebuchadnezzar's sudden demise provides an irrefutable lesson.

> Just because a legislator may be successfully carrying out the functions of his office, and is held in high regard by his constituents, he still does not possess ultimate authority.

As the Creator of the universe and everyone and everything in it, ultimate authority rests with Jesus Christ, and no other. Succeeding in the rough and tumble world of politics is not easy, and once success is attained there is a very strong temptation to conclude that "I" did it, and that "I" hold ultimate authority over what goes on. As mentioned in Chapter Three, we are neither "The masters of our fate" nor "The captains of our soul."

There's No "I" In SERVE

Jesus' statement during His trial to Rome's chief attorney and financial advisor, Pontius Pilate, is one that is accepted by all Christians, but for one reason or another, civil rulers (as well as everyone else!) fall prey to the temptation to make daily decisions without considering whether they conform to the authority of God's Word.

You would have no authority over Me unless it had been given you from above.   JOHN 19.11

We must not forget this:

> We are members of Christ's Kingdom (not our own), and any mental or physical abilities we may have were given to us by Jesus to use to advance His Kingdom (not ours).

The fascinating story of Nebuchadnezzar epitomizes the self-adulation that is an all-too-common trait of non-Christian civil rulers. It could be said that nominal narcissism should be expected among Christians, since we acknowledge that we have been created in the image of God and called to bring about His will "on earth as it is in heaven." [4] However, there is a huge difference between a healthy self-esteem and an esteem that is elitist. On the one hand, we should see ourselves as members of Christ's Team (Kingdom) who are serving Him by living in accordance with His inerrant Instruction Manual. On the other hand, we may be tempted to see ourselves as unique superstars doing our own thing as we lead the masses in whatever direction we choose. Nebuchadnezzar's example makes it clear that each of us, civil ruler or not, should be on guard against letting our nominal narcissism become nefarious.

> *How great are His signs! And how mighty His wonders! His Kingdom is an everlasting kingdom, and His dominion is from generation to generation.*
> DANIEL 4.3

17th century Bible scholar Matthew Poole portrays the king as having "excessive pride and being an epicurean," but notes that these words of Nebuchadnezzar show the

Lord can "make the stoutest hearts to stoop, and do Him homage." [5] Daniel had previously stated that God "will set up a Kingdom which will never be destroyed." [6] Luke also says that Jesus, "will reign over the house of Judah forever, and of His Kingdom there will be no end." [7] As Christians, it's easy to recognize that everything that happens in the world happens because the God we worship is controlling and directing world events. After all, what benefit would it be to worship a god who needs to turn to us for wisdom!

Yet—

> Until we move beyond the recognition that Christ is King of the earth and have a realization of what this means, our worldview and the accompanying impact of our lifestyle on our culture will remain minimal.

Unless our recognition becomes realization, portions of Scripture, such as the following words of Paul, will, at best, only serve to comfort us, instead of guiding us in our Christian walk.

> *And we know that all things work together for good to those who love God, to those who are called according to His purpose.* ROMANS 8.28

Such words as these should energize and embolden us with a humble confidence to take ground for Christ's Kingdom in all that we do. With the psalmist we should proclaim,

> *This was the LORD's doing; it is marvelous in our eyes. This is the day the LORD has made; we will rejoice and be glad in it.* PSALM 118.23

How awesome are Your works! Through the greatness of Your power Your enemies shall submit themselves to You. All the earth shall worship You and sing praises to You. PSALM 66.3-4

In order to be effective servants on Christ's Team, we need to concentrate on fulfilling our God-ordained roles of prophet, priest and king. As we fill these three roles we image Christ, who modeled them during His earthly ministry.

- PROPHET – Proclaiming the gospel, being salt and light and instructing fellow Christians in how to carry out the Bible's cultural agenda
- PRIEST – Interceding in prayer and providing counsel for our brothers and sisters in Christ
- KING – Ruling over ourselves, our families, vocations, and civil government in a Godly manner and bringing every area of our influence under the dominion of Christ.[8]

Renowned Bible scholar Matthew Henry comments on the superiority of Christ's Kingdom over man-centered kingdoms:

Other reigns are confined to one generation and other dynasties to a few generations, but God's dominion is from "generation to generation." [9]

Compare Christ's "everlasting" Kingdom to the lengths of non-Christian kingdoms, which, in many instances last only a generation or two. America's present constitutional government is the historical exception, having lasted for more than 200 years. However, only for the first 100 years or so, was America governed according to the biblical principles upon which it was founded. America's turning away from those principles points to the necessity for us to repent of our lethargy and nonchalant attitude toward our culture. We have every reason to do so, and no biblical reason not to do so.

When Civil Rulers View Man as Being Sovereign

Non-Christian civil rulers attempt to fulfill their role by providing "womb to tomb" security (funded by tax dollars, of course), and those who object are, in effect, proclaimed to be "atheists of the state" and are "excommunicated" from having any role in leadership (by losing their job, or worse).

Our confidence comes from being promised that Christ's power and will are irresistible and that the "inhabitants of the earth and the armies of heaven" stand ready to bring about His will "on earth, as it is in heaven."

America's founders understood this and they also knew that civil liberty begins with the civil government's enforcement of God's required sanctions. This is why they established three branches of government instead of one, and created a system of checks and balances in the legislative, judicial and executive branches to serve as a safeguard against the formation of a tyrannical central government by any one of the branches.

When Civil Rulers View God as Being Sovereign

As the saying goes, "Success breeds success," and that is exactly what civil governments based upon God's Word breed, because it is in His Word *only* that we find the *true* way to govern ourselves! This is why we can take the following words to the bank:

*Blessed is the nation whose God is the LORD, the
people He has chosen as His own inheritance.*

Psalm 33.12

*For unto us a Child is born, unto us a Son is given;
and the government will be upon His shoulder. And
His name will be called Wonderful Counselor,
Mighty God, Everlasting Father, Prince of Peace. Of
the increase of His government and peace there will
be no end, upon the throne of David and over His
kingdom, to order it and establish it with judgment
and justice from that time forward, even forever. The
zeal of the Lord of hosts will perform this.*

Isaiah 9.6-7

The Old Testament has no shortage of object lessons, and
if we pay attention to them we won't have the misfortune
of repeating the mistakes of the Jews and suffering similar
punishments. In the center of Israel, culturally speaking, was
the dwelling place of God's glory-cloud. God was in the midst
of this cloud, and it resided first in the Tabernacle [10] and later
in the Temple. [11] Inside the Temple was the Holy of Holies,
where once a year the high priest entered to offer a blood
sacrifice for the nation. Inside the Holy of Holies was the Ark
of the Covenant, which contained the two tablets of God's
covenant law. All of this imagery and ceremony pointed to
the importance of having God's law at the center of society.
This is how God manifested Himself to mankind in those
days. Today, He manifests Himself through the Bible and the
sacraments of baptism and the Lord's Supper.

*The revealed law of God is the cornerstone of a culture
and should be at the forefront of every legislator's and
judge's decision-making.*

180

Listen carefully to Isaiah's divinely inspired counsel to his wayward neighbors:

> *Woe unto them that decree unrighteous decrees, and*
> *that write grievousness which they have prescribed:*
> *To turn aside the needy from judgment, and to take*
> *away the right from the poor of my people, that*
> *widows may be their prey, and that they may rob the*
> *fatherless!*   ISAIAH 10.1-2

Clearly, the Bible must be our "political textbook." We must replace the state's sovereignty with God's sovereignty. In doing this we must exhibit a charitable manner. Peter counsels, "For it is the will of God that with well doing you may put to silence the ignorance of foolish men." [12] As discussed in Chapter Three, the issue is not which political party a candidate belongs to, but rather what is the source of the legislator's ultimate authority when it comes to supporting or opposing legislation.

I saw a dream which made me afraid.   DANIEL 4.5

This statement shows that those who don't fear God will be frightened by Him. Henry points out how these details of what would happen to the king attest to God's sovereign control of His creation, otherwise there would be no way for Him to bring about this dream in all of its aspects.

> *He was told of them, and of the issue of them, before*
> *they came to pass, that, when they did come to pass,*
> *by comparing them with the prediction of them,*
> *he might see, and say, that they were the Lord's*
> *doing, and might be brought to believe that there is*
> *a divine revelation in the world, as well as a divine*
> *Providence, and that the works of God agree with*
> *His word.* [13]

Nebuchadnezzar had been king for more than 20 years,[14] was a seasoned combat veteran and no doubt had guards posted outside his bedroom and throughout his palace, yet "a dream" scared him. Henry remarks

God can reach the greatest of men with His terrors even when they are most secure, and think themselves at rest and flourishing. [15]

... his [Daniel's] name is Belteshazzar, according to the name of my god. DANIEL 4.8

Even though Nebuchadnezzar had praised God for being "great," His wonders "mighty," and His kingdom "everlasting," [16] the way in which he refers to Daniel reveals that his true god is spelled with a lower case "g." Nebuchadnezzar is arrogant enough to admit that Bel is "my god." At best, Nebuchadnezzar must be appreciating Daniel's God as simply the foremost magician, but he will soon find out first-hand that the distinctive difference between Jehovah and all false gods is not in being magical, but in being in sovereign control of His creation. In today's parlance, the triune God of Scripture is the "real deal."

The king shows by his actions that in order for non-Christians to trade their false gods for the one, true God, they, like everyone else, must be recipients of a supernatural heart transplant. [17] Regardless of his previous statement that Jehovah is the "God of gods, the Lord of kings," [18] Nebuchadnezzar proves by his actions that those words were insincere and that he considers all gods as more or less equal.

... behold, a tree in the midst of the earth ...
DANIEL 4.10

In Scripture, "trees" often refer to men. The prophet Ezekiel describes the king of Assyria and Pharaoh, king of Egypt, as "great cedars." Henry explains Daniel's metaphor:

> *His dignity and eminency above all his neighbors were signified by the height of this tree, which was exceeding great.* [19]

Henry points out that this "tree" was not only impressive to look at but provided protection and provision: "The kings of the earth are to their subjects as a shadow of a great tree."[20] In regard to "provision," Henry observes,

> *The Assyrian was compared to a "cedar,"* [21] *which affords shadow only; but this tree here had much fruit ... This mighty monarch, it should seem by this, not only was great, but did good."* [22]

Henry also notes,

> *Worldly prosperity in its highest degree is a very uncertain thing; it is no uncommon thing for those that have lived in the greatest pomp and power to be stripped of all that which they trusted to and gloried in.* [23]

> *Its fruit abundant ...*   DANIEL 4.12

This verse makes the point that even an evil civil ruler (tyrant) is to be preferred to no ruler (anarchy). Calvin clarifies the meaning of the imagery:

*God appointed the existence of governments in the
world for this purpose – to be like trees on whose
fruits all men feed, and under whose shadow they
rest. ... Tyrants endeavor to extinguish the whole
light of equity and justice, and to mingle all things;
but the Lord meanwhile restrains them in a secret
and wonderful manner, and thus they are compelled
to act usefully to the human race, whether they will
or not.* [24]

*Chop down the tree and cut off its branches ...
nevertheless leave the stump and roots in the earth.*
DANIEL 4.14-15

Jehovah is instructing His angel ("a watcher") to cut
Nebuchadnezzar's kingdom down to its stump, but to leave
the stump so he and it can be restored after "seven years."
Henry replies,

*God in judgment remembers mercy; and may yet
have good things in store for those whose condition
seems most forbidding* [25]

*Let his heart be changed from that of a man, let him
be given the heart of a beast.*   DANIEL 4.16

During those seven years, Nebuchadnezzar would
maintain his human form, but would be reduced to living like
an animal on all fours and without human understanding.
While the king's punishment was severe, at least he was allowed
to live and eventually be restored to lead his countrymen. In
other cases, rulers who arrogantly acted as though *they* alone
were responsible for their successes were killed by opposing
rulers.

Listen to Ezekiel's prophecy against the ungodly king of Tyre.

> *Because your heart is lifted up, and you say, "I am god, I sit in the seat of gods, in the midst of the seas," yet you are a man, and not a god. Because you have set your heart as the heart of a god, behold, therefore, I will bring strangers against you, the most terrible of the nations; and they shall draw their swords, against the beauty of your wisdom, and defile your splendor. ...Will you still say to him before he slays you, "I am a god"? But you will be a man, and not a god in the hand of him who slaps you.* EZEKIEL 28.2, 6-7, 9

> *In order that the living may know that the Most High rules in the kingdom of men, giving it to whomever He will, and sets over it the lowest of men.* DANIEL 4.17

The "kingdoms of the world will become the kingdom of the Lord," [26] and until that happens Christ will continue to show ungodly kings that He is in charge and will give the kingdoms of men to whomever He will. As Asaph sings

> *He puts down one, and exalts another.* PSALM 75.7

Calvin comments,

> *Men cannot ascribe even the slightest merit to themselves without detracting from God's praise.* [27]

Mary sings,

185

*He has put down the mighty from their thrones, and
exalted the lonely.*   LUKE 1.52

Paul adds,

*For there is no authority except from God, and the
authorities that exist are appointed by God.*
ROMANS 13.1

Samuel proclaims,

*He raises the poor from the dust and lifts the beggar
from the ash heap, to set them among the princes
and make them inherit the throne of glory.*
1 SAMUEL 2.8

Some of the notable men that God has raised from
seemingly ignoble status include these:

- Joseph, from being sold into slavery by his jealous
  brothers —GENESIS 37
- Moses, from being rescued in a basket in the Nile river
  —EXODUS 2
- David, from being a poor shepherd boy —1 SAMUEL 16
- Daniel, from the lion's den —DANIEL 6

Poole talks about the king's high opinion of himself:

*Nebuchadnezzar and his flatterers conceited he was
god in earth, independent and unaccountable to any;
and though he had notions of a supreme God, yet
he confined [God's] government to heaven. ...But
the great God will make all men know he rules all
in earth too, and sets up at His pleasure whom He*

will, and plucks them down again. ... as He took the kingdom from Saul and gave it to David.

PSALM 78.70-71) [28]

Ezra exclaims,

Now therefore, thus shall you say to My servant David, "Thus says the LORD of hosts: 'I took you from the sheepfold, from following the sheep, to be ruler over My people Israel. And I have been with you wherever you have gone, and have cut off all your enemies from before you, and have made you a name like the name of the great men who are on earth.'" 1 CHRONICLES 17.7-8

A Word to Voters

Daniel reluctantly gives the king the interpretation of his dream. Henry explains why Daniel's concern for his king is legitimate:

Though Nebuchadnezzar was an idolater, a persecutor, and an oppressor of the people of God, yet he was, at present, Daniel's prince; and therefore, though Daniel foresees, and is not going to foretell, ill concerning him, he dares not wish ill to him. [29]

This portion of Scripture not only is a lesson in humility for civil rulers, but now becomes a lesson for citizens, as well.

God appoints our rulers, and they are His ministers to us for either "good," if we have been obedient to serve Christ's Kingdom according to God's will, or for "bad" if we have been disobedient and/or lethargic in our service. [30]

187

Calvin remarks that if we fail to have an attitude of respect for the office of our legislators and judges, "we will not only rebel against the civil ruler, but against God himself." [31]

God Is the Giver of *All* We Have
(And He can take it away as quickly as He gave it!)

Because he had elevated his own self-esteem above that of the rest of mankind, Nebuchadnezzar would be made to live below the level of the most destitute of humans. Poole speaks to the difficulty that non-Christians have with learning this lesson, since humility is a Christian character trait:

> *How hard is it for lofty princes to learn this lesson, that God is the giver of all they have, and will call them to account severely for all they do, and make the kings and kingdoms of the world to know that they are His, and not theirs, and that their tenure is but at the will of the Lord solely, who can alter and alienate the property of all their enjoyments, being the high Lord paramount above all!* [32]

The example of Nebuchadnezzar's trials illustrates the lengths to which God will go in order to get His message through our sin-hardened and prideful mindset. Were we not sinners, all that would be necessary would be for us to be told, "This is the way, walk in it,"[33] but we are sinners and therefore God will deal with us as severely as we dictate through our continued disobedience. Poole pronounces, "If princes will not learn and know this, God will beat it into them." [34]

Consider the following two notable examples:

- Manasseh, who was "bound with bronze fetters and carried into Babylonian captivity."

*Now when he was in affliction, he implored the Lord
his God, and humbled himself greatly before the God
of his fathers, and prayed to Him; and He received
his entreaty, heard his supplication, and brought him
back to Jerusalem into his kingdom. Then Manasseh
knew that the LORD was God.*

2 CHRONICLES 33.12-13

• David

*Before I was afflicted I went astray, but now I keep
Your word ... It is good for me that I have been
afflicted, that I may learn Your statutes.*

PSALM 119.67, 71

May we all "heed the rod" of God's judgment as we study
what the Bible teaches about the responsibilities of civil rulers
to carry out God's decrees, as well as the responsibilities of
citizens to obey them; and may we voluntarily repent from
our wayward paths and conform our decisions and actions
to God's principles before it is necessary for Him to "appoint
His action" against us! [35] Poole reminds us that

*God's message always gets through, whether it results in
godly repentance and a more holy lifestyle, or whether it
results in our storing up wrath for the day of judgment.* [36]

*Though Nebuchadnezzar never proved a convert,
yet God made him acknowledge this truth upon his
restoration.* [37]

*...your kingdom shall be assured to you, after you
come to know that Heaven [God] rules.*

DANIEL 4.26

Calvin comments on the work of the Holy Spirit:

Nebuchadnezzar would never have acquired this knowledge of his own accord, unless he had been touched by the secret movement of the Spirit. [38]

Calvin continues:

God's chastisements do not profit unless they work inwardly by His Spirit. ... For otherwise they would not attempt to raise themselves, unless they were utterly blind in the midst of their darkness. But when they are dragged into the light they feel their own nothingness and utter vanity. For whatever we are, this depends on God's grace, which sustains us every moment, and supplies us with new vigor. Hence it is our duty to depend upon God only; because as soon as He withdraws His hand and the virtue of His Spirit, we vanish away. In God we are anything He pleases, in ourselves we are nothing. [39]

But our God is in heaven; He does whatever He pleases. PSALM 115.3

God's law mirrors His perfect justice:

At the end of the twelve months he was walking about the royal palace of Babylon. DANIEL 4.29

The longsuffering of God is seen here in that from the interpretation of the king's dream by Daniel to the beginning of its fulfillment, Nebuchadnezzar was given a full year to repent and to "break off his sins." [10] God's patience in this instance was similar to His treatment of the evil king Ahab:

So it was, when Ahab heard those words, that
he tore his clothes and put sackcloth on his body,
and fasted and lay in sackcloth, and went about
mourning. And the word of the LORD came to
Elijah the Tishbite, saying, "See how Ahab
has humbled himself before Me! Because he has
humbled himself before Me, I will not bring the
calamity in his days. In the days of his son I will
bring the calamity on his house.   1 KINGS 21.27-29

Jesus tells us that in regard to King Ahab's wife Jezebel, "I gave her time to repent of her sexual immorality, but she did not repent." [41] Unfortunately for the citizens of his kingdom, Nebuchadnezzar didn't take advantage of this year to repent. Perhaps he thought that in the days, weeks, and months after Daniel's interpretation, God was going to overlook his deserved punishment. As history proves time and again, to have such an attitude is a big mistake!

When God speaks, it's not a question of whether it will happen, but when.

Is not this great Babylon, that I have built for a royal
dwelling by my mighty power and for the honor of
my majesty?   DANIEL 4.30

Henry observes,

Pride and conceit are sins that most easily beset great
men, who have great things in the world. They are
apt to take the glory to themselves which is due to
God only. [42]

King Solomon also addresses this issue:
Unless the Lord builds the house, they labor in

191

vain who build it; unless the Lord guards the city, the watchman stays awake in vain. PSALM 127.1

Poole adds these thoughts:

The manner of proud tyrants is to engross all honor to themselves; moreover he attributes nothing to the signal goodness of God to him, but takes all to himself. Now God, that resists the proud, presently falls upon him, and down he comes while he stood crowing and pruning his attractive feathers. [43]

Henry concludes the point:

Nebuchadnezzar would be more than a man, and therefore God justly makes him less than a man, and puts him on a level with the beasts, [him] who set up for a rival with his Maker. [44]

While the word was still in the king's mouth. DANIEL 4.31

Where do you rank in the civil ruler's Hall of Fame? Compare your accomplishments and length of office to King Nebuchadnezzar's and see what his fame (apart from God) got him.

Even though God is way more patient toward us than we deserve, when His judgment comes, it comes! Four startling examples are the sudden and swift deaths of King Herod, Ananias, Sapphira, and Elymas. As you refresh your memory about these four people, remember that these are real events about real people. The triune God of the Bible really doesn't like disobedience, and in His perfect timing, He really judges it. [45]

The Sudden and Swift Judgment of God

HEROD

Now Herod had been very angry with the people of Tyre and Sidon; but they came to him with one accord, and having made Blastus, the king's personal aide, their friend, they asked for peace, because their country was supplied with food by the king's country.

So on a set day Herod, arrayed in royal apparel, sat on his throne and gave an oration to them. And the people kept shouting, "The voice of a god and not of a man!" Then immediately an angel of the Lord struck him, because he did not give glory to God. And he was eaten by worms and died. But the word of God grew and multiplied.   ACTS 12.20-24

ANANIAS

But a certain man named Ananias, with Sapphira his wife, sold a possession. And he kept back part of the proceeds, his wife also being aware of it, and brought a certain part and laid it at the apostles' feet. But Peter said, "Ananias, why has Satan filled your heart to lie to the Holy Spirit and keep back part of the price of the land for yourself? While it remained, was it not your own? And after it was sold, was it not in your own control? Why have you conceived this thing in your heart? You have not lied to men but to God." Then Ananias, hearing these words, fell down and breathed his last. So great fear came upon all those who heard these things.
                                    ACTS 5.1-5

SAPPHIRA

Now it was about three hours later when his wife came in, not knowing what had happened. And Peter asked her, "Tell me whether you sold the land for so much?" She said, "Yes, for so much." Then Peter said to her, "How is it that you have agreed together to test the Spirit of the Lord? Look, the feet of those who have buried your husband are at the door, and they will carry you out." Then immediately she fell down at his feet and breathed her last. And the young men came in and found her dead, and carrying her out, buried her by her husband.   ACTS 5.7-10

(continued)

The Sudden and Swift Judgment of God *(cont.)*

ELYMAS (BAR-JESUS)

Now when they had gone through the island to Paphos, they found a certain sorcerer, a false prophet, a Jew whose name was Bar-Jesus, who was with the proconsul, Sergius Paulus, an intelligent man. This man called for Barnabas and Saul and sought to hear the word of God. But Elymas the sorcerer (for so his name is translated) withstood them, seeking to turn the proconsul away from the faith. Then Saul, who also is called Paul, filled with the Holy Spirit, looked intently at him and said, "O full of all deceit and all fraud, you son of the devil, you enemy of all righteousness, will you not cease perverting the straight ways of the Lord?

ACTS 13.6-10

As we go about our daily duties, we should not foolishly assume that today will be pretty much the same as yesterday.

And he thought within himself, saying, "What shall I do, since I have no room to store my crops?" So he said, "I will do this: I will pull down my barns and build greater, and there I will store all my crops and my goods. And I will say to my soul, 'Soul, you have many goods laid up for many years; take your ease; eat, drink, and be merry.'" LUKE 12.17-19

And at the end of the time I, Nebuchadnezzar, lifted my eyes to heaven, and my understanding returned to me; and I blessed the Most High and praised and honored Him who lives forever. DANIEL 4.34

Poole writes that it was God who gave Nebuchadnezzar, and us, "the understanding to consider his sad state, and the causes of it." [46]

Even though Christians and non-Christians can reason and use logic, any reasoning that does not conform to biblical principles is vain and will sooner or later prove faulty. For example, does the educational curriculum you have selected for your children include this critical cornerstone of knowing how to incorporate biblical principles into our daily decision-making? If it doesn't you are not fulfilling your parental role of properly educating your children. [47]

A cornerstone of one's education should be explicit and specific instruction and training in how to bring glory and honor to God through our worldview and lifestyle.

And all the inhabitants of the earth are reputed as nothing. He does according to His will in the army of heaven and among the inhabitants of the earth. No one can restrain His hand or say to Him, "What have You done?" ...
Now I, Nebuchadnezzar, praise and extol and honor the King of heaven, all of whose works are truth, and His ways justice. And those who walk in pride He is able to put down. DANIEL 4.35,37

With the lessons of King Nebuchadnezzar's rise, fall and rise fresh in your mind, it may be well to review the various ideas that Satan attempts to implant in the minds of civil rulers of all ages. Remember, he and his fallen angels know they have been defeated, and their worst nightmare is that Christians will realize that and begin living and governing themselves according to God's will, instead of his will. Satan and his co-horts hope to buy time through such tactics. The truth, however, is that no one can delay Christ's victorious return to judge the inhabitants of the earth. Between now and then He will continue to reward and build up civil governments who honor Him and rule according to His laws, and punish and cast down those who dishonor Him by ruling according to their own imaginations. So, once again, here are some of Satan's favorite mental tactics for civil rulers: Read them and beware.

- ✔ Having no high regard for words, since they don't believe in Jesus, "the Word who is God." [48] This means that they will say whatever they think their constituents want to hear, and while they may sound like they mean it, sincerity is the farthest thing from their mind.
- ✔ Viewing God's rule as being confined to heaven.
- ✔ Putting their priorities ahead of God's.
- ✔ Thinking of themselves as being "elite" and "superior" to the general population.
- ✔ Attributing all of their successes to themselves and their efforts, skills and intelligence.
- ✔ Thinking they are beyond punishment and that they can talk their way out of unpleasant consequences.

Christian Legislative Building Blocks

Just because a legislator may be successfully carrying out the functions of his office, and is held in high regard by his constituents, he still does not possess ultimate authority.

We are members of Christ's Kingdom (not our own), and any mental or physical abilities we may have were given to us by Jesus to use to advance His Kingdom (not ours).

A cornerstone of one's education should be explicit and specific instruction and training in how to bring glory and honor to God through our worldview and lifestyle.

Our confidence comes from being promised that Christ's power and will are irresistible and the "inhabitants of the earth and the armies of heaven" stand ready to bring about His will "on earth, as it is in heaven."

The revealed law of God is the cornerstone of a culture and should be at the forefront of every legislator's and judge's decision-making.

God appoints our rulers, and they are His ministers to us either for "good," if we have been obedient to serve Christ's Kingdom according to God's will, or for "bad" if we have been disobedient and/or lethargic in our service. [49]

God's message always gets through, whether it results in godly repentance and a more holy lifestyle, or whether it results in our storing up wrath for the day of judgment. [50]

When God speaks, it's not a question of whether it will happen, but when

Where do you rank in the civil ruler's Hall of Fame? Compare your accomplishments and length of office to King Nebuchadnezzar's and see what his fame (apart from God) got him.

Until we move beyond the recognition that Christ is King of the earth and have a realization of what this means, our worldview and the accompanying impact our lifestyle has on our culture will remain minimal.

NOTES

1 1 Corinthians 1.18
2 Romans 1.18
3 John 1.1
4 Matthew 6.10
5 Poole, Matthew, *Matthew Poole's Commentary*, Vol. II, Psalm – Malachi, (MacDonald), p.824
6 Daniel 2.44
7 Luke 1.32-33
8 See Hanson, Buddy, *Bottom Line Theology: A Bible Study Feast for Those Who Only Have Time for a Sandwich*, (Hanson Group)
9 Henry, Matthew, *Matthew Henry's Commentary: Isaiah to Malachi*, Vol. IV, (MacDonald), p.1045
10 Exodus 40.34
11 1 Kings 8.1-66
12 1 Peter 2.15
13 Henry, *op.cit.*, p.1045
14 Ezekiel 29.17
15 Henry, *op.cit.*, p.1046
16 Daniel 4.3
17 Jeremiah 2.11; 32.39
18 Daniel 2.47
19 Henry, *op.cit.*, p.1047
20 Henry, *op.cit.*, p.1047
21 Ezekiel 31.6
22 Henry, *op.cit.*, p.1047
23 Henry, *op.cit.*, p.1048
24 Calvin, John, *Daniel*, (Banner of Truth Trust, 1561, 1995), p.256
25 Henry, *op.cit.*, p.1048
26 Revelation 11.15
27 Calvin, *op.cit*, p.264
28 Poole, *op.cit.*, p.822
29 Henry, *op.cit.*, p.1050
30 Romans 13.1-7
31 Calvin, *op.cit.*, p.269
32 Poole, *op.cit.*, p.823
33 Isaiah 30.21
34 Poole, *op.cit.*, p.823
35 Micah 6.9
36 Poole, *op.cit.*, p. 823
37 Daniel 4:37
38 Calvin, *op.cit.*, p.277
39 Calvin, *op.cit.*, p.297
40 Daniel 4.27-29
41 Revelation 2.21
42 Henry, *op.cit.*, p.1051
43 Poole, op.cit., p.824
44 Henry, *op.cit.*, p.1052
45 See Hanson, Buddy, *This Is Not A Drill: Real Lessons for Real People from the Real God, Through His Prophets (TBA, Hanson Group) and On How to Live and Govern Ourselves Really!*, (TBA, Hanson Group)
46 Poole, *op.cit.*, p.824
47 Deuteronomy 6.4-6
48 John 1.1
49 Romans 13.1-7
50 Job 36.13; Romans 2:5; Deut. 21:34

CASE STUDY 2

CHURCH & STATE:
DISTINCT SPHERES, RELATED MISSION

THERE IS A LOT OF CONFUSION ABOUT THE SEPARATION OF CHURCH and state. One reason for this stems from the rewriting of history in the public school textbooks to distort the clear intentions of our founding fathers. Another reason is the activist bent of the Supreme Court, which has set precedents based upon political interests instead of upon the original intent of the Constitution. Such an erroneous view sees the church and state as two distinct and non-cooperating institutions.

While the church expects its members to present a godly testimony to the world (being "salt and light"), the state expects citizens to be law-abiding and peaceful. Both the church and state are accountable to God for their origin and authority. As the chronicler teaches, "The chief priest is over you in all matters of Jehovah, and ... the ruler of the house of Judah in all the King's matters." [1] Both must confess, "The Lord is our Lawgiver!" [2] The state has the God-given power to use the sword to defend its citizens from outside aggression,[3] and to keep us safe from criminals by administering swift justice according to the sure and certain terms of Biblical law.[4] It also has the responsibility to protect the personal liberty of its citizens by keeping the total of the taxes it collects less than 10 percent of a person's net income.[5] To do its job effectively, the civil government should derive its laws from biblical laws and the principles contained in the case laws of Exodus that follow the Ten Commandments.

In Jesus' view there is no such thing
as a "sacred realm" and a "secular realm."

After all, it is Christianity that promises racial harmony, while evolution promises continued warfare between groups. The German philosopher Hegel (not our Creator God) taught that there will be continuous cycles of thesis-antithesis-synthesis. The Bible's message is simple: Obey God and He will bless us.

See, I have set before you today life and prosperity,
and death and adversity; in that I command you
today to love the Lord your God, to walk in His
ways and to keep His commandments and His
statutes and His judgments, that you may live and
multiply, and the Lord your God may bless you ...
I have set before you life and death, the blessing and
the curse. So choose life in order that you may live,
you and your descendants, by loving the Lord your
God, by obeying His voice, and by holding fast to
Him; for this is your life and the length
of your days.   DEUTERONOMY 30.15-16, 19-20

Civil Rulers who vote for unbiblical legislation should be called to account by their congregations. American Vision President Gary DeMar writes, "We will not see restoration of civil government until we see the restoration of the Church."[6]

The Proper Role of Civil Government

In Old Testament Israel there was a separation of priest and king, and between the temple and the palace. Contrary to the prevalent misconception among many of our brothers and sisters,

> *Israel had a harmony of church and state under God, not a union of the two.*

Both the civil and the ecclesiastical realms operated according to God's laws. How could we expect it to be otherwise? If God is not in control of the events outside of our homes and churches, how can it be imagined that He is in charge of events inside them? Indeed, if Jesus is not Lord of all, He is not Lord at all.

The church is to set forth the Word of our Lord and Savior so that society will have a clear direction and trustworthy guidance, while the state bases its civil code upon our King. Church members should be taught to take care of the education and welfare of each other instead of letting the state usurp this responsibility. This clear separation of powers and responsibilities is evident in Old Testament Israel where there was a separation of priest and king, and of temple and palace.

Moses was Israel's civil ruler, and Aaron was her priest, as from Israel's very beginning God kept the civil and ecclesiastical offices separate. [7] This truth is seen in the prophet Zechariah's statement, "These are the two anointed ones, who stand beside the Lord of the whole earth." [8] The "two anointed ones" are the Kings and Priests. Here are the names of some of them:

KING	PRIEST
Moses	Aaron
Joshua	Eleazar
David	Abiathar
Solomon	Zadok
Hezekiah	Azariah
Zerubbabel	Joshua

Similarities between the Church and State
1. They are both from God, are "ministers of God," and shall give account of their administrations to God.
2. Both must observe the law and commandments of God, and both have specific directions from Scripture to guide them.
3. Both are "fathers" and ought to be honored and obeyed, according to the fifth commandment.
4. Both are appointed for the glory of God and the good of mankind.
5. Each complements the other.

Differences between the Church and State
1. In their ultimate goal, the civil rulers bring about temporal peace; the Church offers salvation and eternal peace.
2. The State executes capital offenders; the Church excommunicates unrepentant and disobedient members. [9]

Moses teaches that when civil rulers do not base their decisions on God's Word, they and their constituents will be punished:

> *You shall not pervert justice; you shall not show partiality, nor take a bribe, for a bribe blinds the eyes of the wise and twists the words of the righteous.*

*You shall follow what is altogether just, that you may
live and inherit the land which the Lord your God is
giving you.*   DEUTERONOMY 16.19-20

Paul instructs civil rulers to govern "wholeheartedly, as
for the Lord." [10]

It is imperative that we incorporate God's instructions
into our self-governing actions because our heart is
"full of evil" [11] and in order to properly serve God and
present a Godly testimony for Him we need to "put off
our former conduct" and "put on the new man." [12]

Unless and until we incorporate biblical principles into
our daily decision-making we will be "like a city that is
broken down, without walls." [13]

*Let every soul be subject to the governing author-
ities. For there is no authority except from God,
and the authorities that exist are appointed by God.
Therefore, whoever resists the authority resists the
ordinance of God, and those who resist will bring
judgment on themselves. For rulers are not a terror
to good works, but to evil. Do you want to be
unafraid of the authority? Do what is good, and you
will have praise from the same. For he is God's
minister to you for good. But if you do evil, be
afraid; for he does not bear the sword in vain; for he
is God's minister, an avenger to execute wrath on
him who practices evil.*   ROMANS 13.1-5

ALL the Word for ALL of life

203

The Proper Role of Judges

Jehoshaphat makes it clear that since the judges were God's ministers, they were to "image Him" by ruling according to His laws, and that He was with them when they rendered judgment:

> *And he appointed judges in the land in all the*
> *fortified cities of Judah, city by city. And he said to*
> *the judges, "Consider what you are doing, for you*
> *do not judge for man, but for the Lord who is with*
> *you when you render judgment. Now then let the*
> *fear of the Lord be upon you: be very careful what*
> *you do, for the Lord our God will have no part in*
> *unrighteousness, or partiality, or the taking of a*
> *bribe."* 2 CHRONICLES 19.5-7

It can be seen in these verses that King Jehoshaphat was instituting the biblical model of self-government by requiring each city to judge its own cases. (Verse 8 adds that there was a "Supreme Court" in Jerusalem that could be appealed to by individuals who weren't happy with the local ruling.)

That the realms of church and state have distinct responsibilities is clearly brought out in Scripture. The first example of the state's overreaching its jurisdiction and assuming a religious function happened approximately 1,000 years before the birth of Christ. The Israelites had appointed Saul as their first earthly king (ending their theocracy). [14] During their war with the Philistines, Saul's army was greatly outnumbered and Samuel had promised to come and perform a worship service. However, Samuel's arrival was delayed, and when Saul began to see his ranks deserting, he decided to perform the worship service himself. As soon as the service concluded, Samuel arrived and said to Saul:

*You have acted foolishly; you have not kept the
commandment of the LORD your God, which
He commanded you, for the LORD would have
established your kingdom over Israel forever. But
now your kingdom shall not endure. The LORD has
sought out a man after His own heart...*

I SAMUEL 13.13-14

Several hundred years later, Judah's King Uzziah also overstepped the bounds of civil authority. He became king at the age of sixteen. "He did right in the sight of the Lord" and Jerusalem was greatly blessed because of it. At the pinnacle of his career, however, he became proud and acted unfaithfully toward the Lord by entering the temple and burning incense on the altar. When the priest, Azariah, and 80 other priests entered the temple and found King Uzziah, Azariah said, "It is not for you to burn incense to the Lord, but for the priests, the sons of Aaron who are consecrated to burn incense. Get out of the sanctuary, for you have been unfaithful, and will have no honor from the Lord God." Uzziah, however, became enraged and God struck him with leprosy.[15]

Many of today's American Marxists, who enjoy liberty and claim status under the mantle of multicultural and political correctness, would gasp at King David's statement that Christ is the head of the State:

*Now therefore, O Kings, show discernment; take
warning, O judges of the earth. Worship the Lord
with reverence, and rejoice with trembling, do
homage to the Son, Lest He become angry, and
you perish in the way, for His wrath may soon be
kindled.* PSALM 2.10-12

205

*Once the State
leaves its biblical
moorings, its
objective is no
longer peace
and order; but is
primarily fiscal.*

Some would have us believe that the First Amendment calls for a "separation of God and state," to the extent that every mention of God should be removed from the civil sphere. The truth, however, is that the First Amendment simply states, "Congress shall make no law respecting an establishment of religion, or prohibiting the free exercise thereof…" All this means is that there will be no state church, which is what the founders were avoiding, having lived under the domination of the Church of England. So, instead of disestablishing the church, the purpose of the First Amendment is to protect it and to protect citizens from the possibility that Congress might establish a "national" church. [16]

The following chart shows six areas where the parallel ministries of the church and the state should work together to keep society running smoothly.

Comparing the Spheres of Church and State

Church	State
1. Minister of Grace/Excommunication	1. Minister of Justice/Excellence
2. Expose Evil	2. Restrain Evil
3. Teach God's Law	3. Enforce God's Law
4. Funded by God's social tax—the tithe	4. Financed by God's civil tax—the head tax
5. Church courts	5. Civil courts
6. Welfare	6. Warfare

If we base legislation on man's principles (even conservative man's principles) God will not bless us.

206

With such a stark contrast in values and ethics it should be apparent that the idea of a "neutral secular state" is nonfunctional. King David, in passing his throne to Solomon, advised him to

> *Keep His statutes, His commandments, His judgments, and His testimonies, as it is written in the Law of Moses, that you may prosper in all that you do and wherever you turn.*   1 KINGS 2.3

Paul provides the complementary Christian standard:

> *Do not be conformed to this world, but be transformed by the renewing of your mind, that you may prove what the will of God is, that which is good and acceptable and perfect.*   ROMANS 12.2

Socialism Leads to State Oppression

Socialism is an entire system that is built on theft. Various welfare economic systems are constantly being proposed to correct the inequity between the haves and the have-nots. In order to achieve this goal, valuable personal income has been stolen through excessive taxes of all kinds, including the ungodly practice of taxing property. However, history shows that whether the system is communism or socialism, the only people who are helped are the rulers and bureaucrats. The reason these systems are destined to failure is because they are contrary to God's rules. Welfare handouts encourage sloth, as does the gambling mindset in which a person attempts to accumulate wealth without working and earning it. Paul warned about this kind of attitude by saying, "If any would not work, neither should he eat." [17]

The information in this section was taken from Buddy Hanson's The Christian Civil Ruler's Handbook (pp.26-28), and Choose This Day: God's Instructions on How to Select Leaders (pp.63-96).

207

Christian Legislative Building Blocks

It is imperative that we incorporate God's instructions into our self-governing actions because our heart is "full of evil" [18] and in order to properly serve God and present a godly testimony for Him we need to "put off our former conduct" and "put on the new man." [19]

Israel had a harmony of church and state under God, not a union of the two.

ALL the Word for ALL of life

In Jesus' view there is no such thing as a "sacred realm" and a "secular realm" of society.

Once the State leaves its biblical moorings, its objective is no longer peace and order; it is primarily fiscal.

If we base legislation on man's principles (even conservative man's principles) God will not bless us.

208

NOTES

1 2 Chronicles 19.11

2 Isaiah 33.22; James 4.12

3 Romans 13.1-7

4 Deuteronomy 16.20; Proverbs 21.3

5 1 Samuel 8.11-18

6 DeMar, Gary, *God and Government*, Vol. III, (American Vision Press), p.112

[Judgment begins at the household of God.]

7 See Hanson, Buddy, *God's Ten Words: Practical Applications from the Ten Commandments* (Hanson Group, 2002), bhanson@graceandlaw.com

8 Zechariah 4.14

9 Gillespie, George, *Aaron's Rod Blossoming* (Sprinkle

Pub., 1985), pp.85-87

10 Colossians 3.23

11 Ecclesiastes 9.3

12 Ephesians 4.22-23

13 Proverbs 25.28

14 1 Samuel 9 - 11

15 2 Chronicles 26.3-5, 9-10,16-21

16 See "Letter From Plymouth Rock," Vol.10, Number 2

17 2 Thessalonians 3.10

18 Ecclesiastes 9.3

19 Ephesians 4.22-24

CASE STUDY 3

And do not be conformed to this world, but be
transformed by the renewing of your mind, that you
may prove what is that good and acceptable and
perfect will of God. ROMANS 12.2

AMERICAN CULTURE IN THE 21ST CENTURY IS OPERATING UNDER the agenda of non-Christians, as it has been doing for more than a century and a half. Every major influential institution has been taken over (by default) by non-Christians. Therefore, any time we turn on the radio or TV or pick up the newspaper, we are hearing and/or seeing the news and views of the day presented by people who hate the principles of the triune God of the Bible.

Such an atmosphere makes it very difficult for Christians to keep non-Christian "viruses" from slipping into our worldview. This "Civil Ruler Model of Behavior" worksheet is provided in an effort to keep you from unwittingly imaging Satan in your daily decision-making (since with every decision we make we are imaging either Christ or Satan).

This simple four-step model provides an objective guide by which you can bring glory and honor to your Lord, Savior and King, Jesus Christ as you make your legislative or judicial decisions.

Each Model begins with the Apostle Paul's reminder that we have been mercifully called into Christ's Kingdom and given the Holy Spirit to guide us into a correct understanding of Scripture. Given this understanding, we can transform culture, instead of conforming our lifestyles to it as we did before our conversion.

Next is a line on which to name the issue that is before you. Following that is a place to identify the sphere of government to which God has given responsibility for this issue. Through these God-appointed self-governing spheres, God works His eternally perfect plan for us to live and govern ourselves. Each has specific accountabilities to God, and no sphere should usurp the responsibilities of another.

After you identify the sphere or spheres to which God has assigned this particular issue (Step One), space is provided to list the pertinent scriptural injunctions (Step Two). As Christians we are commanded to live according to God's opinion, not our opinion. (We're not to repeat what Adam and Eve were guilty of!).

Based on the verses cited as God's opinion, you next describe the biblical course of action that you should take (Step Three). In Step Four you once again refer to the four God-appointed self-governing spheres and briefly describe what continuing actions need to be built into your solution. Following the worksheet are two samples of what a completed worksheet might look like: The first is on "Educating Our Children," and the second is "Civil Law – Settled or Unsettled?" They are probably much longer than the ones you will prepare for your major decisions, but they will provide an idea of how useful such a worksheet can be in thinking through a pending legislative or judicial decision.

The Civil Ruler Model of Behavior

And do not be conformed to this world, but be transformed by the renewing of your mind, that you may prove what is that good and acceptable and perfect will of God.   ROMANS 12.2

THE ISSUE _____

- Step One: To which sphere has God assigned this issue?
  - _____ Self-governing Individual
  - _____ Family
  - _____ Church
  - _____ Civil Ruler

- Step Two: God's Opinion (Scriptures relating to this issue) _____
  _____
  _____
  _____

- Step Three: (Based upon the above Scriptural support), What is the biblical course of action required? _____
  _____
  _____
  _____

- Step Four: Sustaining the Correct Decision
  Once God's counsel is followed by enacting legislation that conforms to God's will, what will be required of each God-appointed self-governing sphere to ensure continued success?

  Civil Government _____

  Individual _____

  Family _____

  Church _____

THE CIVIL RULER MODEL OF BEHAVIOR

*And do not be conformed to this world, but be
transformed by the renewing of your mind, that you
may prove what is that good and acceptable and
perfect will of God.*   ROMANS 12.2

THE ISSUE: *Educating our Children*

- **Step One: Is this an issue that God requires from the**
  ✔   Self-governing Individual
  ✔   Family
  ✔   Church
  _____ Civil Ruler

- **Step Two: God's Opinion** (Scriptures relating to this issue)
    Every Christian agrees that God's Word is "truth." This means that anything, whether it be a family, business, legislative or judicial decision that does not conform to biblical principles is "false." Therefore, if the education your child is receiving is not based upon biblical principles it is a "false" education. If your child is receiving a Christian education he knows who he is (a creature of God), what his purpose is (to bring about God's will on earth as it is in heaven) and how he is supposed to do it (by incorporating the biblical principles he knows into his daily lifestyle). He will also be systematically taught how to defend the faith "in season and out."
    The public (government) schools are not only "false," but they were established to be just that. John Dewey is bold enough to admit this:

> [Teachers are] "the prophets of the true God and the usherer of the true kingdom of God."
>
>   MY PEDAGOGIC CREED

The Humanist magazine adds

> *The battle for mankind's future must be waged and*
> *won in the public school classroom by teachers who*
> *correctly perceive their role as the proselytizers*
> *of a new faith: a religion of humanity ...utilizing a*
> *classroom instead of a pulpit to convey humanist*
> *values in whatever subject they teach.*
>
> THE HUMANIST MAGAZINE,
> JANUARY/FEBRUARY 1983

Why do non-Christians place so much emphasis on the public schools? Listen to the former head of Harvard University's School of Education:

> *Every child in America who enters school at the age*
> *of five is mentally ill, because he comes to school*
> *with allegiance toward our elected officials,*
> *toward our founding fathers, toward our institutions,*
> *toward the preservation of this form of government*
> *...All of that proves the children are sick, because*
> *the truly well individual is the one who has rejected*
> *all of those things and is what I would call the true*
> *international child of the future.* [1]

Public schools were established to turn our children against us and against our beliefs, and in doing so they have become the state's churches! Since everyone is created in God's image, everyone is religious. This need will either be met by teaching our children the true religion and true education, [2] or by having them instructed in the false religion and false education of the public schools. Jesus tells us, "Everyone will be like his teacher." [3] Do we want our children being like their non-Christian public school teachers, or like Christ?

215

Perhaps the following chart will assist you in sharpening your focus to the clear contrast between godly and ungodly educational systems.

Knowledge Contrasted	
True Education	**False Education**
1. King Solomon, "The fear of the LORD is the beginning of knowledge. Proverbs 1.1	1. Kart Marx, "Man is the creature of The natural order only.
2. (Analogical) Thinking God's thoughts after Him. Ephesians 4.23	2. (Unilogical) Thinking man's Thoughts.
3. Regenerate reasoning (with the Holy Spirit). John 16.13	3. Unregenerate reasoning (without the Holy Spirit).
4. Error is the result of sin. 1 John 3.4	4. Errors are decreasing as man's knowledge increases.
5. Absolute truth: Knowledge of certain related facts that are created by our Creator. We can know truth absolutely because God reveals it. Philippians 3.8-10; Colossians 2.2-3	5. Relative truth: Knowledge of random unrelated facts that "just are. If The pursuit of absolute truth fails because All FACTS are needed.
6. Who Are We?A creature of God. Genesis 1.26 Psalm 139.14	6. Who Are We? A biological accident.
7. Life's Purpose: God-centered and honoring lifestyle and worldview, because He is all sufficient.l Colossians 2.8; 1.15-20; Ephesians 4.11-12; Galatians 5.13-14; Matthew 28.19; Genesis 1.26-28	7. Life's Purpose: Man-centered and honoring lifestyle and worldview. because man is seen to be selfsufficient.
8. The natural PLUS the supernatural. Genesis 1.2; 26.13; Romans 1.19-20	8. The natural only (what can be seen, felt, measured, tested).

Knowledge Contrasted (cont.)

9. Biblical justice. 2 Samuel 23.3; 2 Chronicles 19.6-7
10. How to live a) Practical application of biblical truths to an absolute and unchanging value standard. Romans 12.1-2 b) Render unto Caesar only what is his. Romans 13.1-7; 1 Peter 2.13-17 c) Conform culture to God's eternally perfect plan for His creation. Philippians 2.12-16; Matthew 6.10 d) Systematically taught how to defend the faith. 2 Timothy 4.2
11. Personal life of the teacher is allImportant. 1 Thessalonians 2.1-12, Especially v.8; Luke 6.40

9. Poetic justice.
10. How to live a) Practical application of knowledge learned to relative values. b) Render unto Caesar everything he demands. c) Submit to the latest cultural fads. d) Taught that all religions are irrelevant to "real life."
11. Personal life of the teacher is irrelevant and none of our business.

What Does God Say?

Having seen what man's word states about educating our children, let's listen to what God's Word says:

> Thus says the LORD:
> Do not learn the way of the Gentiles;
> Do not be dismayed at the signs of heaven,
> For the Gentiles are dismayed at them.
> For the customs of the peoples are futile.
>
> JEREMIAH 10.2

217

*Do not provoke your children to wrath, but bring
them up in the training and admonition of the Lord.*
                                        EPHESIANS 6.4

*Do not be unequally yoked together with unbeliev-
ers. For what fellowship has righteousness with
lawlessness? And what communion has light with
darkness?*   2 CORINTHIANS 6.14

*My people are destroyed for lack of knowledge.
Because you have rejected knowledge, I also will
reject you from being priest for Me; because you
have forgotten the law of your God, I also will forget
your children.*   HOSEA 4.6

Any curriculum that does not have the law of God as
its centerpiece is not true education. God's Word is the
foundation of how we should live and govern ourselves. It
is our final authority over our conduct and beliefs. The Lord
Himself said, "Whoever has my commands and obeys them,
he is the one who loves me." [4]

• **Step Three:** (Based upon the above Scriptural support),
What is the biblical course of action required?
Are public school teachers likely to teach God's Word,
or criticize it? The answer should be obvious. Not only will
they hide behind the "pluralism" myth: " All religions take
you to heaven," but they will use the "neutrality" myth:
"We can't endorse any particular religious belief." Neither
pluralism nor neutrality is a biblical alternative. So, even
though public schools profess to be "neutral," we know they
are lying, because Genesis 3.15 states that non-Christians
"hate" biblical principles and those who hold to them. Jesus,
in His Great Commission, commands us to "teach them all
things I have commanded you." [5] Is this being taught daily in

the public schools? For example, how about the "fruit of the Spirit": love, joy, peace, longsuffering, kindness, gentleness, self-control? 6 Is it being taught in public schools? Of course not, and even when "values" are taught, they are taught as if they are "common sense," and are not given the authority of being based upon God's Word (i.e., the first four of the Ten Commandments). And, speaking of the Ten Commandments, the first one says,

> *You shall have no other gods before Me ... For I, the LORD your God, am a jealous God..."*
>
> Exodus 20.3,5

It should be clear from this that the public schools are founded upon the principle of breaking this commandment, so our Christian brothers and sisters who say we should not "abandon" the schools, but "reform" them, should be asked: Upon what basis do you hope to "reform" them since their leaders will not allow you to bring biblical principles into the picture? Long story short, God did not ordain government schools, so He won't allow them to be "reformed."

Whether as an individual, family, community, state or nation, we can ill afford to continue to disregard God's counsel. The words of warning that Jehovah spoke through the prophet Hosea to Israel's Northern Kingdom more than 2,700 years ago apply equally to us in 21st century America:

> *My people are destroyed for lack of knowledge.*
> *Because you have rejected knowledge,*
> *I also will reject you from being priest for Me;*
> *Because you have forgotten the law of your God,*
> *I also will forget your children.*
>
> Hosea 4.6

Approximately 400 years earlier, Jehovah spoke similar words to Israel's priest Eli:

> *I said indeed that your house and the house of your father would walk before Me forever. But now the LORD says: «Far be it from Me; for those who honor Me I will honor, and those who despise Me shall be lightly esteemed."*   1 SAMUEL 2.30

How should you educate?

By not seeing God as the Creator, all public school curriculum becomes subjective and existential. This means that there are no sure and certain ideas on how to live and govern ourselves, or even why certain events happen. Studying history is downgraded to a meaningless exercise in memorizing dates. By sending our children to ungodly public schools, we are furthering the myth in our children that "religion" is relegated to Sundays and/or to the inside of our homes, churches, or minds.

Some say, "We have weekly devotionals in our home, and our children attend youth groups at church, plus their weekly Sunday school class and worship services, so they are being taught 'the truth.'" Let's ask them to smell the coffee and tell us if they really believe that three or four hours of biblical instruction each week can contend with 30 hours of non-Christian indoctrination.

Apples & Oranges

Government education has about as much in common with Christian education as apples have with oranges. There is no common ground between the two and the government knows this. [7] It is high time that Christians also acknowledge the chasm between "true" and "false" education. The importance of providing our children with an education in the truth is described by Asaph. He tells the descendants of the wilderness wanderers that God

> ...established a testimony in Jacob, and appointed
> a law in Israel, which He commanded our fathers,
> that they should make them known to their children;
> that the generation to come might know them, the
> children who would be born, that they may arise
> and declare them to their children, that they may set
> their hope in God, and not forget the works of God,
> but keep His commandments; and may not be like
> their fathers, a stubborn and rebellious generation, a
> generation that did not set its heart aright, and
> whose spirit was not faithful to God.   PSALM 78.5-8

This, however, was not done. The fathers did not teach their children to think God's thoughts after Him and to live exclusively according to His ethics. As a result they grew up with a non-Godly worldview, determining "good and evil" according to their own ethical standards.

Teaching our children the fundamentals of Christianity enables them to develop a Christian worldview and to trust in and rely upon God, instead of themselves. The fathers did not teach their children this in Moses' day (though Moses himself taught them and the LORD commended him), [8] it didn't happen in Asaph's day and it isn't happening in our day. Probably 99 percent of the people reading this were sent to public (government) schools by their (well-intentioned) parents. As a consequence of this, only an estimated five percent of adult Christians have a Christian worldview—which goes a long way to explain why the lifestyles of Christians and non-Christians are virtually indistinguishable. It also presents a frightening picture of what will happen to our children, since less than one in ten Christian parents know enough about a

Christian worldview to pass it on. This puts us in not only a shameful, but a most dangerous situation. Paul warns us,

> *We should no longer be children, tossed to and fro*
> *and carried about with every wind of doctrine, by*
> *the trickery of men, in the cunning craftiness of*
> *deceitful plotting, but speaking the truth in love, may*
> *grow up in all things to Him who is the head –*
> *Christion*.   EPHESIANS 4.14-15

By not acknowledging absolute truth, public (government) schools are teaching our children "every wind of doctrine" except the truth. Since they oppose God at every turn, they image their god, Satan, by using "the cunning craftiness of deceitful plotting." Is it any wonder, then, that an estimated 98 percent of our children do not have a Christian worldview.[9] In Jesus' words, "They are mistaken, not knowing the Scriptures nor the power of God." [10] God tells us what His historical reaction is to such a failure of parents to teach their children in His truth:

> *Therefore I was angry with that generation, and said,*
> *"They always go astray in their heart, and they have*
> *not known My ways." So I swore in My wrath,*
> *"They shall not enter My rest."*   HEBREWS 3.10-11

Can Your Child Really Be "Salt & Light" in the Public School?

The question of educating our children is arguably the most important question facing the 21st century church. The 20th century church completely missed the mark and we are suffering the consequences in our fallen culture. There are no biblical reasons for sending your child (or yourself as a teacher/administrator) to the ungodly schools. This is why this issue is so critical: It cuts directly to the heart of our profession of faith. Talk is cheap. Anyone can go on and on about how much they love Jesus, but Jesus tells us to walk our talk. "If you love Me you will keep My commandments."[11] Jesus adds, "You will know them by their fruits." [12]

This means that the only acceptable answer to how we should educate our children can only be found in Scripture. How could it be otherwise? May we never forget who we are and from what we have been mercifully and miraculously rescued. The Lord tells us, "The imagination of man's heart is evil from his youth." [13] Jeremiah adds, "The heart is deceitful above all things, and desperately wicked: who can know it?"[14] Again, Jesus: "Those things which proceed from the mouth come from the heart, and they defile a man." [15] Before our conversion we could only depend on our own knowledge and wisdom, but since our new birth, with the aid of the Holy Spirit we can correctly understand God's revealed wisdom. Why, then, would we want to address any issue in our own faulty and imperfect wisdom, when we have access to God's perfect wisdom? Do we not understand that in following our own thoughts, we are imitating what Eve did by living as though she was god? As Christians, our calling is to re-think God's thoughts. This is why David writes, "In Your light, we see light." [16]

• **Step Four: Sustaining the Correct Decision**
Once God's counsel is followed by enacting legislation that conforms to God's will, to ensure continuing success what will be required from the God-appointed self-governing spheres:

> *Civil Government.* There is no biblical basis for the civil government to be in the education business.

Individual. The education of children is the sole responsibility of the family and church. College and graduate school should be a joint decision among parents, church officers and other disciplers of young adults, and the individual student.

Family. The Father is directly responsible for the education of his children and can delegate the daily educating to the mother and/or Christian day schools.

Church. Churches should strongly consider beginning a Christian day school and/or serving as a coordinating point of homeschool students. An important part of a church budget should be a scholarship fund to pay or help defray the tuition of Christian day schools. The church should also join with other churches to provide an employment clearing-house for teachers, administrators and coaches presently employed in the government (public) schools to help them exit from that situation to one that honors God.

NOTES

1 Pierce, Dr. Chester, cited in "Educating For The New World Order," 1973
2 Deuteronomy 6.6-9
3 Luke 6.40
4 John 14:21
5 Matthew 28.20
6 Galatians 5.22
7 Luke 16.8
8 Deuteronomy 4.5-7
9 George Barna, www.barna.org
10 Matthew 22.29
11 1 John 5.3; 2.3
12 Matthew 7.16
13 Genesis 8.21
14 Jeremiah 17.9
15 Matthew 15.18
16 Psalm 36.9

THE CIVIL RULER MODEL OF BEHAVIOR

*And do not be conformed to this world, but be
transformed by the renewing of your mind, that you
may prove what is that good and acceptable and
perfect will of God.* ROMANS 12.2

THE ISSUE: *Civil Law–Settled or Unsettled?*

• Step One: Is this an issue that God requires from the

_____ Self-governing Individual
_____ Family
_____ Church
__✔__ Civil Ruler

• **Step Two: God's Opinion** (Scriptures relating to this issue)
The term "settled law" is frequently heard in relation to
candidates for the Supreme Court and whether they would
vote to "unsettle" previous "settled" points of law. In most
instances, what is being asked is whether the potential judge
would vote to overturn the Roe v. Wade decision. The sixth
edition of Black's Law Dictionary defines Stare Decisis as the
"policy of courts to stand by precedent and not to disturb
settled point ... where facts are substantially the same ..."
While the intent is to give stability to legal decisions, history
proves that Stare Decisis is by no means an absolute rule. For
example, in the 1896 Plessy v. Ferguson decision, "separate
but equal" settled law was unsettled in 1954. After 58 years
of being "settled law" the court declared,

*We conclude that, in the field of public education,
the doctrine of "separate but equal" has no place.
Separate educational facilities are inherently
unequal. Therefore, we hold that the plaintiffs and*

225

others similarly situated for whom the actions have been brought are, by reason of the segregation complained of, deprived of the equal protection of the laws guaranteed by the Fourteenth Amendment.

So when some decry that we should not "unsettle" Roe v. Wade, they might consider that it has only been "settled" for a little more than half the time as was the "separate but equal" precedent. The question that must be asked by lawyers, judges and legislators who are Christians and who, by definition, believe in absolute ethics, is this: "Why should our civil laws be based upon the ever-changing whims of public opinion?" After all, God's Word tells us,

The heart is deceitful above all things, and desperately wicked; who can know it?
JEREMIAH 17.9

Truly the hearts of the sons of men are full of evil ...
ECCLESIASTES 9.3

...every intent of the thoughts of his heart was only evil continually.
GENESIS 6.5; 8.21

Verses like these point to the urgency of having our civil laws based upon the inerrant and absolute principles of God's Word instead of trusting in man's fallen wisdom. It was undoubtedly in recognition of the sinfulness of man that Alexander Hamilton quoted the famed William Blackstone:

The law...dictated by God Himself, is, of course, superior in obligation to any other. It is binding over all the globe, in all countries, and at all times. No human laws are of any validity if contrary to this. [1]

Fellow signer of the Declaration of Independence, Rufus King, adds,

> *The law established by the Creator ... extends over the whole globe, is everywhere and at all times binding upon mankind ...This is the law of God by which He makes His way known to man and is paramount to all human control.* [2]

For those non-Christians who would reply, "We live in a pluralistic democracy where the will of the people is paramount, which means we must 'unsettle' our 'settled' precedents from time to time," we can only respond that America was founded as a republic, not a democracy, as witnessed by the numerous civil laws that are still in our various local, state and federal law codes. For any doubters, one has only to read the preambles to the various state constitutions to see the Trinitarian language. [3] Another signer of the Declaration of Independence exclaims

> *A simple democracy is the devil's own government.* [4]

The contrast, then, couldn't be clearer between a Christian civil ruler's view of the law and that of a non-Christian. Christians see ethics eternally enmeshed in the concrete Word of God, while non-Christians see all words as being nothing more than putty in the hands of the ruling elite to form agendas and imaginations according to their own biases. Since God's Word is "truth," the Christian civil ruler recognizes that the only way to be certain that we are governing ourselves properly is to conform our civil laws to biblical principles.

Just as the individual, family and church are accountable to govern their actions according to the inerrant Word of

God, so, too are civil rulers, as they submit themselves to their King, Jesus Christ [5]

• **Step Three:** (Based upon the above Scriptural support), **What is the biblical course of action required?**

Neither Christian civil rulers nor Christian citizens should be frustrated at the ungodly antics and perverse social agenda currently being implemented by non-Christian civil rulers. After all, they are simply being consistent with their worldview that they are gods, and are thereby capable of distinguishing right from wrong. [6] The frustration (and the wrath!) of Christian citizens should be directed to civil rulers who profess to be Christians, but who rule as though they were non-Christians. Our attitude toward such "Christian" civil rulers should be to point out to them, in brotherly compassion, the errors of their ways, [7] either directly or through someone else, and if they are truly a Christian they will humbly repent and be grateful that someone corrected their course, just as we should be for someone getting us back on course when we go off track (as all of us imperfect creatures will). If the "Christian" civil ruler displays the ungodly attribute of pride and dismisses our counsel, we should similarly "dismiss" him and begin looking for a genuine Christian to run against him.

Included in the oath taken by members of Congress, and very probably by most state and local officers, is the phrase, "So help me God." The Christian civil rulers (legislators and judges) should recognize that by making such a declaration that they are inviting the wrath of God if they fail to rule in conformity to His laws. [8] Today's civil rulers would be wise in following Judah's King Jehoshaphat's admonition to the judges he appointed:

Take heed to what you are doing, for you do not judge for man but for the LORD, who is with you in the judgment. Now therefore, let the fear of the LORD be upon you; take care and do it, for there is no iniquity with the LORD our God, no partiality, nor taking of bribes. 2 CHRONICLES 19. 6-7

Without Christian civil rulers there will be no justice, because the Bible equates "justice" with "righteousness," and the only way to be righteous is to obey God's law.

Therefore the law is powerless, and justice never goes forth. For the wicked surround the righteous; therefore perverse judgment proceeds. HABAKKUK 1.4

He who justifies the wicked, and he who condemns the just, both of them alike are an abomination to the LORD. PROVERBS 17.15

When Jehovah established an earthly king, [9] he was required to have a copy of His law written in a book so he could read it "all the days of his life:"

Also it shall be, when he sits on the throne of his kingdom, that he shall write for himself a copy of this law in a book, from the one before the priests, the Levites. And it shall be with him, and he shall read it all the days of his life, that he may learn to fear the LORD his God and be careful to observe all the words of this law and these statutes. DEUTERONOMY 17.18-19

The prophet Isaiah provides the model of a Christian judge:

> *The Spirit of the LORD shall rest upon Him, the Spirit of wisdom and understanding, the Spirit of counsel and might, the Spirit of knowledge and of the fear of the LORD. His delight is in the fear of the LORD, and He shall not judge by the sight of His eyes, nor decide by the hearing of His ears; but with righteousness He shall judge the poor, and decide with equity for the meek of the earth; He shall strike the earth with the rod of His mouth, and with the breath of His lips He shall slay the wicked. Righteousness shall be the belt of His loins, and faithfulness the belt of His waist.* ISAIAH 11.2-5

• Step Four: Sustaining the Correct Decision
   Civil Rulers who profess to be Christians should not only be on guard to not pass any legislation that conflicts with the perfect ethic code of the triune God of the Bible, and should work toward removing existing laws that are ungodly.

Civil Government. Make known to your church officers your sincere desire to provide a consistent testimony for your Lord, Savior and King, Jesus Christ, in the halls of the legislature, or on the bench of the courts, or in any other elected or appointed position of public service. Ask them to not be hesitant to offer constructive counsel to help you fulfill your duties in a God-honoring fashion.

Individual. Find out whether your civil rulers who profess to be Christians are taking their profession of faith seriously, and if they are not, approach them directly or through someone else to find out if their reason for so acting is intentional or unintentional. Ask your church officers to provide training for current civil rulers and candidates on how to biblically fulfill the duties of their office.

Family. Since only the father should vote in the household, hold frequent discussions about current civil rulers and candidates to determine who will provide the best biblical representation.

Church. In offering a small group study on how to biblically fulfill the role of civil ruler, inform the attendees that the principles enabling a legislator or a judge to carry out his duties to the glory and honor of God are identical with the principles by which they fulfill their duties in their professions. It would be highly hypocritical for us to demand from civil rulers a ethical standard different from the one under which we are operating in our vocations, classrooms, and homes.

NOTES

1 Hamilton, Alexander, *The Papers of Alexander Hamilton*, Vol.I, p.87, February 23, 1775, quoting William Blackstone's *Commentaries on the Laws of England*, Robert Bell, 1771, Harold C. Syrett, ed., (Columbia University Press, 1961) Vol. I, p.41

2 King, Rufus, *The Life and Correspondence of Rufus King*, Vol. VI, p.276, Charles King, ed., (G.P. Putnam's Sons, 1900)

3 See Appendix Three. "In Their Own Words," *EXIT Strategy: A Handbook to Exponentially Improve Your Service for God*, Buddy Hanson, (Hanson Group, 2005), p.275

4 *The Letters of Benjamin Rush*, Vol. I, p.454 L.H. Butterfield, ed., (Princeton University Press, 1951)

5 Philippians 2.6-11; Ephesians 1.20-22; Psalm 110.1; Acts 2.32-36; Daniel 7.13-14; Revelation 1.5; 17.14; 19.16

6 Genesis 3.5

7 Matthew 18. 15-18

8 Deuteronomy 5.11

9 1 Samuel 8

Christian Legislative Building Blocks

Instead of listing the key points from this Case Study, I thought it more valuable to provide a visual illustration for how Christians should deal with any of the various cultural issues of today. Unless "The Foundational Five Building Blocks for Dealing with Any Issue" are understood and agreed upon, it will be or little use to attempt to implement a biblical solution, because that solution will not have the infrastructure it needs to sustain itself.

The first Building Block is **God's Word,** which is true and brings success. The second Building Block is **Man's Word,** which is false and brings failure. Since our thoughts "are only evil continuously," [1] and our hearts, "deceitful above all else and beyond understanding," [2] and every sin "comes from our heart," [3] we must recognize that our logic, common sense and pragmatism will only end in failure. This means that we have a big problem, but God provides us with a bigger solution in the third Building Block. His **Supernatural Solution** is for us to rethink His perfect and inerrant revealed thoughts, instead of relying upon our false thoughts. King David tells us that it is in His light that we see light. [4] When Isaiah records Jehovah's words, "Come now, let us reason together," [5] the meaning is not that we sit down on one side of the table, with God on the other side, and we begin to brainstorm ideas on how to improve our culture. God doesn't need our ideas, we need His ideas. So when we "reason together" with Him, we are simply being good listeners, then active obeyers as we incorporate His truths into our worldview and lifestyle. Only by doing this are we able to "cast down every thought that exalts itself against the knowledge of God." [6]

The fourth Building Block is **Divine Resources** to assist us in bringing about "His will on earth as it is in heaven."[7] Each member of the Trinity provides invaluable assistance to us. The second Person of the Trinity, Jesus, is the Word incarnate. The apostle John tells us that He "became flesh and lived among us." [8] His words and lifestyle demonstrate how we should live and govern ourselves, and they also give us His promises to bless our obedience to His laws, or to discipline us for our disobedience. The third Person of the Trinity, the Holy Spirit, writes God's law on our hearts and motivates us to learn and obey God's Word. The first Person of the Trinity, God the Father, communicates to us through His Word and our prayers. He promises to hear "anything we ask" that conforms to His will [9] and to not listen to or answer any prayer or petition that does not conform to His will. [10] For example, suppose a husband lost his job and was having difficulty finding another one and couldn't pay the rent or buy groceries or clothes for his children. Apparently at the end of his rope, he offers the following prayer:

> *Father, as you know, I am in a terrible predicament. I can't find any work and can't pay my bills. Forgive me for this petition, but I see no other solution. Help me to rob a bank so I can have enough money to carry me through until I get back on my feet. I promise to never do this again, and I also promise to pay back all of the money. I'm just in a desperate position and know of no other way to provide for my family.*

The Foundational Five Building Blocks

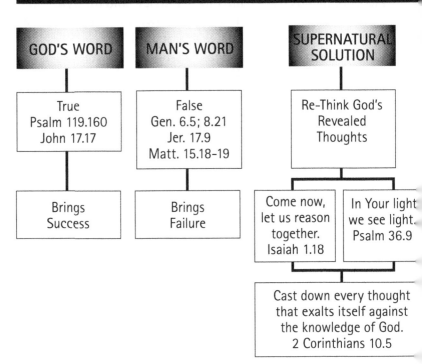

GOD'S WORD	MAN'S WORD	SUPERNATURAL SOLUTION
True Psalm 119.160 John 17.17	False Gen. 6.5; 8.21 Jer. 17.9 Matt. 15.18–19	Re-Think God's Revealed Thoughts
Brings Success	Brings Failure	Come now, let us reason together. Isaiah 1.18 — In Your light we see light. Psalm 36.9

Cast down every thought that exalts itself against the knowledge of God. 2 Corinthians 10.5

or Dealing with Any Issue

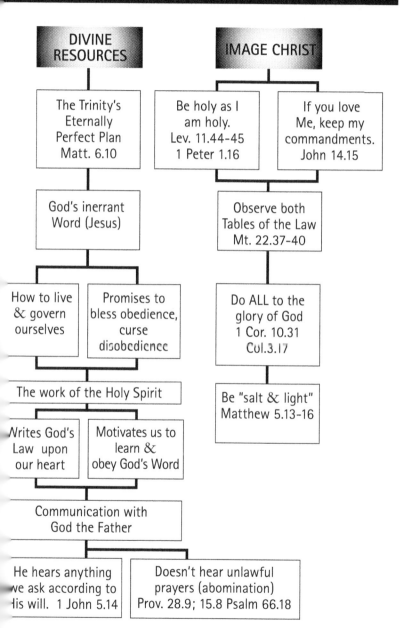

DIVINE RESOURCES

The Trinity's Eternally Perfect Plan Matt. 6.10

God's inerrant Word (Jesus)

How to live & govern ourselves

Promises to bless obedience, curse disobedience

The work of the Holy Spirit

Writes God's Law upon our heart

Motivates us to learn & obey God's Word

Communication with God the Father

He hears anything we ask according to His will. 1 John 5.14

Doesn't hear unlawful prayers (abomination) Prov. 28.9; 15.8 Psalm 66.18

IMAGE CHRIST

Be holy as I am holy. Lev. 11.44-45 1 Peter 1.16

If you love Me, keep my commandments. John 14.15

Observe both Tables of the Law Mt. 22.37-40

Do ALL to the glory of God 1 Cor. 10.31 Col.3.17

Be "salt & light" Matthew 5.13-16

Would God answer such a prayer? Of course not. Regardless of how sincere and well-intended the husband was in asking for "help," his request goes directly against the eighth commandment to "not steal." So, obviously, this prayer does not conform to God's will. One of the sample worksheets in this case study was "Educating Our Children." There are numerous Christian parents who sincerely believe that the public schools can be reformed and no doubt pray that God will bring this about. However, as we all know, "The road to hell is paved with good intentions."

The fifth Building Block is to **Image Christ**. At any point in time we are either imaging Christ or Satan. There is no other alternative. Jesus commands us to "be holy as I am holy." [11] Jesus also tells us that we prove our love for Him by "keeping His commandments." [12] No matter where we are, and no matter what we are doing, whether in our homes, our vocation, the halls of the legislature ... anywhere, we are commanded to "do all to the glory of God." [13] This is how we become "salt and light" to our non-Christian neighbors. [14]

By keeping these "Foundational Five Building Blocks," fresh in our memories, we will have a biblical framework within which to correctly tackle any cultural issue that faces us.

NOTES

1 Genesis 6.5; 8.21
2 Jeremiah 17.9
3 Matthew 15.18-19
4 Psalm 36.9
5 Isaiah 1.18
6 2 Corinthians 10.5
7 Matthew 6.10
8 John 1.14
9 1 John 5.14
10 Proverbs 28.9; 15.8; Psalm 66.18
11 Leviticus 11.44-45; 1 Peter 1.16
12 John 14.15
13 1 Corinthians 10.31; Colossians 3.17
14 Matthew 5.13-16

CASE STUDY 4

WHOSE MONEY IS IT?
*We've Come a Long Way
Since Col. Davy Crockett*

SPENDING BY THE CIVIL GOVERNMENT IS OUT OF CONTROL AS politicians attempt to "buy votes" by adding programs and services that the Bible says are supposed to be provided for by individuals, families and churches. Such politicians need to be replaced by statesmen like Col. Davy Crockett, who understood that each Congressman must be guided and constrained by the principles in the Constitution.

Christians continue to be judged by God in the form of ever-higher taxes because we either refuse to elect Christians as our civil rulers, or else elect Christians who disobey and disrespect God's commands because of an inadequate Christian worldview. Such a misunderstanding of how to apply the biblical principles they so staunchly profess to believe has resulted in their being poor stewards of the resources of their constituents. While many states are in the midst of a budgetary crisis, perhaps no single example highlights the problem more dramatically than foreign aid. It is estimated that 75 percent of our annual $13 billion foreign aid dollars goes to ungodly countries. Even though most U.N. members vote against America on at least two out of every three votes, Congress continues to lavish our hard-earned tax dollars on the likes of:

Egypt	$2,000,000,000 (79% votes against U.S.A.)
Jordan	$192,814,000 (71% votes against U.S.A.)
India	$143,699,000 (81% votes against U.S.A.)
Pakistan	$6,721,000 (75% votes against U.S.A.)

Such a flagrant disregard for the eighth commandment ("thou shall not steal") has not always been a hallmark of civil rulers. The following story from *The Life of Colonel David Crockett* by Edward S. Elis, 1884, illustrates the necessity of churches to train would-be civil rulers in a thorough Christian worldview so that, once elected, they will represent their communities and/or states in a God-honoring fashion. The narration of Davy Crockett's compelling story follows:

"I was one day in the lobby of the House of Representatives when a bill was taken up appropriating money for the benefit of a widow of a distinguished naval officer. It seemed that everybody favored it. The Speaker was just about to put the question when Crockett arose. Everybody expected, of course, that he was going to make a speech in support of the bill. He commenced:

"'Mr. Speaker, I have as much respect for the memory of the deceased, and as much sympathy for the suffering of the living, if suffering there be, as any man in this House; but we must not permit our respect for the dead or sympathy for a part of the living to lead us into an act of injustice to the balance of the living. I will not go into an argument to prove that Congress has no power under the Constitution to appropriate this money as an act of charity. Every member upon this floor knows it.

"'Mr. Speaker, I am the poorest man on this floor. I cannot vote for this bill, but I will give one week's pay to the object, and if every member of Congress will do the same, it will amount to more than the bill asks.'

"He took his seat. Nobody replied. The bill was put upon its passage, and instead of passing unanimously, as was generally supposed, and as no doubt it would have, but for the speech, it received but few votes and was lost. Like many others, I desired the passage of the bill, and felt outraged at its defeat. ... I went early to his room the next morning and ... I broke in upon him rather abruptly, asking him what the devil had possessed him to make that speech and defeat that bill yesterday. Without turning his head or looking up from his work, he replied, 'I will answer your question. But thereby hangs a tale, and one of considerable length, to which you will have to listen.' I listened and this is the tale that I heard.

We have the right, as individuals, to give away as much of our own money as we please in charity; but as members of Congress we have no right so to appropriate a dollar of the public money.

"'Several years ago I was one evening standing on the steps of the Capitol with some other members of Congress, when our attention was attracted by a great light over in Georgetown. It was evidently a large fire. We jumped into a hack and drove over as fast as we could. When we got there, I went to work and I never worked as hard in my life as I did there for several hours. But, in spite of all that could be done, many houses were burned and many families made houseless, and, besides, some of them had lost all but the clothes they had on. The weather was very cold, and when I saw so many women and children suffering, I felt that something ought to be done for them, and everybody else seemed to feel the same way.

"The next morning a bill was introduced appropriating $20,000 for their relief. We put aside all other business and rushed it through as soon as it could be done. I said everybody felt as I did. That was not quite so; for, though they perhaps sympathized as deeply with the sufferers as I did, there were a few of the members who did not think we had the right to indulge our sympathy or excite our charity at the expense of anybody but ourselves. They opposed the bill, and upon its passage demanded the yeas and nays. The yeas and nays were recorded, and my name appeared on the journals in favor of the bill.

"The next summer, when it began to be time to think about election, I concluded I would take a scout around among the boys of my district. I had no opposition there, but, as the election was some time off, I did not know what might turn up, and I thought it was best to let the boys know that I had not forgot them, and that going to Congress had not made me too proud to go to see them.

"So I put a couple of shirts and a few twists of tobacco into my saddlebags and put out. I had been out about a week and had found things going very smoothly, when, riding one day in a part of my district in which I was more of a stranger than any other, I saw a man in a field plowing and coming toward the road. I gauged my gait so that we should meet as he came to the fence. As he came up I spoke to the man. He replied politely, but, as I thought, rather coldly, and was about turning his horse for another furrow when I said to him: "Don't be in such a hurry my friend; I want to have a little talk with you, and get better acquainted." He replied: "I am very busy, and have but little time to talk, but if it does not take too long, I will listen to what you have to say."

"'I began: "Well, friend, I am one of those unfortunate beings called candidates, and ..."

"Yes, I know you; you are Colonel Crockett, I have seen you once before, and voted for you the last time you were elected. I suppose you are out electioneering now, but you had better not waste your time or mine. I shall not vote for you again."

"This was a sockdolager (a conclusive heavy blow). I begged him to tell me what was the matter. "Well, Colonel, it is hardly worthwhile to waste time or words upon it. I do not see how it can be mended, but you gave a vote last winter which shows that either you have not the capacity to understand the Constitution, or that you are wanting the honesty and firmness to be guided by it. In either case you are not the man to represent me. But I beg your pardon for expressing it in that way. I did not intend to avail myself of the privilege of the constituent to speak plainly to a candidate for the purpose of insulting or wounding you. I intend by it only to say that your understanding of the Constitution is very different from mine; and I will say to you what, but for my rudeness, I should not have said, that I believe you to be honest. ... But an understanding of the Constitution different from mine I cannot overlook, because

the Constitution, to be worth anything, must be held sacred, and rigidly observed in all its provisions. The man who wields power and misinterprets it is the more dangerous the more honest he is.'

"I admit the truth of all you say, but there must be some mistake about it, for I do not remember that I gave any vote last winter upon any constitutional question."
"No Colonel, there's no mistake. Though I live here in the backwoods and seldom go from home, I take the papers from Washington and read very carefully all the proceedings of Congress. My papers say that last winter you voted for a bill to appropriate $20,000 to some sufferers by fire in Georgetown. Is that true?"
"Certainly it is, and I thought that was the last vote which anybody in the world would have found fault with."

> *"Well, Colonel, where do you find in the Constitution any authority to give away the public money to charity?"*

"Here was another sockdolager; for, when I began to think about it, I could not remember a thing in the Constitution that authorized it. I found I must take another tack, so I said, "Well, my friend, I may as well own up. You have got me there. But certainly nobody will complain that a great and rich country like ours should give the insignificant sum of $20,000 to relieve women and children, particularly with a full and overflowing Treasury; and I am sure, if you had been there, you would have done just as I did."

"It is not the amount, Colonel, that I complain of; it is the principle. In the first place, the government ought to have in the Treasury no more than enough for its legitimate purposes. But that has nothing to do with the question. The power of collecting and disbursing money at pleasure is the most dangerous power that can be entrusted to man, particularly under our system of collecting revenue by a tariff, which reaches every man in the country, no matter how poor he may be, and the poorer he is the more he pays in proportion to his means.

"So you see, that while you are contributing to relieve one, you are drawing it from thousands who are even worse off than he. If you had the right to give anything, the amount was simply a matter of discretion with you, and you had as much right to give $20,000,000 as $20,000. If you have the right to give to one, you have the right to give to all; and as the Constitution neither defines charity nor stipulates the amount, you are at liberty to give to any and everything which you believe, or profess to believe, is a charity, and to any amount you may think proper. You will very easily perceive what a wide door this would open for fraud and corruption and favoritism, on the one hand, and for robbing the people on the other.

> "No, Colonel, Congress has no right to give charity. Individual members may give as much of their own money as they please, but they have no right to touch a dollar of the public money for that purpose.

"There are about two hundred and fifty members of Congress. If they had shown their sympathy for the suffers by contributing each one week's pay, it would have made over $13,000. There are plenty of wealthy men in Washington, who could have given $20,000 without depriving themselves. The congressmen chose to keep their own money, which, if reports are true, some of them spend not very creditably; and the people about Washington no doubt applauded you for giving what was not yours to give, thus relieving them of the necessity of giving.

> "The people have delegated to Congress, by the Constitution, the power to do certain things. To do these, it is authorized to collect and pay moneys, and for nothing else. Everything beyond this is usurpation, and a violation of the constitution.

"... So you see, Colonel, you have violated the Constitution in what I consider a vital point. It is a precedent fraught with danger to the country, for

> when Congress once begins to stretch its power beyond the limits of the Constitution, there is no limit to it, and no security for the people.

243

"I have no doubt you acted honestly, but that does not make it any better...and you see that I cannot vote for you."

"Well, my friend," I said, "you hit the nail upon the head when you said I had not sense enough to understand the Constitution. I have heard many speeches in Congress about the powers of Congress, but what you have said here at your plow has got more hard, sound sense in it than all the fine speeches I ever heard. If I had ever taken the view of it that you have, I would have put my head into the fire before I would have given that vote; and if you will forgive me and vote for me again, if I ever vote for another unconstitutional law I wish I may be shot. ... I must know your name." "My name is Bunce." "Not Horatio Bunce?" "Yes." "Well, Mr. Bunce, I never saw you before ... but I know you very well. ... "

"It was one of the luckiest hits of my life that I met that man. He mingled but little with the public, but was widely known for his remarkable intelligence, incorruptible integrity, and for a heart brimful and running over with kindness and benevolence, which showed themselves not only in words but in acts. ...Mr. Bunce converted me politically. He came nearer converting me religiously than I had ever been before ...if everyone who professes to be a Christian lived and acted and enjoyed it as he does, the religion of Christ would take the world by storm.

"Now sir,' concluded Crockett, 'you know why I made that speech yesterday.'"

This appeared in The COUNSEL of Chalcedon, July/August 1991, and is used with permission www.chalcedon.org/counsel 866.299.6567.

Christian Legislative Building Blocks

We have the right, as individuals, to give away as much of our own money as we please in charity; but as members of Congress we have no right so to appropriate a dollar of the public money.

The people have delegated to Congress, by the Constitution, the power to do certain things. To do these, it is authorized to collect and pay moneys, and for nothing else. Everything beyond this is usurpation, and a violation of the Constitution.

"Well, Colonel, where do you find in the Constitution any authority to give away the public money to charity?"

"No, Colonel, Congress has no right to give charity. Individual members may give as much of their own money as they please, but they have no right to touch a dollar of the public money for that purpose."

The Constitution, to be worth anything, must be held sacred, and rigidly observed in all its provisions. The man who wields power and misinterprets it is the more dangerous the more honest he is.

When Congress once begins to stretch its power beyond the limits of the Constitution, there is no limit to it, and no security for the people.

245

CASE STUDY 5

A CHRISTIAN PERSPECTIVE ON JUST WAR

William Einwechter

WAR BY ITS VERY NATURE IS A SPECTACLE OF VIOLENCE, DESTRUCTION, suffering, and death. War is filled with many horrors and is a great human tragedy. War tends to unleash the worst of human passions: hate, vengeance, wicked ambition, cruelty, base desires, and blood-lust. Erasmus was fond of the adage of Pindar: "Sweet is war to him who knows it not." Or as those who do know war testify: "War is hell." These things being true, how could a Christian ever be in favor of war?

The undeniable fact of history is that war is a common condition in human affairs. From the earliest days of man's existence, he has been at war with his fellow man. How has the church responded to the fact of war? There have been two basic stands concerning war among Christians and their particular church denominations: pacifism and just war. Pacifists declare that all war is evil and contrary to the principles of Jesus and the New Testament. Hence, Christian participation in war is forbidden. Just war adherents believe that a war may be just if it meets certain criteria. If the war is just, then a Christian may participate in it. The purpose of this article is to summarize and defend the just war position.

Introduction to the Just War Position

The teaching of the Bible leads the Christian to presuppose the possibility of a just war. There are five arguments that show that war is not necessarily sinful (though, of course, a particular war may be), and that war can indeed be the righteous response to evil.

First, God, through the inspired words of Scripture, depicts Himself as a "man of war" engaged in battle against His enemies (Ex. 15:3-9; Isa. 42:13). The Lord reveals that He is "mighty in battle" (i.e. warfare; Ps. 24:8). He describes Himself as using weapons of war (e.g., the sword and arrows; Deut. 32:41-42) to take vengeance on His enemies. If warfare is always evil and the warrior is always acting sinfully when wielding his weapons, then God could not depict His nature and ways by reference to war. The fact that God so extensively associates Himself with war and the warrior indicates that war can be just.[1] The Messiah, the Lord Jesus, is also depicted as a warrior engaged in battle in both the Old and New Testaments (Ps. 110; Rev. 19:11-21).

Second, God commanded Israel to engage in war and went forth with His people to give them victory in battle. This included the charge to destroy the Canaanites and the commands related to the defense of the land of Palestine against invaders and oppressors (e.g., Judg. 4:6-7; 6:11-17; 1 Chron. 14:8-17). God cannot command His people to do that which is intrinsically evil.

Third, the Lord gave specific instructions on the conduct of war in His revealed law (Deut. 20:1-20). All of the laws of God are just. Therefore, it follows that war itself is just if the laws of God concerning it are followed.

Fourth, men of God, such as Abraham, Moses, Joshua, Gideon, and David, engaged in warfare with God's approval and help. Furthermore, the New Testament specifically endorses the warfare of these men as examples of faith in God and what faith can accomplish (Heb. 11:33-34).

Fifth, the New Testament does not repeal the Old Testament law in regard to war, and specifically upholds, in principle, the civil magistrates' authority to go to war. The sword that is given by the Lord to the civil ruler, which he does not wield in vain as God's minister, is a weapon of war and a symbol of warfare (Rom. 13:1-4). Additionally, Jesus, John the Baptist, and Peter did not call soldiers who believed in God to leave their profession of arms (Luke 7:9; 3:14; Acts 10).

The just war position recognizes that every war comes about because of the evil in the heart of man (cf. James 4:1-2). If we lived in a world where all men sought to love God and their neighbor there would be no war. However, the truth is that wicked men yet abound and seek to tyrannize other men and nations through their weapons and armies. It is the righteous duty of civil rulers to act to stop the rapine and murder of their people by wicked assailants and restore peace (1 Tim. 2:2). So, even though the genesis of war is found in the evil of man, the taking up of arms to stop that evil can be righteous.[2]

The principles of the just war position that have been formulated by the Christian church have their root in the teaching of Ambrose, Augustine, and Aquinas. These men sought to address the issue of war from a Christian perspective. In seeking the answer to the question of when a war can be considered just, they employed the Bible and classical ideals of just war that had been developed by Greek and Roman thinkers. The Old Testament revelation concerning warfare was central to their thinking, as was the general biblical revelation of the standards of God's moral law, but they also found significant insight into the nature of just war from men like Cicero. Holmes provides a summary of Cicero's view:

The pagan Cicero provides the first organized statement of a just war theory. In the ideal state where law is based on right reason rather than utility, (1) the only just cause for war is the defense of national honor and safety, (2) war is a last resort when all negotiations fail, (3) it must be formally declared, in order to give due warning, (4) the purpose may not be conquest or power, but the securing of a just peace, (5) prisoners and all who surrender should be spared, and (6) only those who are legally soldiers should be involved (De Republica iii. 22-29; De Officiis i. 11-12).[3]

Augustine rejected Cicero's ideal state as unrealistic, and did not believe that natural law or universal reason could provide the basis for peace and justice.[4] Nevertheless, he and others saw much that was true in the classical just war formulation and adapted it, with modifications, to coincide with biblical ethics. More in line with the classical emphasis on natural law and reason was Thomas Aquinas. Holmes states that according to Aquinas: "A just war...is one that is governed by laws which derive from natural law, and hence from the eternal law of God."[5]

Regardless of the contribution to just war principles that was made by Greek and Roman philosophers and statesmen, the Christian view on just war must ultimately be derived from the Scriptures, which alone are the final rule of faith and practice.

Statement of Just War Principles

A war can be considered just if the following standards are met.[6]

The war is conducted by legitimate civil authority

The authority to go to war resides in the state alone; no other institution or individual can commit a nation to war. Each nation needs to constitutionally designate who has the authority to define and formally declare war.

The truth that only duly constituted civil authority may wage war is based on the biblical teaching concerning the state. In distinction from the institutions of the family and church,

God has given the state the responsibility and authority to restrain and punish evil by means of force. As God's minister, the civil magistrate is charged with protecting the person and property of those under his authority from evildoers (Rom. 13:1-6; 1 Pet. 2:14). The ruler should so act and govern that the citizens may live in peace, secure from threats to their well-being from criminals, domestic and foreign (1 Tim. 2:1). Justice and the protection of individual rights and liberties is the work of civil government (Deut. 16:18-20).

The restraint of evildoers and the maintaining of justice, peace, and liberty may require the civil government to go to war. The sword, which is the biblical symbol of the state's authority to enforce criminal law and to punish evildoers to the point of death, if necessary, is also a weapon of war. That is, the state's authority to defend its citizens includes both the police and military functions. There is no essential difference between police force and military force: one is employed against enemies of justice within and the other to enemies of justice without. The power of the sword extends to taking the life of a murderer and the lives of enemy soldiers in war.

Therefore, war is an extension of the biblical duty of civil government to protect its citizens by punishing evildoers who strike at their lives and liberties. In war, the evildoers are those of another state who act unjustly at the command and authority of their civil rulers.

The war is based on a just cause

If the state is the minister of God for justice, then it can only wage war to uphold justice and avenge evil. Thus, a just war is one that is fought for the purpose of defending life and property, vindicating justice, and reestablishing peace. A just war is a response to evil; it is an act of defense against international criminal activity (as defined by God's law); it is a resistance to lawlessness and a terror to evildoers.

Augustine said that war can be waged justly as a defense against aggression and for the protection of life and liberty. He also believed that war, on certain occasions, could be fought because of wrongs inflicted on a nation through economic or other means. Thus, war should only be waged to vindicate justice. The goal of war, taught Augustine, was the restoration of international peace.[7]

Calvinist political thinker Johannes Althusius (1557-1638), in his important work *Politica*, states:

> There are seven just causes for declaring and waging war. The **first** cause is the recovery of things taken away through violence by another people. The **second** cause is the defense against violence inflicted by another, and the repulsion of it. The **third** cause is the necessity for preserving liberty, privileges, rights, peace, and tranquility, and for defending the true religion. The **fourth** cause occurs when a foreign people deny peaceful transit through its province without good reason. The **fifth** cause occurs when subjects rise up against their prince and lord, do not fulfill their pledged word, and are not willing to obey him, although they have been admonished many times. The **sixth** cause is contumacy, which occurs when any prince, lord, or city has so contemptuously and repeatedly scorned the decisions of courts that justice cannot be otherwise administered and defended. The **seventh** just cause of war occurs when agreements are not implemented by the other party, when he does not keep his promises, and when tyranny is practiced upon subjects.[8]

It is significant to note that in Althusius' seven just causes for war, the first four refer to the just causes of war between nations and the last three to the just causes of civil war. In another place in *Politica*, Althusius restates these same causes under five headings:

The causes of war that rely upon the right are (1) defense of liberty and of one's rights, and repulsion of a launched attack, (2) defense of the pure religion, (3) recovery of properties unjustly seized, (4) denial of justice, and (5) conspiracy with an enemy, and rebellion....[9]

Finally, he summarizes just cause under two headings: But these causes can easily be reduced to two, the first is defense and the other vindication. The former repulses and the latter vindicates injury launched against God, the commonwealth, its subjects, or the church. I understand defense to be either of your own nation or of another.... Vindication is a legitimate cause for war when a judgment and recovery of what has been seized has not yet taken place.[10]

Jonathan Edwards, one of America's greatest theologians, demonstrated that "he held to the just war tradition and considered it sometimes obligatory for the Christian to bear arms."[11] In a sermon on 1 Kings 8:44-45, "A People of God may be called of God to go forth to war against their Enemies," Edwards gives his views on what constitutes a just cause for war. McDermott encapsulates Edwards' teaching in the sermon as follows:

In the remainder of the sermon Edwards outlined the circumstances in which a professing people may feel justified in going to war: (1) when the rights of a public society are invaded and the preservation of the community requires it; and (2) when a people are obliged by a "Just alliance or Covenant" contracted with another people for their "mutual defense and Preservation."[12]

253

In summary of Edwards' view on just cause for war, McDermott writes:

> *Military force is justified, thought Edwards, when the "rights and privileges of a people are threatened," or "when the preservation of the Community or Publick society so requires it." If "injurious and bloody enemies" molest and endanger a society, it is the "duty" of government to undertake that society's defense by the use of force. This follows "from the Law of self-Preservation."*[13]

The Christian consensus is that a war is only just when its cause is to defend the life, liberty, and property of a people who are being assaulted by an aggressor. In defending against the crimes of a belligerent foe, a just war is also the punishment of evildoers and a vindication of justice. As Dabney states: "Defensive war is, then, righteous, and only a defensive war."[14]

Defensive war is supported by Scripture. The case law of Exodus 22:2-4 that authorizes deadly force in self-defense against a dangerous intruder, also, by application, authorizes the use of deadly force in national defense against those who invade or attack the lives, liberties, and properties of the people. National defense in warfare is the exercise of the right of self-defense collectively by citizens under the authority and direction of the civil magistrate. The laws of war given in Deuteronomy 20 authorize war in national defense.[15] Abraham's rescue of Lot (Gen. 14) and Israel's wars of defense against the hostile nations around them (cf. Judges, 1 and 2 Samuel, and 1 and 2 Kings) indicate God's approval and sanction on defensive war. Proverbs 24:11-12 and 31:8-9 would justify a stronger nation going to the aid of a weaker nation to defend it against wicked aggression,[16] while texts such as Psalm 15:4 would require a nation to defend a nation with whom it has a "just alliance" for mutual defense when that nation is attacked (cf. Josh. 10).

Christians may participate in a war only if it is based in a just cause—to defend life, liberty, and property against evil aggression. In regard to Christian participation in war, Carnell states:

"Of course, it is needful that the government be on the side of righteousness before a Christian can conscientiously fight. And while it may be complex to determine when a government is the defender and not the aggressor — for motives are infinitely compounded with the subtleties of propaganda and emotion — nevertheless the principle is incontestable that a Christian may not fight in either a preventive or an aggressive war."[17]

In summary, there are three kinds of war that are just: (1) wars of defense against aggression; (2) wars to help and defend an ally or weaker nation from aggression; (3) civil wars to overthrow rank tyranny and oppression by the rulers[18] or to put down evil insurrection.

The war is waged with right intention

Not only must the cause be just, the just cause must be the reason why a nation goes to war. The intention must be justice and the restoration of peace and not national honor or development. Often, a "just cause" is just a cover for national or political ambitions. Augustine wisely pointed out that nations often go to war for no more than political and economic reasons. Political reasons include the desire for power, conquest, personal glory and national pride, and solutions to domestic problems. Economic reasons include the acquisition of new wealth, territory, natural resources, and access to trade routes and ports.[19]

The essence of this principle is that the nation waging war is doing so in the pursuit of justice and not for reasons of self-interest or aggrandizement.[20] Mosely contends that "a just war cannot be considered to be just if reasons of national interest are paramount or overwhelm the pretext of fighting aggression."[21]

The Bible teaches that the intent behind our actions is morally determinative (Matt. 6:1-5, 16; 1 Cor. 3:13; 10:31; 13:1-3; James 4:1-3). The true nature of human conduct is determined by our motive, so that even that which in itself may be right becomes evil when the purpose behind the action is self-centered. Apparent good conduct has often been only a cloak for evil. So a war is only just if the true intent is the glory of God (1 Cor. 10:31) through the suppression evil aggression and the establishment of peace and justice.

The war is undertaken only as a last resort.

All non-violent means and options for the redress of grievances and the establishment of justice between nations should seriously be tried and at an end before the use of deadly force can be justified. Althusius stated: "Just cause for waging war occurs when all other remedies have first been exhausted and peace and justice cannot otherwise be obtained."[22] He further explained:

> *This authority to undertake war ought not to be employed by the magistrate unless all other remedies have failed, and there is no other way to repel an attack upon his subjects, to avoid and vindicate injustice to them, or to obtain peace and tranquillity in the realm.... But before undertaking war a*

*magistrate should check his own judgment and
reasoning, and offer prayers to God to arouse and
direct the spirit and mind of his subjects and himself
to the well-being, utility, and necessity of the church
and community, and to avoid all rashness and
injustice....*[23]

The Scriptures support the concept that ultimate sanctions should not be pursued until other options for reconciliation and redress have been exhausted (cf. Matt. 18:15-17). The Bible condemns those who are hasty and rash in their actions because they exalt folly (Prov. 14:29). When one contemplates the misery and suffering that war brings, it is certainly folly to go to war when the injury can be made right without war. The law of God instructs Israel to offer terms of peace to an enemy city (Deut. 20:10-15) before attacking it; only after the offer is rejected can Israel begin hostilities. Rushdoony gives the following explanation of this law:

*...[biblical] military law requires that, prior to an
attack, or rather, a declaration of war, an offer of
peace be extended to the enemy. The offer of peace
cannot be an offer to compromise. The cause, if it be
just, must be maintained; the enemy must yield to
gain peace.*[24]

Rushdoony reminds us that peace should not be secured at the price of justice. The principle that war should be a last resort does not mean that we are required to negotiate a base peace that leaves aggression and tyranny unopposed. To abandon justice in the name of peace ultimately is to lose both.

The war is fought on the basis of a reasonable chance of success.

Before war is pursued there must be a careful calculation to determine if a nation has the strength and resources to win the war. If not, the commencement of military action should either be abandoned or postponed until the nation is ready. It is considered unjust to commit soldiers to die and to subject citizens to the deprivations, sorrows, and horrors of war in a vain undertaking.

The Word of God generally supports this principle of the just war position. In Luke 14:28-32, Jesus teaches the folly of those who begin something without considering if they have what is necessary to finish it. He specifically speaks of the wisdom of a king who does not go to war unless he calculates that he has a good chance of success. If the king determines that he cannot win the war, according to Jesus, he shows prudence by sending ambassadors to the leader of the army coming against him to seek conditions of peace. Also relevant is the word of the prophet Jeremiah where he called on Judah to not resist (fight) the Babylonians who were coming to conquer them because it was futile to go to war against them. It was futile because God had decreed judgment against the wicked rulers and people of Judah.

But there are questions concerning this principle of just war doctrine. These questions are aptly raised by Mosely:

> The next principle is that of reasonable success. This
> is another necessary condition for waging just war,
> but again is insufficient by itself. Given just cause
> and right intention, the just war theory asserts that
> there must be a reasonable probability of success.
> The principle of reasonable success is consequential
> in that the costs and benefits of a campaign must
> be calculated. However, the concept of weighing
> benefits poses moral as well as practical problems as

evinced in the following questions. Should one not go to the aid of a people or declare war if there is no conceivable chance of success? Is it right to comply with aggression because the costs of not complying are too prohibitive? Is it not sometimes morally necessary to stand up to a bullying larger force, as the Finns did when Russia invaded in 1940...? Besides, posturing for defense may sometimes make aggression itself too costly, even for a much stronger side. However, the thrust of the principle of reasonable success emphasizes that human life and economic resources should not be wasted in what would obviously be an uneven match. For a nation threatened by invasion, other forms of retaliation or defense may be available, such as civil disobedience, or even forming alliances with other small nations to equalize the odds. Historically, many nations have overcome the probability of defeat: the fight may seem hopeless, but a charismatic leader or rousing speech can sometimes be enough to stir a people into fighting with all their will.[25]

And a factor that Mosely does not mention is the power of God granting victory against seemingly impossible odds to a people who obey and trust in Him—as He did repeatedly for Israel.

The war has the establishment of a superior peace as its goal.

This principle raises the issue of proportionality and states that war should not be waged unless the good that may reasonably be expected from taking up arms is greater than the evil to be redressed and the evils that may result from the conflict. To state it in another way, the peace that is sought through going to war must be preferable to the peace that would have prevailed if the war had not been fought. And again, the overall death and devastation anticipated by the war should be outweighed by the good that hopefully will result.

Proportionality also is applied to the conduct of the war. The force used in actual combat should not go beyond that which is necessary to achieve the goals of the war.

The legal principle of lex talionis (the law of retalia-tion) calls for proportionality in sentencing criminals—the punishment must fit the crime. It was given to judges to enable them to carry out their duties as God's ministers of vengeance on evildoers. As a just war is waged for the suppression of evil and visiting God's judgment on evildoers it seems proper to apply the principle of lex talionis to warfare, at least in the general sense of proportionality.

The laws of war given in Deuteronomy 20 raise interesting questions concerning proportionality. These laws suggest that there is a dear price to pay if you are a tyrant or the aggressor nation in a war. The retribution for unjustly starting a war should be so terrible that anyone will think twice before committing this awful crime. If death is a necessary sanction to restrain men from murder, what should be the penalty for those rulers who through their lust for power and fame bring death and suffering to multitudes by aggressive wars? Rushdoony's answer is to the point: "...if warfare is to punish and/or destroy evil, the work of restoration requires that this be done, that an evil order be overthrown, and, in some cases, some or many people be executed."[26]

The war is waged with proper discrimination between combatants and non-combatants.

This principle of just war states that civilians and civilian industry and property are not to be deliberately targeted nor abused, and that all due care should be taken to minimize collateral damage to civilian life and property. In other words, non-combatants are to be granted immunity from attack by the armies waging the war. Military personnel and military industry should be the sole objects of military operations.

However, if a civilian engages in hostile actions, he becomes a combatant, regardless of his non-military status, and becomes a legitimate target. Also, when a soldier is captured and disarmed he ceases to be a combatant and, though he may be kept as a prisoner of war until the end of the war, he must be treated properly and cared for if wounded.

Biblical law supports the concept of discriminating between military and non-military targets. In the laws relating to the conduct of war given in Deuteronomy 20, all women and children[27] are to be spared from the sword, and all fruit-bearing trees are to be spared from the ax. These laws stand against the concept of "total war."

According to the doctrine of total war, anyone or anything of the nation that you are at war with is a legitimate target (e.g., civilians or civilian targets), if the targeting of these will weaken the enemy's resources and will to fight. Total war is evil for it leads to the wanton slaughter of women and children and to the wholesale destruction of homes, farms, and industries—all of which biblical law forbids.

Concluding Observations on Just War

The principles of just war are distinguished between those that justify when one may go to war (*jus ad bellum*) and those that govern how a war is to be waged (jus in bello). The jus ad bellum principles are that war must be waged by a legitimate civil authority, have a just cause, be fought with right intention, as a last resort, when there is probability of success, and when the good to be achieved is greater than the suffering brought about by the war. The jus in bello principles are the need to make proper discrimination between military and non-military targets, to fight with right intention (i.e., a just peace, thus avoiding acts of war that will ultimately hinder peace), and to seek proportional good from the tactics and methods employed in the war (i.e., no tactic should be used unless the good expected from its use is greater than the evil caused).

The just war doctrine rejects the mindless patriotism of "my country right or wrong" and challenges the citizens to make a moral judgment concerning the wars their nation fights. If a citizen believes that the war is unjust he needs to refrain from participation in or support of the war. The just war position logically entails the righteousness of conscientious objection against unjust wars: "since war is to be waged in a just cause only, and normally, in defense of homeland and of justice, the right of conscientious objection means that one has the moral right to refuse support to an ungodly war."[28]

King Solomon says that there is a "time for war" (Eccl. 3:8), indicating what all wise men understand: going to war is sometimes necessary to withstand the wickedness of aggressive rulers and nations that murder, pillage, rape, steal, and tyrannize others. Rushdoony explains:

> Similarly, physical resistance, whether in the form of warfare or personal resistance to murderous attack, or the attempts of evil men to overwhelm us, is a godly stand and by no means wrong. In an evil world, such resistance is often necessary; it is an unpleasant and ugly necessity, but not an evil. David could thank God for teaching him to war successfully (II Sam. 22:35; Ps. 18:34; 144:1). In an evil world, God requires men to stand in terms of His word and law.[29]

Warfare is a part also of a sinful order, but no less right under godly circumstances, and the right of the sword is by no means withheld because war belongs to the state of sin. Hardly an aspect of our lives can be separated from this sinful order in any full sense, but the law [of God] speaks to covenant-keepers in a sinful world, not to men in heaven.[30]

The fundamental essence of a Christian perspective on just war is encapsulated in the following statements by Dabney and Carnell:

> *Defensive war is, then, righteous, and only defensive war. Aggressive war is wholesale robbery and murder. If the magistrate is armed with righteous power to destroy the domestic murderer, a fortiori he has the right to destroy these alien murderers, committing the crime wholesale. The "Peace Society" used to argue that all war is sinful, from the horrors of war. They are enormous. But common sense would rather argue from this the guilt of the perpetrators and the right of punishing it in some appropriate way. Who may do it if not the magistrate? But war should only be defensive. As soon as the invader is disarmed, his life should be spared; especially as individual invaders are usually private subjects of the invading sovereign, who have little option about their own acts as private soldiers. It is scarcely needful to add that the Scriptures of both Testaments expressly teach the righteousness of the patriot soldier's profession. The Apostle, in Heb. ii [11], teaches that the valor of the defensive soldier is one of the noble fruits of religious faith, a principle he ascribes to the inworking of God himself. A moment's reflection shows that the rightfulness of capital punishment stands or falls with the lawfulness of defensive war.[31]*

Defensive warfare is simply the use of a national police force to destroy gangsterism on an international scale. The soldier is in exactly the same position as the civil officer at the scene of a bank robbery. Each must put down perversity with force. War is the last expedient to which a nation can turn when its survival is threatened by those bent on world domination and the lust for power. There is no doubt but that war is a terrible thing, almost too awful to speak of without tears in our voices. But the consequence of not matching force with force within the collective ego is infinitely less bearable. We will destroy the very securities within which men can preach and hear the Word of Life; we will betray all of the forms that guarantee our basic freedoms; and, worst of all, we will commit a sin against the very God who has ordained that Christian citizens be subject to those who have been placed in civil office as a praise to the good and a terror to the evil.[32]

This article originally appeared in The Christian Statesman, *Vol. 146, No. 4 (July- August 2003), and is reprinted here by permission of the National Reform Association.*

NOTES

1 To understand the strength of this point we only need to reflect on how it would be impossible (and utterly abhorrent) for God to depict Himself and His ways by calling Himself a liar, a murderer, or a thief. All of these reflect the violation of the righteous law of God and could never be associated with God in any way. Yet, God repeatedly aligns Himself with war and the warrior. This is proof that war can be righteous and just.

2 The depiction of God as a warrior is based on His opposition to the evil of man. He wars against sin and wickedness.

3 Arthur F. Holmes, "Just War Criteria," in Baker's Dictionary of Christian Ethics, ed. Carl F. H. Henry (Grand Rapids: Baker Book House, 1973), p. 359

4 *Ibid.*

5 *Ibid.*

6 Due to man's sinful state and moral weakness it is not likely that any nation will adhere fully to all these standards in any given war. Even the most conscientious nation will fall short to one degree or another. But this fact does not nullify the truth of the just war position any more than the inability of married couples to live up fully to God's standards for home and family nullifies the truth

of the righteousness of the biblical teaching for the home.

7 See Frederick O. Bonkovsky, *International Norms and National Policy* (Grand Rapids: William B. Eerdmans Publishing Co., 1980), pp. 52-57; and Ronald H. Bainton, *Christian Attitudes Towards War and Peace* (New York: Abingdon Press, 1960), pp. 95-99.

8 Johannes Althusius, *Politica*, an abridged translation of *Politics Methodically Set Forth and Illustrated with Sacred and Profane Examples* (1614), ed. and trans. by Frederick S. Carney (Indianapolis: Liberty Fund, 1995), pp. 88-89.

9 *Ibid.*, p. 187.

10 *Ibid.*

11 Gerald R. McDermott, *One Holy and Happy Society: The Public Theology of Jonathan Edwards* (University Park, PA: The Pennsylvania State University Press, 1992), p. 74.

12 *Ibid.*

13 *Ibid.*, p. 133.

14 R. L. Dabney, *The Practical Philosophy* (Harrisonburg, VA: Sprinkle Publications, [1897] 1984), p. 437.

15 Since these laws (except for 20:16-18 which repeats earlier legislation concerning the destruction of the Canaanites) are different than the ones given concerning the war for the conquering of Canaan, and since Israel was not given any more land than Canaan to conquer, the purpose of these laws was to guide Israel when they went to war in self-defense.

16 The decision to go to the defense of a weaker nation when there exists no prior just alliance is problematic and must be approached with great caution and wisdom. Definitely, the decision must be based on a request for help from the weaker nation, on the application of the principles of just war, and on a consideration of any other biblical teaching relevant to the specific request.

17 Edward J. Carnell, *The Case for Biblical Christianity* (Grand Rapids: William B. Eerdmans Publishing Co., 1969), p. 134. Among those who believe that defense is the only just cause for war are some who would reject the view that all preventive wars are necessarily unjust. Mosely writes: "Self-defense against physical aggression, therefore, is putatively the only sufficient reason for just cause. Nonetheless, the principle of self-defense can be extrapolated to anticipate probable acts of aggression, as well as in assisting others against an oppressive government or from another external threat (interventionism).

Therefore, it is commonly held that aggressive war is only permissible if its purpose is to retaliate against a wrong already committed (e.g., to pursue and punish an aggressor), or to pre-empt an anticipated attack" (Alex Mosely, "Just War Theory" in *The Internet Encyclopedia of Philosophy*, 2001, at http://www.utm.edu/research/iep/j/justwar.htm).

18 The legitimate authority to resist would reside in the lesser magistrates that lead the people against the tyranny.

19 Bonkovsky, *International Norms and National Policy*, p. 55.

20 Mosely, "Just War Theory."

21 *Ibid.*

22 Althusius, *Politica*, p. 88.

23 *Ibid.*, p. 188.

24 Rousas John Rushdoony, *The Institutes of Biblical Law* (Phillipsburg, NJ: Presbyterian and Reformed Publishing Co., 1973), pp. 278-279.

25 Mosely, "Just War Theory."

26 Rushdoony, *The Institutes of Biblical Law*, p. 279 (italics in original).

27 Since in Israel the specified age for soldiers was 20 years and up (Num. 1:3; 26:2), it can be deduced that according to biblical law all young men under the age of 20 were to be spared.

28 Rushdoony, *The Institutes of Biblical Law*, p. 280

29 *Ibid.*, p. 121.
30 *Ibid.*, pp. 404-405.
31 Dabney, *The Practical Philosophy*, p. 437.

32 Carnell, *The Case for Biblical Christianity*, p. 136.

Christian Legislative Building Blocks

Statement of Just War Principles

The war is conducted by legitimate civil authority.

The war is waged with right intention.

The war is undertaken only as a last resort.

The war has the establishment of a superior peace as its goal.

The war is waged with proper discrimination between combatants and non-combatants.

The war is based on a just cause.

CASE STUDY 6

BIBLICAL PRINCIPLES OF CIVIL GOVERNMENT

THIS CONCLUDING CASE STUDY PROVIDES A QUICK REFERENCE for Civil Rulers on seven topics which they will very likely have to discuss. It is hoped that these Bible verses will prove helpful in building a Christian response to questions from their constituents, their peers, and the media.

God is in Sovereign Control over the Nations

God, who made the world and everything in it, since He is Lord of heaven and earth, does not dwell in temples made with hands. ACTS 17.24

From these the coastland peoples of the Gentiles were separated into their lands, everyone according to his language, according to their families, into their nations. GENESIS 10.5

The earth is the LORD's, and all its fullness, the world and those who dwell therein. PSALM 24.1

While the word was still in the king's mouth, a voice fell from heaven: "King Nebuchadnezzar, to you it is spoken: the kingdom has departed from you! And they shall drive you from men, and your dwelling shall be with the beasts of the field. They shall make you eat grass like oxen; and seven times shall pass

*over you, until you know that the Most High rules
in the kingdom of men, and gives it to whomever He
chooses."*

*That very hour the word was fulfilled concerning
Nebuchadnezzar; he was driven from men and ate
grass like oxen; his body was wet with the dew of
heaven till his hair had grown like eagles' feathers
and his nails like birds' claws. And at the end of the
time I, Nebuchadnezzar, lifted my eyes to heaven,
and my understanding returned to me; and I blessed
the Most High and praised and honored Him who
lives forever:*

*For His dominion is an everlasting dominion,
And His kingdom is from generation to
generation.
All the inhabitants of the earth are reputed as
nothing;
He does according to His will in the army of
heaven
And among the inhabitants of the earth.
No one can restrain His hand
Or say to Him, "What have You done?"*

*At the same time my reason returned to me, and for
the glory of my kingdom, my honor and splendor
returned to me. My counselors and nobles restored
to me, I was restored to my kingdom, and excellent
majesty was added to me. Now I, Nebuchadnezzar,
praise and extol and honor the King of heaven, all of
whose works are truth, and His ways justice. And
those who walk in pride He is able to put down.*

DANIEL 4.28-34

*And Jesus came and spoke to them, saying, "All
authority has been given to Me in heaven and on
earth.*   MATTHEW 28.18

*Jesus answered, "You could have no power at
all against Me unless it had been given you from
above."*   JOHN 19.11

*Therefore God also has highly exalted Him and given
Him the name which is above every name, that at
the name of Jesus every knee should bow, of those
in heaven, and of those on earth, and of those under
the earth, and that every tongue should confess that
Jesus Christ is Lord, to the glory of God the Father.*
                                        PHILIPPIANS 2.9-11

*[Jesus] Who has gone into heaven and is at the right
hand of God, angels and authorities and powers
having been made subject to Him.*   1 PETER 3.22

God Will Not Give His Glory to Another

You shall have no other gods before Me.
                                        EXODUS 20.3

*I am the LORD, that is My name; and My glory I
will not give to another, nor My praise to carved
images.*   ISAIAH 42.8

*I am the First and I am the Last; besides Me there
is no God. And who can proclaim as I do? Then let
him declare it and set it in order for Me, since I
appointed the ancient people. And the things that are
coming and shall come, let them show these to them.*
                                        ISAIAH 44.6-7

God Selects Civil Rulers
(Good Civil Rulers to Bless Obedient Societies;
Bad Civil Rulers to Curse Disobedient Societies)

Let every soul be subject to the governing author-
ities. For there is no authority except from God, and
the authorities that exist are appointed by God.
ROMANS 13.1

By Me kings reign, and rulers decree justice.
PROVERBS 8.15

The Most High rules in the kingdom of men, gives it
to whomever He will, and sets over it the lowest of
men. DANIEL 4.17

However the LORD God of Israel chose me [David]
above all the house of my father to be king over
Israel forever, for He has chosen Judah to be the
ruler. And of the house of Judah, the house of my
father, and among the sons of my father, He was
pleased with me to make me king over all Israel. And
of all my sons (for the LORD has given me many
sons) He has chosen my son Solomon to sit on the
throne of the kingdom of the LORD over Israel.
1 CHRONICLES 28.4-5

And He changes the times and the seasons; He
removes kings and raises up kings; He gives wisdom
to the wise and knowledge to those who have
understanding. DANIEL 2.21

Then [King Nebuchadnezzar] was driven from the
sons of men, his heart was made like the beasts, and
his dwelling was with the wild donkeys. They fed

272

*him with grass like oxen, and his body was wet with
the dew of heaven, till he knew that the Most High
God rules in the kingdom of men, and appoints
over it whomever He chooses.*　　　DANIEL 5.21

*For [Christ] must reign till He has put all enemies
under His feet.*　　　1 CORINTHIANS 15.25

*And He is before all things, and in Him all things
consist.*　　　COLOSSIANS 1.17

*And the people kept shouting, "The voice of a god
and not of a man!" Then immediately an angel of the
Lord struck [King Herod], because he did not give
glory to God. And he was eaten by worms and died.*
　　　ACTS 12.22-23

*For unto us a Child is born, unto us a Son is given;
and the government will be upon His shoulder. And
His name will be called Wonderful, Counselor,
Mighty God, Everlasting Father, Prince of Peace. Of
the increase of His government and peace there will
be no end, upon the throne of David and over His
kingdom, to order it and establish it with judgment
and justice from that time forward, even forever. The
zeal of the Lord of hosts will perform this.*
　　　ISAIAH 9.6-7

*They set up kings, but not by Me; they made princes,
but I did not acknowledge them.*　　　HOSEA 8.4

*The king's heart is in the hand of the LORD, like the
rivers of water; He turns it wherever He wishes.*
　　　PROVERBS 21.1

It's OK to be a Civil Ruler

And Pharaoh said to his servants, "Can we find such a one as this, a man in whom is the Spirit of God?" Then Pharaoh said to Joseph, "Inasmuch as God has shown you all this, there is no one as discerning and wise as you. You shall be over my house, and all my people shall be ruled according to your word; only in regard to the throne will I be greater than you." And Pharaoh said to Joseph, "See, I have set you over all the land of Egypt."

Then Pharaoh took his signet ring off his hand and put it on Joseph's hand; and he clothed him in garments of fine linen and put a gold chain around his neck. And he had him ride in the second chariot which he had; and they cried out before him, "Bow the knee!" So he set him over all the land of Egypt. Pharaoh also said to Joseph, "I am Pharaoh, and without your consent no man may lift his hand or foot in all the land of Egypt." And Pharaoh called Joseph's name Zaphnath-Paaneah. And he gave him as a wife Asenath, the daughter of Poti-Pherah priest of On. So Joseph went out over all the land of Egypt. Genesis 41.38-45 And King Ahasuerus imposed tribute on the land and on the islands of the sea. Now all the acts of his power and his might, and the account of the greatness of Mordecai, to which the king advanced him, are they not written in the book of the chronicles of the kings of Media and Persia? For Mordecai the Jew was second to King Ahasuerus, and was great among the Jews and well received by the multitude of his brethren, seeking the good of his people and speaking peace to all his countrymen. ESTHER 10.1-3

274

*Then the king promoted Daniel and gave him many
great gifts; and he made him ruler over the whole
province of Babylon, and chief administrator over
all the wise men of Babylon. Also Daniel petitioned
the king, and he set Shadrach, Meshach, and Abed-
Nego over the affairs of the province of Babylon; but
Daniel sat in the gate of the king.* DANIEL 2.48-49

Civil Rulers Must Rule According to God's Word

*Why do the nations rage, and the people plot a vain
thing? The kings of the earth set themselves, and the
rulers take counsel together, against the LORD and
against His Anointed, saying, "Let us break Their
bonds in pieces and cast away their cords from us."*

*He who sits in the heavens shall laugh; the Lord
shall hold them in derision. Then He shall speak to
them in His wrath, and distress them in His deep
displeasure: "Yet I have set My King on My holy hill
of Zion."*

*"I will declare the decree: the LORD has said to
Me, 'You are My Son, today I have begotten You.
Ask of Me, and I will give You the nations for
Your inheritance, and the ends of the earth for Your
possession. You shall break them with a rod of iron;
You shall dash them to pieces like a potter's
vessel.'"*

*Now therefore, be wise, O kings; be instructed,
you judges of the earth. Serve the LORD with fear.
And rejoice with trembling. Kiss the Son, lest He be
angry, and you perish in the way, when His wrath
is kindled but a little. Blessed are all those who put
their trust in Him* PSALM 2

The wicked shall be turned into hell, and all the nations that forget God.   PSALM 9.17

But God is the Judge: He puts down one, and exalts another.   PSALM 75.7

He has put down the mighty from their thrones, and exalted the lowly.   LUKE 1.52

But Peter and the other apostles answered and said: "We ought to obey God rather than men.   ACTS 5.29

Shadrach, Meshach, and Abed-Nego answered and said to the king, "O Nebuchadnezzar, we have no need to answer you in this matter. If that is the case, our God whom we serve is able to deliver us from the burning fiery furnace, and He will deliver us from your hand, O king. But if not, let it be known to you, O king, that we do not serve your gods, nor will we worship the gold image which you have set up."   DANIEL 3.16-18

And God spoke all these words, saying: "I am the LORD your God, who brought you out of the land of Egypt, out of the house of bondage. "You shall have no other gods before Me.
"You shall not make for yourself a carved image— any likeness of anything that is in heaven above, or that is in the earth beneath, or that is in the water under the earth; you shall not bow down to them nor serve them. For I, the LORD your God, am a jealous God, visiting the iniquity of the fathers upon the children to the third and fourth generations of those who hate Me, but showing mercy to thousands, to those who love Me and keep My commandments.

276

"You shall not take the name of the LORD your God in vain, for the LORD will not hold him guiltless who takes His name in vain. EXODUS 20.1-7

Because of all the evil of the children of Israel and the children of Judah, which they have done to provoke Me to anger—they, their kings, their princes, their priests, their prophets, the men of Judah, and the inhabitants of Jerusalem. And they have turned to Me the back, and not the face; though I taught them, rising up early and teaching them, yet they have not listened to receive instruction. But they set their abominations in the house which is called by My name, to defile it. And they built the high places of Baal which are in the Valley of the Son of Hinnom, to cause their sons and their daughters to pass through the fire to Molech, which I did not command them, nor did it come into My mind that they should do this abomination, to cause Judah to sin. JEREMIAH 32.32-35

For the terrible one is brought to nothing, the scornful one is consumed, and all who watch for iniquity are cut off—Who make a man an offender by a word, and lay a snare for him who reproves in the gate, and turn aside the just by empty words. ISAIAH 29.20-21

The instant I speak concerning a nation and concerning a kingdom, to pluck up, to pull down, and to destroy it, if that nation against whom I have spoken turns from its evil, I will relent of the disaster that I thought to bring upon it. And the instant I speak concerning a nation and concerning a kingdom, to build and to plant it, if it does evil in

*My sight so that it does not obey My voice, then I
will relent concerning the good with which I said I
would benefit it.* JEREMIAH 18.7-10

*For do I now persuade men, or God? Or do I seek to
please men? For if I still pleased men, I would not be
a bondservant of Christ.* GALATIANS 1.10

*Also it shall be, when [a civil ruler] sits on the throne
of his kingdom, that he shall write for himself a copy
of this law in a book, from the one before the priests,
the Levites. And it shall be with him, and he shall
read it all the days of his life, that he may learn to
fear the LORD his God and be careful to observe
all the words of this law and these statutes, that his
heart may not be lifted above his brethren, that he
may not turn aside from the commandment to the
right hand or to the left, and that he may prolong his
days in his kingdom, he and his children in the midst
of Israel.* DEUTERONOMY 17.18-20

*And in vain they worship Me, [or govern] teaching
as doctrines the commandments of men. For laying
aside the commandment of God, you hold the
tradition of men.* MARK 7.7-8

PROVIDE JUSTICE

*For the word of the LORD is right, and all His work
is done in truth. He loves righteousness and justice;
the earth is full of the goodness of the LORD.*
PSALM 33.4-5

*But if our unrighteousness demonstrates the right-
eousness of God, what shall we say? Is God unjust
who inflicts wrath? (I speak as a man.)* ROMANS 3.5

Woe to him who builds his house by unrighteousness and his chambers by injustice, who uses his neighbor's service without wages and gives him nothing for his work.   JEREMIAH 22.13

If there is a dispute between men, and they come to court, that the judges may judge them, and they justify the righteous and condemn the wicked.
                                                DEUTERONOMY 25.1

You shall do no injustice in judgment. You shall not be partial to the poor, nor honor the person of the mighty. In righteousness you shall judge your neighbor.   LEVITICUS 19.15

Defend the poor and fatherless; do justice to the afflicted and needy. Deliver the poor and needy; free them from the hand of the wicked.   PSALM 82.3-4

Then I commanded your judges at that time, saying, "Hear the cases between your brethren, and judge righteously between a man and his brother or the stranger who is with him. You shall not show partiality in judgment; you shall hear the small as well as the great; you shall not be afraid in any man's presence, for the judgment is God's. The case that is too hard for you, bring to me, and I will hear it."
                                                DEUTERONOMY 1.16-17

Learn to do good; seek justice, rebuke the oppressor; defend the fatherless, plead for the widow.
                                                ISAIAH 1.17

For there is no partiality with God.   ROMANS 2.11

DEFENSE

*If the thief is found breaking in, and he is struck so
that he dies, there shall be no guilt for his bloodshed.
If the sun has risen on him, there shall be guilt for his
bloodshed. He should make full restitution; if he has
nothing, then he shall be sold for his theft. If the theft
is certainly found alive in his hand, whether it is an
ox or donkey or sheep, he shall restore double.*

EXODUS 22.2-4

*When you go out to battle against your enemies, and
see horses and chariots and people more numerous
than you, do not be afraid of them; for the LORD
your God is with you, who brought you up from
the land of Egypt. So it shall be, when you are on
the verge of battle, that the priest shall approach
and speak to the people. And he shall say to them,
"Hear, O Israel: Today you are on the verge of battle
with your enemies. Do not let your heart faint, do
not be afraid, and do not tremble or be terrified
because of them; for the LORD your God is He
who goes with you, to fight for you against your
enemies, to save you." Then the officers shall speak
to the people, saying: "What man is there who has
built a new house and has not dedicated it? Let him
go and return to his house, lest he die in the battle
and another man dedicate it. Also what man is there
who has planted a vineyard and has not eaten of it?
Let him go and return to his house, lest he die in
the battle and another man eat of it. And what man
is there who is betrothed to a woman and has not
married her? Let him go and return to his house, lest
he die in the battle and another man marry her."*

The officers shall speak further to the people, and say, "What man is there who is fearful and fainthearted? Let him go and return to his house, lest the heart of his brethren faint like his heart." And so it shall be, when the officers have finished speaking to the people, that they shall make captains of the armies to lead the people.

When you go near a city to fight against it, then proclaim an offer of peace to it. And it shall be that if they accept your offer of peace, and open to you, then all the people who are found in it shall be placed under tribute to you, and serve you. Now if the city will not make peace with you, but war against you, then you shall besiege it. And when the LORD your God delivers it into your hands, you shall strike every male in it with the edge of the sword. But the women, the little ones, the livestock, and all that is in the city, all its spoil, you shall plunder for yourself; and you shall eat the enemies' plunder which the LORD your God gives you. Thus you shall do to all the cities which are very far from you, which are not of the cities of these nations.

But of the cities of these peoples which the LORD your God gives you as an inheritance, you shall let nothing that breathes remain alive, but you shall utterly destroy them: the Hittite and the Amorite and the Canaanite and the Perizzite and the Hivite and the Jebusite, just as the LORD your God has commanded you, lest they teach you to do according to all their abominations which they have done for their gods, and you sin against the LORD your God. When you besiege a city for a long time, while making war against it to take it, you shall not destroy its trees by wielding an ax against them; if you can eat of them, do not cut them down to use *in the siege, for the tree of the field is man's food. Only the trees which you know are not trees for food you may destroy and cut down, to build siegeworks against the city that makes war with you, until it is subdued.* DEUTERONOMY 20.1-20

Civil Ruler's Duty toward Citizens...Personal Liberty

For rulers are not a terror to good works, but to evil. Do you want to be unafraid of the authority? Do what is good, and you will have praise from the same. For he is God's minister to you for good. But if you do evil, be afraid; for he does not bear the sword in vain; for he is God's minister, an avenger to execute wrath on him who practices evil. ROMANS 13.3-4

You shall not murder. EXODUS 20.13

Whoever sheds man's blood, by man his blood shall be shed; for in the image of God He made man. GENESIS 9.6

He who strikes a man so that he dies shall surely be put to death. However, if he did not lie in wait, but God delivered him into his hand, then I will appoint for you a place where he may flee. "But if a man acts with premeditation against his neighbor, to kill him by treachery, you shall take him from My altar, that he may die. EXODUS 21.12-14

Moreover the prince shall not take any of the people's inheritance by evicting them from their property; he shall provide an inheritance for his sons

from his own property, so that none of My people
may be scattered from his property.   EZEKIEL 46.18

So you shall dwell with us, and the land shall be
before you. Dwell and trade in it, and acquire
possessions for yourselves in it.   GENESIS 34.10

For the Scripture says, "You shall not muzzle an ox
while it treads out the grain," and, "The laborer is
worthy of his wages."   1 TIMOTHY 5.18

Citizens Duty toward Civil Rulers...Honor

PRAY

Therefore I exhort first of all that supplications,
prayers, intercessions, and giving of thanks be made
for all men, for kings and all who are in authority,
that we may lead a quiet and peaceable life in all
godliness and reverence.   1 TIMOTHY 2.1-2

And seek the peace of the city where I have caused
you to be carried away captive, and pray to the
LORD for it; for in its peace you will have peace.
                                    JEREMIAH 29.7

SPEAK NO EVIL

You shall not revile God, nor curse a ruler of your
people.   EXODUS 22.28

Honor all people. Love the brotherhood. Fear God.
Honor the king.   PETER 2.17

COOPERATE WITH THEM

*Remind them to be subject to rulers and authorities,
to obey, to be ready for every good work, to speak
evil of no one, to be peaceable, gentle, showing all
humility to all men.* TITUS 3.1-2

*Therefore submit yourselves to every ordinance
of man for the Lord's sake, whether to the king as
supreme, or to governors, as to those who are sent by
him for the punishment of evildoers and for the
praise of those who do good. For this is the will of
God, that by doing good you may put to silence the
ignorance of foolish men—as free, yet not using
liberty as a cloak for vice, but as bondservants
of God.* 1 PETER 2.13-16

*For because of this you also pay taxes, for they are
God's ministers attending continually to this very
thing. Render therefore to all their due: taxes to
whom taxes are due, customs to whom customs, fear
to whom fear, honor to whom honor.*
ROMANS 13.6-7

*"Render therefore to Caesar the things that are
Caesar's, and to God the things that are God's."*
MATTHEW 22.21

PROVIDE GODLY COUNSEL & A GODLY LIFESTYLE

*You are the salt of the earth; but if the salt loses its
flavor, how shall it be seasoned? It is then good for
nothing but to be thrown out and trampled
underfoot by men. You are the light of the world.
A city that is set on a hill cannot be hidden. Nor do*

*they light a lamp and put it under a basket, but
on a lampstand, and it gives light to all who are in
the house. Let your light so shine before men, that
they may see your good works and glorify your
Father in heaven.* MATTHEW 5.13-16

Christian Legislative Building Blocks

God is in Sovereign Control over the Nations

God Will Not Give His Glory to Another

God selects the Civil Rulers (Good Civil Rulers to Bless Obedient Societies; Bad Civil Rulers to Curse Disobedient Societies)

It's OK to be a Civil Ruler

Civil Rulers Must Rule According to God's Word

Civil Rulers' Duty Toward Citizens ...Personal Liberty

Citizens Duty Toward Civil Rulers ...Honor

APPENDIX

THE CHRISTIAN VOTE

And the Winner is ...

The primary purpose of most people when they go to vote is either to get their candidate elected, or to keep another candidate from getting elected. So, they vote either "for" or "against" candidates. Since only one in four Christians votes, perhaps their primary purpose is to "grin and bear" whatever the results happen to be.

Do three out of four Christians sit out elections because they are apathetic and are not concerned about the downward spiral of our culture? I don't think so. In fact, I believe the opposite is true: they are smart enough to realize that there is no substantive difference between most candidates. Therefore they conclude it doesn't make any difference who wins.

Such a conclusion, however, is unbiblical to its core. Why would Christians set out to discredit and dishonor their God? The answer could well be that they don't do it intentionally, but rather rationally and for pragmatic reasons. Our culture is disintegrating and Christians are not voting because they are not taking the time to step back from the hustle and bustle of daily activities to filter their decision-making through the Biblical principles they profess to believe. Add to this, pastors who are more afraid of the IRS than of God, and never preach or teach their congregations how to carry out their civil duties in a Biblical manner; the result is a religion of which only our non-Christian opponents can be proud. Today's typical church focuses on Bible study (for apparently nothing more than to accumulate spiritual warm fuzzies to get someone through difficult times), prayer (with seldom a focus on "living out" their prayer requests), foreign missions (its easier telling someone else how to live, than doing so ourselves) and the end times. (While we spend time speculating on what *may happen*, non-Christians are taking over what *is happening* in our culture).

What Scripture commands Christians and our pastors and Bible teachers to focus on is how we can demonstrate God's will through our daily actions and decisions. We are not called to bring about specific results. That's what God does. He's in the results business; we're in the obedience business. While it is true that He graciously and mercifully works through us to "Christianize" the earth, a brief look through Scripture will show that He often does so in some very un-rational and un-pragmatic ways (e.g., the parting of the Jordan River, raining down food from the skies, etc.).

We must remember that we are in our present fallen condition because Eve decided to disregard God's advice. In approaching the next election with the mindset of "determining the winners" we are merely imitating Eve's attitude of not depending upon God's wisdom and counsel.

Our role as Christians is simple: it's to vote for the best Biblically qualified candidate, and then watch God go to work. If there are no Biblically qualified candidates, our task is to approach our pastor and church officers and encourage them to begin a training program to raise up such candidates. It must be realized that the Democrats and Republicans don't offer candidates who can best be described as "dumb" and "dumber" for no reason! They want to discourage intelligent voters to the point that they will sit out the elections. They could care less if only 25 percent of the population votes. They are only concerned about the power and influence that comes from winning. It is our duty to raise up Christian candidates who can then use their power to influence a return of our culture to the Biblical principles upon which it was founded.

Of RINOs, DINOs and CINOs

Many people do not vote along straight party lines. Instead they vote along ideological lines, which usually includes candidates from both major parties. Such voters usually think that either liberals or conservatives hold the answer to our culture's problems.

However, from a Christian point of view, society's problems have been brought about because of liberals and conservatives. The reason for this is that only God's Word is true, which means that any candidate who does not conform his decisions to Biblical principles is making a faulty (untrue) decision. When viewed from this perspective there emerge three types of candidates:

RINOs   Republicans In Name Only (otherwise
            known as liberal Republicans)
DINOs   Democrats In Name Only (otherwise known
            as conservative Democrats)
CINOs   Christians In Name Only (from either party)

The difference between CINOs and the RINOs & DINOs is one of intention. RINOs & DINOs know full well what they're doing. They have determined that they are in a district where if they are going to get elected they have to belong to a particular party. Even though that party doesn't reflect their agenda, they run under its name, get elected, then vote with the other party's agenda. Everything is carried out by design and intention.

CINOs, on the other hand, don't set out to intentionally disobey God. They make it a priority to obey Him inside their homes and churches, and in some cases even teach Sunday

School. Unfortunately, they fail to give a second thought about applying His principles to their everyday legislative decisions. Because of their overall moral character they honor God when it comes to issues relating to the Second Table of the Law (honor those in authority, don't kill, steal, cheat, covet, etc.). However, they dishonor God when they give the reasons for voting and legislating the way they do. For example, instead of admitting that the reason they voted for a Marriage amendment is that "God says so," they desert (apostatize) from their faith by abandoning the First Table of the Law (commandments 1-4) and using the euphemism, "It's a traditional value for marriage to be between one man and one woman."

While these Legislators profess to be Christians, they legislate as Christians In Name Only, with the consequence that their votes often conform to unbiblical principles –possibly without their realizing it. If their congregation and their church officers were obedient to Jesus' teaching in Matthew 18, these CINOs would be counseled about their inconsistent behavior so they could correct it. But sadly, most pastors are more concerned about church growth than about discipling their members. If America's original pastors had had the attitude of today's pastors, America would still be an English colony. King George would not have had to refer to "that Presbyterian revolt," because such self-centered wimpy Pastors would have sheepishly taught that there was a "separation of God and the state."

There is no reason for America Christians to continue to live as though we served a defeated God, or to act as though we were second-class citizens. Our Lord, Savior and King has been "given the nations for His inheritance, and the ends of the earth for His possession." (Psalm 2:8) He has further appointed us to bring about His will "on earth as it is in heaven" (Matthew 6.10). May we be about the business of serving our sovereign God by campaigning and voting for Christians, then not being hesitant to counsel them to legislate like "Cs," (Christians) not CINOs.

Taxes, Taxes and More Taxes

Why is it that no matter what the election, or who is running, the recurring theme is, "With a little more taxes we can solve your problems"? The answer is that we continue to elect politicians instead of statesmen. The civil government has no revenue except what we give to it through our taxes. Tax revenues give politicians the opportunity to "buy" votes by funneling a portion of that money back into their districts. Politicians don't have principles, they only have offices they are elected to, and they will do practically anything to stay in that office. This explains why they are self-centered in their policy decisions.

Statesmen, on the other hand, are others-centered in their policy decisions, and they act on principles. They're honest; they do what they say they will do. They prefer to under-promise and over-perform, which is exactly opposite of the behavior of politicians.

It will be only when we begin to elect statesmen that we will stop hearing the constant demand for more taxes. Statesmen recognize the distinction between two forms of civil government: a representative republic and a pure democracy. The pledge of allegiance to the flag includes the phrase, "and to the republic for which it stands"; however for most of the last one hundred years America has been deliberately walking away from our republic roots and toward a pure democracy. The consequences of this have been ominous as we have gone from working 20 days per year to pay off our taxes (in 1900) to 120 days (today). In addition to losing a lot of money to the civil government (which has done an excellent job of wasting much of it), with increased taxation we have experienced the accompanying loss of personal liberties. Of course this is just what the State wants: a dependent citizenry that pays more and more for more and more services--services we could and should be providing ourselves. Personal liberty and income are not the only things at risk. History shows that our very country is on slippery ice. An 18th century Scottish history professor, Alexander Tyler, is reported to have said this about the fall of the Athenian Republic, which happened more than 2,000 years ago:

> A democracy cannot exist as a permanent form of government. It can only exist until the voters discover that they can vote themselves largesse [generous gifts] from the public treasury. From that moment on, the majority always votes for the candidates promising the most benefits from the public treasury, with the result that a democracy always collapses over loose fiscal policy, [which is] always followed by a dictatorship.
>
> The average age of the world's greatest civilizations has been two hundred years. These nations have progressed through this sequence. From bondage to spiritual faith; from spiritual faith to great courage; from courage to liberty; from liberty to abundance, from abundance to complacency; from complacency to apathy, from apathy to dependence, from dependence back into bondage.

The choice during each election is up to us. Do we want to continue to support and vote for candidates who cater to our self-centered desires to "get something for nothing," mainly by robbing another district's tax revenues for the benefit of our community? Or will we, by electing statesmen, recapture the vision of our country's founders, who gave us the best and most affluent country in the history of the world? Will we have a pure democracy where we are at the ever-changing whims of the tyranny of the 51 percent, or a representative republic where statesmen legislate on the basis of what's best for their constituents, instead of lining their pockets?

Praise God we live in a country where we can freely campaign and vote for statesmen. May we do so before we lose that privilege by becoming dependent upon self-centered politicians.

Preparing to Live With a Down-Sized Central Government

So far we have noted that the primary purpose of Christians at the polls is to vote for the most Biblically qualified candidate and let God handle the results. Our attitude in approaching the voting booth is not different from what it should be when we do anything else ... bring glory and honor to the One who graciously and mercifully called us into His family. We have also discussed the necessity of electing not just Christians, but Christians who legislate according to Biblical principles. As we have all observed, CINOs (Christians In Name Only) do not vote differently from conservative non-Christians, and are therefore part of society's problem, not its solution. Then we observed that the reason we continue to hear the cry for "just a little more taxes" is because that is how politicians think, and unless and until we begin electing statesmen, our pocketbooks and our personal liberty will continue to be raided by the self-serving non-Christian State.

In this concluding section we ask this question: What would we do if the State suddenly said, "We've had enough of your complaints. Beginning with next year's fiscal budget we are going to eliminate all social services and stop funding education and prisons (which in my home state, Alabama, represents 84 percent of the budget). Let's see if you can do any better than we can with your 84 percent tax reduction!"

Our first reaction might well be something like, "Hot

diggity dog!" But after that initial euphoria, what would be our plan to "take over" these social services? Scripture is not silent about the responsibility of the God-ordained self-governing spheres of the individual, family and church to provide these services, so we should be able to handle them, right? Pardon my sounding political, but the answer is, "Right, according to Scripture, but not-so-fast in terms of realistic expectations." In order for civilization to work according to God's instructions, we have to follow His instructions, and that includes tithing. In short, the work of the Kingdom must be financed. It should be easy to conclude that with our 84 percent tax reduction we could all tithe (10 percent of our net income) and still have plenty of money left over. That's true, and that's God's point about being self-governing people.

What is also true, however, is that our pastors and church officers must begin to instruct us specifically in how to apply Biblical principles to all areas of our lives. One of the ramifications of this is that as we assume control of the education of our youth, we must teach a specific Biblical curriculum. Simply using the existing Godless textbooks and adding a prayer or two during the day will not result in producing a generation that's ready to "enlarge the area of [their] tent." (Isaiah 54.2)

Is it likely that the State will call our bluff by turning social services back to citizens? Probably no more likely than being flooded out when it had never rained, or having one of the fiercest armies become confused and destroy themselves before attacking us. But this doesn't mean that we shouldn't be preparing ourselves to take back services the civil government has no Biblical mandate to provide.

There are several reasons why today's church fails to explicitly instruct its members in how to live for God. Some churches may do so because of a misunderstanding, others intentionally; but either way is unacceptable in God's eyes.

The first question we need to ask our pastor and church officers is, "Whose will are you obeying, God's or Caesar's? Since 1952, churches have had the option (!) of incorporating. The First Amendment to the US Constitution guarantees tax-exempt status (and freedom to preach all of God's Word as it applies to all of our culture). The unbiblical invention of incorporation has relegated the church to the status of a moralistic social club of the State, having as its top priority serving Caesar's every political whim.

As Christians, we are the only people on the face of the earth that know how to live correctly. This is not an arrogant statement, since we didn't invent the rules, but were enabled to understand God's rules via the grace of the Holy Spirit. There is therefore no more damaging blow that can be used against us by non-Christians than to convince us that our wisdom should be privatized and kept inside our churches and homes. (This is exactly what they have accomplished through the IRS incorporation.) The battle lines for our culture war could not be clearer:

God says Jesus Rules Over *All Things*

> And God the Father put all things under Jesus' feet
> and gave Him to be head over all things to the
> church...that in all things He may have the
> preeminence.   EPHESIANS 1.22; COLOSSIANS 1.18

Caesar says Jesus Rules Only Over Your Heart

> Everything for the State; nothing outside the State;
> nothing against the State. (Mussolini) The State
> embraces everything, and nothing has value outside
> the State. The State creates the right. (Franklin
> Delano Roosevelt)

Answers to the following three questions will help you determine whether your church is serving God in all things, or in only the ways Caesar allows:

• **QUESTION 1**	May the church discuss the positions of candidates on various cultural issues, making recommendations about which candidates best reflect Biblical principles?
CAESAR'S COMMAND	The church must limit its comments to describing the positions of candidates on issues and is prohibited from making voting recommendations.
GOD'S COMMAND	Who will rise up for Me against the wicked? Who will take a stand for Me against evildoers? PSALM 94.16
	Who knows whether you have come to the kingdom for such a time as this? ESTHER 4.14
• **QUESTION 2**	May the church "put its money where its mouth is" and contribute to candidate campaigns and/or cover the expenses of a candidate's appearance at the church?
CAESAR'S COMMAND	The church is not authorized to help any candidate in any financial manner.

GOD'S COMMAND   The laborer is worthy of his wages.
LUKE 10.7

Woe to him...who uses his neighbor's service without wages and gives him nothing for his work.   JEREMIAH 22.13

• QUESTION 3   May the church distribute written statements (including advertisements and/or editorials in church bulletins and newsletters) advocating the election or defeat of candidates?

CAESAR'S COMMAND   The church is muzzled by the State from endorsing one candidate over another in any printed format.

GOD'S COMMAND   They have not wholly followed Me, except Caleb...and Joshua.
NUMBERS 32.11,12

Take heed that the light that is in you is not darkness.   LUKE 11.35

Does Caesar's Command Allow Your Church to Obey God?

You are the salt of the earth; but if the salt loses its flavor, how shall it be seasoned? It is then good for nothing but to be thrown out and trampled under foot by men.   MATTHEW 5.13-16

I would hope that by now you are you disturbed and ashamed that your church is "limited," "prohibited," "not

297

authorized," and "muzzled" from teaching God's principles on our various cultural issues. The Bible is on our side and God is in our corner on these issues. The question is, "Will we continue to trust in our wisdom and ability, or depend upon His perfect wisdom and divinely revealed instructions for living?"

BIBLIOGRAPHY

Bastiat, Frederic
  The Law
  Foundation for
  Economic Education

Calvin, John
  Daniel
  Banner of Truth Trust

Clausewitz, Karl Von, War
  Politics and Power
  Regnery

DeMar, Gary
  God and Government, Vol. III
  American Vision Press

Einwechter, William
  A Conquering Faith
  Chalcedon Foundation

Federer, William J.
  America's God and Country:
  Encyclopedia of Quotations
  Amerisearch

Gillespie, George
  Aaron's Rod Blossoming
  Sprinkle Publishing

Hanson, Buddy
  This Is Not A Drill: Real Lessons
  for Real People from the Real
  God, Through His prophets,
  On How to Live and Govern
  ourselves Really!
  Hanson Group

Hanson, Buddy
  God's Ten Words: Practical
  Applications from the Ten
  Commandments
  Hanson Group

Hanson, Buddy
  Bottom Line Theology: A Bible
  Study Feast for Those Who only
  Have Time for a Sandwich
  Hanson Group

Hanson, Buddy
  EXIT Strategy: How To
  Exponentially Increase Your
  Service To God
  Hanson Group

Hanson, Buddy
  What's Scripture Got To Do
  With It?
  Hanson Group

Hanson, Buddy
It's Time to Un-Quo the Status
Hanson Group

Hanson, Buddy
Choose This Day: God's Instructions on How to Select Leaders
Hanson Group

Hanson, Buddy
The Christian Civil Ruler's Handbook
Hanson Group

Henry, Matthew
Matthew Henry's Commentary: Isaiah to Malachi, Vol. IV
MacDonald Publishing

Machiavelli, Niccolo
The Prince
Norton Critical Edition

Machiavelli, Niccolo
The Prince
Signet Classics

Miller, Sen. Zell
A National Party No More: The Conscious of a Conservative Democrat
Stroud and Hall

Poole, Matthew
Matthew Poole's Commentary, Vol. II, Psalm – Malachi
MacDonald Publishing

Rushdoony, R.J.
Institutes of Biblical Law
P & R Publishing

Shakespeare, William
"The Taming of the Shrew"

Stein, Leo
Hitler Came For Me
Pelican

Thornton, John Wingate
The Pulpit of the American Revolution 1860
Burt Franklin

Warren, Robert Penn
All The King's Men
Harvest Books

Wines, Rev. E.C.
The Roots of the American Republic Study Guide
by Rev. Paul R. McDade
The Plymouth Rock Foundation

Young, E. J.
Genesis Three
Hagefen Publishing

God's Ten Words
PRACTICAL APPLICATIONS FROM
THE TEN COMMANDMENTS

"WHY DOES HUMANITY NEED GOD'S LAW?" FIRST AND FOREMOST IT
serves as a mirror to show us as we really are (fallen and filthy
in God's sight), not as we may imagine we are (not quite perfect,
but not as bad as others). This helps us to recognize our need of
repenting and placing our faith in Christ's words and work.

The principles contained in the Ten Commandments provide
a prescription for not only stopping our culture's decline, but
of restoring it to God's will. Each Commandment includes a
section on what civilization was like before the influence of that
Commandment, plus a review and practical application. Comments
from many of the most respected biblical scholars are included.

Choose This Day
GOD'S INSTRUCTIONS ON HOW TO SELECT LEADERS

AMERICA NEEDS LEADERS AND CHOOSE THIS DAY GIVES GOD'S FORMULA
for selecting them. The civil government policy-making table, like
everything else, belongs to God, not man. It should be noted that
we're not umpires who "calls'em as we sees'em" when it comes to
making our daily decisions, but rather we're players who follow
what our coach (God, through His Word) tells us to do. God's duty
is to "call the shots," our duty is to obediently follow His game
plan. So for Christians to have a goal of being an equal partner
in setting society's policies is to greatly demean God. It is exactly
because of our refusal to be "salt and light" to our communities
that we have lost not only our seat at culture's table, but the entire
table, and getting it back won't be easy. Still, it can be done and as
soon as we have secured one seat, we need to begin working on a
second seat, and then a third, until we have recaptured them all.

THE CHRISTIAN CIVIL RULER'S HANDBOOK

As important as it is to elect Christian civil rulers (legislators and judges), this is only the first step. Unless the Christians we elect to office have a developed Christian worldview, they will govern no differently than a non-Christian conservative. The Handbook provides a quick read for busy legislators on how to rule according to God's will, instead of according to their own imagination of how God might want them to govern.

Two appendices extend the practical applications discussed in the Handbook. The first one answers common objections regarding religion and politics, and the second one is a multiple choice test on the U.S. Constitution (with an answer key) that Home Schoolers like to use. Get a copy for your Civil Rulers!

BOTTOM LINE THEOLOGY
A BIBLE STUDY FEAST FOR THOSE
WHO ONLY HAVE TIME FOR A SANDWICH

If Bible study could be thought of as a meal there would be several very wholesome full meals available, complete with veggies, bread and beverage. However, when these lengthy books are boiled down to the bottom line you will find that the biblical principles that they teach and those that BLT teaches are the same, because there is only one Bible! The advantage that BLT offers is that you won't use up most of your time in searching for the biblical principles in which you are interested. So, if your current schedule necessitates that you grab a fast spiritual sandwich, then BLT is the Bible study for you. Each of the thirteen sections gets directly to the heart of the Biblical principles discussed.

DAILY BLT
A DAILY ARSENAL OF GODLY AMMUNITION
TO HELP YOU TAKE GROUND FOR GOD'S KINGDOM

DAILY BLT IS UNIQUE IN THAT IT GIVES PRACTICAL TOOLS TO USE according to the way that best fits your personality and schedule. Each Day has three 2-page sections, and depending upon your schedule you can use one (15-minutes), two (30 minutes), or all three (45-minutes) of these 2-page sections. Since Sunday is a Sabbath Day Rest in the Lord, fourteen additional pages are provided.

MAKING YOUR DAILY READS
VOL. I, II & III
HOW TO READ THE DEFENSE OF YOUR OPPONENTS'
OBJECTIONS TO CHRISTIANITY AND MAKE THE RIGHT CALL TO
UPHOLD THE FAITH

MAKING YOUR DAILY READS PROVIDES 52 "READS," FOR THE various objections the reader is likely to encounter on a daily basis. The READS are categorized into five "audibles:"

R One religion is as good as another
E God doesn't know everything, besides eternity is where Jesus wins
A Apologetics; defending the faith against common objections
D God is dead when it comes to "real life" issues.
S The State is exempt from God's authority.

Each audible begins with a Scouting Report that sets the theme for the section. Following that is one READ for each week with a page for the reader to re-write the READ in their own words, and spend the entire week practicing it. As a bonus, a short course in apologetics is included in an appendix.

THY WILL BE DONE ON EARTH
HEAVENLY INSIGHTS FOR DOWN-TO-EARTH LIVING FROM THE PROPHET ISAIAH

ISAIAH'S "FIFTH GOSPEL" IS THE MOST QUOTED OLD TESTAMENT BOOK in the New Testament. Isaiah's message offers valuable insights on how to best deal with the situations and circumstances in which we find ourselves. Pastor and author Martyn Lloyd-Jones writes, "[Isaiah] is relevant because it is a book that deals with men and women in their relationships to God ... this is not merely a contemporary message, it is the message of God for the condition of humanity at all times and in all places."

FLOWERS
FOR THE
CHRISTIAN WORLDVIEW GARDEN

NOT QUITE SURE WHAT A CHRISTIAN WORLDVIEW IS? IF SO, YOU'RE NOT alone. Only one in twenty Christian adults knows the answer. The seven chapters of FLOWERS discuss the various aspects of a developed Christian worldview. All Christians have one or more of these aspects included in their Worldview Garden, but God desires that we have all seven, because the more "flowers" we have, the less "weeds" we will have. The elements of a developed Christian worldview are:

From Him, through Him and to Him are all things. ROMANS 11.36
Lean not on your own understanding. PROVERBS 3.5
Obedience brings blessings. LEVITICUS 26; DEUTERONOMY 28
Word of God is true. PSALM 119.160
Exhibit humility. Matthew 23.12
Repent. EZEKIEL 14.6
Saved to succeed, not secede. PSALM 2.8

WHAT'S SCRIPTURE GOT TO DO WITH IT?
CONNECTING YOUR SPIRITUAL DOTS FOR A MORE MEANINGFUL LIFE

EVERY CHRISTIAN COULD LIST CORE BIBLICAL TRUTHS IN WHICH HE unquestionably believes. Unfortunately, few of us incorporate these beliefs into our lifestyle. How is it with you? Does your lifestyle consistently demonstrate the "answers" you say that the Bible has to life's questions? Are you being salt and light to those with whom you come into contact, or has your salt lost its savor, and is good for nothing else but to be trampled under foot?

Many of us have a lot of "Spiritual Dots" (core Christian beliefs) floating around inside our mind that for one reason or another we have not connected to our everyday lifestyle. What's Scripture Got To Do With It? will raise your awareness of those particular Spiritual Dots and stresses the urgency to live in accordance with them.

ITS TIME TO UN-QUO THE STATUS
HOW TO NORMALIZE THE PRESENT ABNORMAL CULTURE OF A NON-CHRISTIAN, UPSIDE-DOWN WORLD AND TURN IT RIGHTSIDE UP WITH CHRISTIAN PRINCIPLES

WHAT DOES BEING A CHRISTIAN MEAN? SHOULD OUR LIFESTYLE REALLY be different than that of a non-Christian? And what about our culture: Is "tweaking it" a little with Christian values about the best we can expect, or should we strive to completely transform it? It's Time to Un-Quo the Status addresses these issues by discussing four overarching questions:

- Who Are We & What Are We Supposed To Do?
- Should Christians Be Seen & Not Heard?
- How To Take Ground For Christ's Kingdom
- The Absolute & Positive Hope For The Earth

EXIT STRATEGY
A HANDBOOK TO EXPONENTIALLY
IMPROVE YOUR SERVICE FOR GOD

IF YOU'VE BEEN ITCHING FOR AN ANTIDOTE FOR THE RAMPANT SPIRITUAL anemia that exists throughout your community, *EXIT Strategy* provides the scratch. Each reader will be able to evaluate a book they're about to buy, or a study they're thinking of joining with thirteen Door Opener worksheets that quickly identify whether they will be involved in simply another form of church "busyness," or in an activity that will help them grow in their personal holiness.

While every Christian knows we must obey God, *EXIT Strategy* clarifies that in order to obey God in the way God prefers, we must first know and understand His Word. This is achieved through the exclusive Door Opener worksheets, plus the complete Westminster Larger Catechism (196 questions).

THIS IS NOT A DRILL
REAL LESSONS FOR REAL PEOPLE FROM THE
REAL GOD, THROUGH HIS PROPHETS,
ON HOW TO LIVE AND GOVERN OURSELVES, REALLY!

THIS IS NOT A DRILL IS DESIGNED TO BE A RESOURCE BOOK FOR YOU and your family (and hopefully even a small group study with your friends). With this in mind, the format has been designed more along that of a textbook, than a novel. To help you understand the historical circumstances to which each prophet is speaking, the content is divided into three sections:
- History & Hypocrisy: Conforming ourselves to the world
- Habits: Reforming ourselves to the Word, and
- Holiness or Holocaust? Blessings or Curses: God's sovereignty in History and Prophecy

JUST BECAUSE JESUS SAVES YOU FROM THE FIRE IT DOESN'T MEAN YOU GET TO DRIVE THE FIRE TRUCK!

HOW THE "ME FIRST" BRAND OF CHRISTIANITY IS IN FACT "NO Christianity" at all, and why our Culture will continue to unravel unless and until we "Seek first the Kingdom of God," (Matthew 6.33) by abandoning the idea of there being a God, and begin dealing with the reality of God and the responsibilities that are connected to being a Christian. Fire Truck assists you in

- Answering the question: "Am I getting the job done, as a Christian?" by explaining what you have been called into Christ's Kingdom to accomplish, and by helping you develop a "vision" of how to live as a Christian. We should not forget that God isn't interested that we know His will, but that we do His will.
- Making the non-negotiable attitude change from "What's in this for me?" to "What's in this for Christ's Kingdom?"
- Exchanging subjective conservative moralism for objective Christian reality.
- Developing the awareness and understanding of how a God-oriented lifestyle is superior to a man oriented lifestyle.
- Striving for consistency in your Christian walk, not complacency.

RETURN TO SINNER
ARE YOUR DAILY DECISIONS
BETRAYING YOUR CHRISTIAN TESTIMONY?

- What does it mean to be a Christian?
- What is it like to "image" Jesus in what we think, say and do?
- What changes need to be made in the worldview and lifestyle of a new Christian from the worldview and lifestyle he had before his conversion?

If a non-Christian were to ask any Christian these typical questions, he would likely receive some impressive answers. However, when the non-Christian begins to try to find Christian neighbors who are living according to the answers he receives, he may very well conclude that "all of this town's Christians must have gone on vacation." RETURN describes how to "love the Lord your God with your whole heart," and live your life in a God-honoring manner.

HOW TO DE-PROGRAM YOURSELF
FROM ALL OF THE BLASPHEMOUS IDEAS
YOU LEARNED IN PUBLIC SCHOOL

FOR MORE THAN 160 YEARS AMERICAN EDUCATORS HAVE BEEN TURNING out Marxist "Manchurian Candidates," who have been subtly indoctrinated to respond to cultural issues in ungodly ways, all the while thinking that they are "card carrying Christians." The operative word here is "think," and it is the way they have been taught to think (or not think) that is the brilliance of the public (government) school movement, and the shame of Pastors to allow their God to be systematically blasphemed on a daily basis.

If you think that it is beyond the realm of possibilities that your "strings" are being pulled in order for you to make your daily decisions according to the non-Christian worldview cultural agenda that is currently in vogue, read this book F-A-S-T!

Buddy Hanson, President of the Christian Policy Network, and Director of the Christian Worldview Resources Center frequently speaks to Churches Homeschool organizations and civic groups about the necessity of applying biblical principles to every situations, circumstances and decision-making. "There are many fine organizations presenting the descriptions about how a Christian worldview should differ from a non-Christian one, but that's only half of the equation. Our focus is to present God's prescriptions to reform our culture. Christianity is not an intellectual trip, but a world-transforming trip as Jesus commands us to live-out our faith and bring about 'God's will on earth as it is in heaven.'" (MATTHEW 6.10)

For pricing and ordering information contact:*
The Hanson Group
bhanson@graceandlaw.com
2 Windsor Drive, Tuscaloosa, AL 35404
205.454.1442

Bookstores can also order through Ingram Distributors
* Quantity discounts available

CPSIA information can be obtained at www.ICGtesting.com
Printed in the USA
BVOW11s1426020914

365187BV00026B/474/P